THE TRANSFER OF UNDERTAKINGS IN THE PUBLIC SECTOR

Employment and European Union Law Series

Series editors:

Colin Bourn, Jeff Kenner and Alan Neal
University of Leicester

Already published:

Trends in European Social Policy
edited by Jeff Kenner

The Transfer of Undertakings in the Public Sector

Edited by

Colin Bourn

Ashgate

DARTMOUTH

Aldershot • Brookfield USA • Singapore • Sydney

Published by
Dartmouth Publishing Company Limited
Ashgate Publishing Limited
Gower House
Croft Road
Aldershot
Hampshire GU11 3HR
England

Ashgate Publishing Company
Old Post Road
Brookfield
Vermont 05036
USA

Ashgate website: http://www.ashgate.com

British Library Cataloguing in Publication Data
The transfer of undertakings in the public sector. -
(Employment and European Union law series)
1. Labor contracts - Great Britain 2. Labor laws and legislation - Great Britain
I. Bourn, Colin
346.4'1'024

Library of Congress Catalog Card Number: 99-75455

ISBN 1 84014 772 5

Printed in Great Britain by
Antony Rowe Ltd, Chippenham, Wiltshire

Contents

Biographical Notes on Authors

Catherine Bailey is a graduate of the Law and Employment Relations programme in the University of Leicester. She is Legal Officer with Rother District Council, where she has had extensive responsibilities for transfers related matters.

Colin Bourn is a Director of the International Centre for Management, Law and Industrial Relations in the Faculty of Law in the University of Leicester and also practises as a barrister, specialising in employment issues. He has published many articles on employment matters and is the joint author of *Anti-Discrimination Law in Britain*, Sweet and Maxwell, 3rd edn., 1996.

Karl Larrad is a graduate of the Law and Employment Relations programme in the University of Leicester. He is a solicitor and Legal Officer, Kirklees Metropolitan Council, where he has had extensive responsibilities for transfers related matters.

Pascale Lorber is a graduate of the Law and Employment Relations programme in the University of Leicester. She is now a Lecturer in Law at the University of Leicester, where she has specialised in issues of information, consultation and participation at work, on which she has published several articles.

Stephen Hardy is Lecturer in Law in the Department of Social Work and Law in the University of Salford. He undertook a Ph.D. in this area and is joint author of *TUPE and CCT Business transfers: UK Labour Market Views*, Staffordshire Law School, 1997.

Paul Thorpe is a graduate of the Law and Employment Relations programme in the University of Leicester. He is Personnel Officer, Barnsley District Council, where he has had extensive responsibilities for transfers related matters.

Preface

The aim of this book is to provide an assessment of the way in which the Acquired Rights Directive has functioned in Britain and in particular how it has had impact upon the public sector. The book draws together contributions written from a legal and a human resource perspective. It is hoped that it will be of value to those attempting to grapple with the implications of the Directive and that it will provide an insight into the likely impact of the amending Directive 98/50/EC agreed at the Cardiff Council in June 1998. This volume has had a long gestation period, awaiting the resolution of issues in the case law, such as the *Suzen* and *Wilson* cases, as well as agreement in the Council on a revised and amended Acquired Rights Directive. In the event, the major uncertainties about the scope of the transfers regime and the capacity of employers to vary terms and conditions of employment have reached some resolution, with the text of the revised Directive available, so that this volume is able to present an analysis which may have a longer life than has been possible hitherto in this fast moving field.

Several of the chapters in this book started life as dissertations written for the masters programmes in Law and Employment Relations and in European Union law which are offered by the International Centre for Management, Law and Industrial Relations in the University of Leicester. It forms the second volume in a series based upon research undertaken by staff members in the International Centre and by participants in the two masters programmes which it offers. As the progammes in Law and Employment Relations and in European Union Law are offered in a distance learning format, they attract mature professional students who often bring a great depth of experience to their research projects. It is that combination of practical experience, personal interest and academic knowledge which often leads to the selection of projects which are of considerable practical, as well as theoretical, interest. It is with the hope that this book will be of interest to those involved in the practice of business reorganisations and the transfer of undertakings, as well as to the academic community, that this book is offered as a contribution to the growing literature on these matters.

This book is the second to be published in a series of volumes emanating from the International Centre for Management, Law and Industrial Relations in the University of Leicester, which draw together the fruits of research in the fields of interest of the Centre, principally, employment law and European Union law. The series will include monographs, collected essays and conference papers which reflect the diversity of work currently being undertaken.

The law is as stated at 31st March, 1999

Colin Bourn
Leicester, 1999

List of Tables

Table of Cases

Table of European Community Legislative Instruments

Table of European Community Legislative Instruments

EC Treaty Articles

Directives

Table of Statutes

Table of Statutes

Table of Statutory Instruments

Table of Statutory Instruments

1. Introduction: the Scope of the Public Sector

Colin Bourn

The focus of this volume is the impact of the Acquired Rights Directive upon the public sector and it seems appropriate therefore to give some brief analysis of what is meant by that term in this context. As the transfers regime is a matter of Community law, the most relevant approach to this issue is offered by Community law. Article 189 of the EC Treaty places upon the Member States an obligation to implement the requirements set out in directives. In the absence of full implementation in accord with the current interpretation of the directive by the European Court of Justice, an individual upon whom the directive confers unconditional and precise rights may rely, as against the state, upon the provisions of the relevant directive, once the date for implementation has passed.[1] In *Becker v Finanzamt Munster-Innenstadt*,[2] the Court of Justice held that

> 'It would be incompatible with the binding effect which Article 189 ascribes to directives to exclude in principle the possibility of the obligations imposed by them being relied upon by the persons concerned, particularly in cases in which the Community authorities have, by means of a directive, placed Member states under a duty to adopt a certain course of action. The effectiveness of such a measure would be diminished if persons were prevented from relying upon it in proceedings before a court and national courts were prevented from relying on it and were prevented from taking it into consideration as an element of Community law. Consequently, a Member state which has not adopted the implementing measures required by the directive within the

1 *Becker v Finanzamt Munster-Innenstadt* C-8/81[1982] ECR 53.

2 Note 1.

> prescribed period may not plead, as against individuals, its own failure to perform the obligations which the directive entails.
>
> Thus, wherever the provisions of a directive appear, as far as their subject matter is concerned, to be sufficiently unconditional and sufficiently precise, these provisions may, in the absence of implementing measures adopted within the prescribed period, be relied upon as against any national provision which is incompatible with the directive or in so far as the provisions define rights which individuals are able to assert against the state.'

In *Becker* two strands of reasoning can be perceived, that of the necessity to ensure the effectiveness of Community law and the assertion that states should not be able to profit from their own failure to implement the provisions of a directive. It is this latter argument which underpins the judgment in the later case of *Marshall v Southampton and South West Hampshire Health Authority,*[3] that directives may be relied upon against the state, in view of the latter's failure to fulfil its obligation to implement the directive in question. Directives may not be relied upon against private persons, whether natural or legal, who bear no responsibility for implementing Community obligations, which means to say that directives can only be of direct vertical direct. *Marshall* also decided that directives could be relied upon against the state in whatever capacity it was acting, whether as public authority or as employer. That this opened a gap between the legal position of employees in the public and private sectors was held not to be determinative, in that the state may repair this fault by implementing the directive correctly. The limitation of the direct effect of directives to matters in which a state entity is the defendant was confirmed in *Facini Dori v Recreb Sr.*[4]

Whilst the Court of Justice in *Marshall* relied upon the classification by the Court of Appeal of the respondent health authority as a public authority, no general proposition was advanced as to the boundaries of the state. Specific findings have been made that tax authorities,[5] local and regional authorities[6] and police authorities[7] are, like health authorities in *Marshall*, emanations of the state. In *Foster v British Gas plc*[8] the Court of Justice had to decide whether

3 C-152/84, [1986] IRLR 140 ECJ, [1983] IRLR 237.

4 C-91/92 [1995] All E.R. (E.C.) 1.

5 *Becker v Finanzamt Munster-Innenstadt* C-8/81[1982] ECR 53.

6 *Fratelli Costanzo v Commune de Milano* C-103/88.

7 *Johnson v Chief Constable of the RUC* C-222/84 [1986] IRLR 263.

8 C-188/89 [1990] IRLR 353 ECJ, [1988] IRLR 354 CA.

a pre-privatisation public utility which had been incorporated as a public company, all the shares of which were still in public ownership, was an emanation of the state. In the process the Court of Justice espoused a general formula to determine the extent of the public sector.

> 'It follows ... that a body, whatever its legal form, which has been made responsible, pursuant to a measure adopted by the state, for providing a public service under the control of the state and has for that purpose special powers beyond those which result from the normal rules applicable in relations between individuals is included in any event among the bodies against which the provisions of a directive capable of having direct effect may be relied upon.'

There is therefore a three part test, namely, (a) is the body providing a public service pursuant to a measure adopted by the state, (b) is it providing a public service under the control of the state and (c) does it have special powers beyond those normally applicable in private relations. These were regarded as cumulative criteria by the Court of Appeal in *Doughty v Rolls Royce plc.*[9] in that whilst the absence of any one might not be fatal, there would need to be 'something else, not contemplated by the formula' to be present for the case to fall within the ambit of the state. In the *Rolls Royce* case, although the firm was at the material time 100% owned by the state and therefore under its control, it was held not to be responsible for providing a public service, nor did it exercise any 'special powers' such as were exercised by British Gas.

The position of post-privatisation public utilities was considered in *Griffin v South West Water Services Ltd.*[10] in which the employer, a wholly owned subsidiary of South West Water plc, successor to the South West Water Authority, was considered to be an emanation of the state to which the Equal Treatment Directive was directly applicable. The question was held to be not whether the employer was under the control of the state, but whether the service it provided was under the control of the state. The legal form of the body was held to be irrelevant, as also was the fact that it is a commercial undertaking not carrying out any of the traditional functions of the state, over which the state has no day-to-day control. As it was conceded that the 'public service condition' and the 'special powers condition' were fulfilled, the body was an emanation of the state where it was providing water and sewage services under the control of the state.

9 [1992] IRLR 126.

10 [1995] IRLR 15 CA.

Whilst the position of nationalised or post-nationalised commercial undertakings was distinguished by the Court of Appeal from that of a voluntary aided school in *NUT v St May's Church of England (Aided) Junior School,*[11] such a school was nonetheless held to be an emanation of the state, even though it is not under the direct control of central government. The inclusive nature of the test in *Foster* is indicated by the way in which bodies which meet the tripartite test 'are included among the bodies against which the provisions of a directive capable of having direct effect may be relied upon'. Thus other bodies may fall within the scope of the state, even though, as in the instant case, not each and every element of the test is fully satisfied. Schiemann L.J. held that it is not appropriate to treat the test as if it were a statutory definition, so that even though he was not convinced that the governing body exercised special powers in providing an education service under the control of the state, the directive was of direct effect.

It is perhaps a chimera to seek for an all-embracing definition of public sector employment,[12] as definitions tend to depend upon their context. Whilst for the purposes of the application of directives having an employment protection function the approach of the ECJ has been inclusive, in the context of the reservation of public sector employment to nationals of the Member States, the Court of Justice has adopted a restrictive approach. In that context public sector employment has been seen as a derogation from the principle of free movement contained in Article 48 and has been restricted to employments which 'involve direct ...[or] indirect participation in the exercise of powers conferred by public law or duties designed to safeguard the general interests of the State or other public authorities.'[13] However, it is the more expansive approach adopted in *Foster* which is material to the application of the ARD, rather than the restrictive free movement case law.

Fredman and Morris consider that the distinctive features of public sector employment[14] stem from two factors, namely the role of government as public authority accountable ultimately to Parliament and the general reliance of government on taxation as a source of revenue. These features are not shared to the same degree in all parts of the public sector, so that there is not an abrupt dividing line between the public and private sectors but a shading effect, with the more peripheral parts of the public sector having much in common with the private sector. The balance of governmental and commercial considerations in employment policy in the public sector is not uniform and

11 [1997] IRLR 242.

12 See Morris and Fredman, Is There a Public/Private Labour Law Divide, *Comparative Labor Law Journal*, 14, (1993), pp. 115-137.

13 C-149/74, *Commission v Belgium*, [1980] ECR 388, [1980] CMLR 413.

14 Note 12 *supra*.

has shifted over time. The notion of the state as a 'model employer'[15] has come under increasing strain in the past twenty years and government contractors are no longer subject to the Fair Wages Resolutions. Private sector management techniques have been imported into the public sector and much service work has been contracted-out, so that the line between the public and private sectors is now blurred. The Next Steps Agencies are quasi-independent of central government, yet exercising a power and providing a public service under the control of central government. Privatised public utilities may be providing such a public service under state control exercised by the various statutory regulators and often require special powers beyond those normal to private relations, as exemplified by the *South West Water* case, even though employment decisions are likely to be driven by commercial considerations. Where a purely service function of a public body, such as cleaning or catering, has been contracted out, it is, on this approach, unlikely to be considered as constituting an emanation of the state subject to vertical direct effect. It is unlikely that such a body is providing a public service pursuant to a measure adopted by the state, though the contract specification may make it under the control of a branch of the state. Neither is it likely that it has special powers beyond those normally applicable in private relations.

Although there can be no doubt that the exercise of governmental functions constitutes the heart of the public sector, such activities are excluded from the scope of the Directive. The question as to whether the exercise of public administrative functions could constitute an economic entity within the Directive was raised in *Henke v Gemeinde Schierke & Verwaltungsgemeinschaft 'Brocken'*[16] in which a number of municipalities created between them a common collective organisation and the original municipalities were dissolved. The mayor's secretary in one of these municipalities, who was not re-enghied by the administrative collectivity, brought an action claiming that her contract of employment had been transferred to the new structure. The German government argued firstly that the Directive should not apply to public authorities in the exercise of their powers, secondly that the activities of public authorities are not comprehended by measures based on Article 100 which concerned measures directly affecting the establishment or functioning of the common market, thirdly that local authorities are governed exclusively by national law and are not part of the Community's economic system and fourthly that the terms 'undertaking' or 'business' are inappropriate to describe

[15] Hepple B. Labour Law and Public Employees in Britain, in *Labour Law and the Community: Perspectives for the 1980's*, Chapter vii, pp.1-20.

[16] [1996] IRLR 701, ECJ.

local authorities.[17] The Court of Justice based itself on the first recital å the preamble to the Directive, holding that

> 'The Directive sets out to protect workers against the potentially unfavourable consequences for them of changes in the structure of undertakings resulting from economic trends at national and community level, through, *inter alia* transfers of undertakings, businesses or parts of businesses to other employers as a result of transfers or mergers.'

The Court also emphasised that in its different language versions the Directive refers to businesses and undertakings, not words apt to describe public administrative functions, which '(e)ven if it is assumed that those activities had aspects of an economic nature, they could only be ancillary.' The 1998 amended Directive has placed this decision on a legislative basis by excluding from the scope of the Directive 'the administrative reorganisation of public administrative authorities or the transfer of administrative functions between public administrative authorities'. The preamble to the amended Directive provides that such clarification does not alter the scope of Directive 77/187/EEC as interpreted by the Court.

However, the fluidity of the boundary between the private and public sectors is demonstrated by the proposals of the Labour administration to privatise air traffic control, which might be seen as having a regulatory rather than commercial function. As with other privatisations, it would, however, be possible to include within the legislation a requirement that TUPE be deemed to apply, even if the view were taken that a governmental function such as air traffic control fell within the *Henke* decision. However, where a public service, such as a local authority planning function, is contracted out to the private sector, although the indicia set out in *Foster* would be satisfied, such a function can be argued to be an inherently administrative function falling within *Henke* and therefore excluded from the provisions of the Directive.

Thus even though the proposed revised Article 1(1)(c) of the Directive expressly includes 'public or private undertakings engaged in economic activities whether or not they are operated for gain', employees in engaged in public administrative functions are presently excluded from the coverage of the Directive. Consequently, the post-*Henke* decision of an Employment Tribunal that TUPE applies to local government reorganisation[18] is, it is submitted, wrong. The merger of NHS Trusts may also fall within *Henke*, so that although the provision of a public health service is clearly within the

17 M. Sargeant, New Doubts about Transfers, *Industrial Law Journal*, 26, 3, p.p. 265-269.

18 *Evans v East Riding of Yorkshire Council* , Hull 18th February, 1997.

public sector, a reorganisation of NHS Trusts may be argued not to attract the protection of the Directive. Clearly the decision in *Henke* could have a considerable effect upon the rights of employees affected by local government or health service reorganisations, affecting not only those engaged in obviously governmental functions, but also those engaged in ancillary activities.

A further blurring of the public/private boundary comes about via the Public Finance Initiative, under which private capital is invested in public facilities in such a way as to avoid the need to increase the public sector borrowing requirement (PSBR). In order that the higher cost of private finance is not to be capitalised and shown against the PSBR, Treasury accounting rules demand that the something is secured other than simply fixed assets. For that reason the PFI is concerned with the provision of fully serviced premises, covering everything other than the specific professional activity, such as, say, the provision of clinical or educational services. Whilst it is likely that such a provision falls within *Foster* so as to constitute an emanation of the state, it is arguable that it also falls within *Henke* and therefore outside the protection of the ARD. Yet a serviced building would seem to be primarily an economic, rather than an administrative, activity and the better view would seem to be that any staff transferred into the new facilities would be covered by TUPE.

The importance of the consideration as to whether direct effect applies as regards the ARD has diminished since the 1993 Trade Union Reform and Employment Rights Act but is still more than nominal, as whilst many disparities between the ARD and the TUPE have been eliminated, some remain. The 1993 Act anticipated many of the arguments put forward by the European Commission in its 1994 Article 169 enforcement proceedings against the UK.[19] The criticisms that UK law, as set out in TUPE, did not apply to transfers not involving the transfer of property, did not embrace non-commercial ventures, did not provide adequate remedies in cases of non-compliance and did not invoke the need for consultations 'with a view to seeking agreement' had, by the time of the hearing of the complaint, either been corrected or alleviated by legislation or by the development of case law. The remaining head of complaint that the obligation to inform and consult was limited to recognised independent trade unions, thus depriving non-union employees of the right to be consulted, was not addressed until the passage of the 1995 Consultation Regulations.[20] The Consultation Regulations

[19] *EC v UK*, C-382/92 [1994] IRLR 392. And see the criticisms made of the UK law in this respect by Hepple, EEC Labour Law in the UK – A New Approach, *Industrial Law Journal*, (1989) 18, 3, pp. 129-133.

[20] Collective Redundancies and Transfer of Undertakings (Protection of Employment) (Amendment) Regulations SI 1995/2587.

can in their original form be criticised as failing to address the need to ensure capable and independent representation for all employees, whilst potentially undermining the role of trade unions and are currently the subject a consultation proposal with a view to their amendment. Thus there remains the possibility of claiming a right under the directly effective Directive, where there remain disparities between its terms and those of the implementing legislation. In such circumstances a claim made against a private sector employer could only succeed in so far as the terms of the domestic legislation were capable of interpretation to give effect to the Directive, without distorting the meaning of the domestic law.[21]

Where a person has suffered loss or damage due to the failure of the state to implement a directive correctly and on time, a damages action against the state is possible, following the principles enunciated in *Francovich and Boniface v Italian Republic*[22] and subsequent cases. Prior to 1993 non-commercial ventures were excluded from TUPE, but the longer limitation period available for a claim made in respect of a breach of statutory duty recently enabled a group of former council workers sponsored by the GMB, Unison and the TGWU to present a claim in respect of their dismissal or employment on less favourable terms between 1982 and 1993 as a consequence of the contracting-out of the functions in which they were employed. In November 1997 the Government conceded in the High Court that the workers were entitled to compensation.

Thus the public sector, although undergoing a process of rapid transition, would appear from the point of view of the application of the ARD, to consist of bodies, in whatever legal form, which are legally responsible for providing a public service under the control of the state and which exercise special powers for that purpose, providing that the functions exercised are not of a purely administrative or governmental type.

The book considers the main issues that have arisen in the application of the ARD to the public sector. In chapter 2 we consider the aims of the Acquired Rights Directive, chapter 3 examines the scope of a 'relevant transfer' under the Directive. In chapter 4 we examine the history and development of CCT. Chapter 5 is concerned with the provision of information to contractors, whilst chapter 6 looks at dismissals and chapter 7 the preservation and variation of terms of employment. Chapter 8 examines the question of pensions in the context of CCT. Chapter 9 is concerned with employee consultation and information processes. In chapter 10 the future of the Directive is considered with an examination of the recently revised text of the Directive.

21 *Marleasing S.A. v La Commercial Internacional de Alimentacion S.A.* C- 106/89 [1990] ECR 1-4135, *Webb v EMO Air Cargo (UK) Ltd* [1993] IRLR 27.

22 C-9/90 [1991] ECR 1-5357, [1993] 2 CMLR 66.

2. The Aims of the Acquired Rights Directive and TUPE

Colin Bourn

In considering the aims and purposes of the Acquired Rights Directive 77/187/EEC it is worth first contemplating the aims of the European Economic Community as set out in Article 2 of the Treaty of Rome, namely that

> 'The Community shall have as its task, by establishing a common market and progressively approximating the economic policies of the Member states, to promote throughout the Community a harmonious development of economic activities, a continuous and balanced expansion, an increase in stability, an accelerated raising of the standard of living and closer relations between the states belonging to it.'

The Community was intended to achieve European political integration via a spillover from the economic integration brought about by the creation of a common market. As Davies[1] expresses the matter

> 'There is no doubt that it is that project (the creation of a common market) which constitutes the heart of the Community undertaking. The free movement of goods, services, labour and capital across the Community and without reference to national boundaries is the rock upon which the Community is presently built.'

The social aims of the Treaty were to be achieved via the creation of a common market, as is clearly implied by the wording of Article 2. Nonetheless, there was a social chapter in the Treaty, namely articles 117-122, of which article 117 provided that

1 Market Integration and Social Policies, Paul Davies, 24 *Industrial Law Journal*, 1, 49-78.

> 'Member States agree upon the need to promote improved working conditions and an improved standard of living for workers, so as to make possible their harmonisation while the improvement is being maintained.
>
> The believe that such a development will ensue not only from the functioning of the common market, which will favour the harmonisation of social systems, but also from the procedures provided for in this Treaty and from the approximation of provisions laid down by law, regulation or administrative action.'

There is a manifest ambiguity in the aims set out in Article 117 and in the means by which those aims are to be achieved. Paragraph 1 states the aims of the Article, which are to promote improved working conditions and an improved standard of living in the process of their harmonisation. This harmonisation is seen in the second paragraph of Article 117, as arising naturally from the process of economic integration through market-led adjustments. Legislative harmonisation occupies a subordinate place, as can be seen by the way in which it is introduced by the phrase "but also".

In the period from 1957-72, dubbed the period of economic neo-liberalism by Hepple,[2] the economic integration of the market predominated with emphasis placed on the free movement and the correction of distortions to competition. As Paul Davies has remarked, the lack of activity in regard to labour law and social matters was

> '...not because the drafters did not expect the Common Market to produce social benefits for workers and citizens of the Member states. On the contrary these benefits were to be delivered through market mechanisms, not legislation.'[3]

In this first period the Community was concerned to lay down what Streit and Mussler term 'framework activities'. This involves the setting out of a framework of non-discriminatory rules within which economic actors may choose, not only between goods and services in a common market but between locations and institutional systems within which to site their activities. In consequence, Streit and Mussler[4] argue that since national rules and

2 B. Hepple, The Crisis in E.C. Labour Law, (1987), 16 *Industrial Law Journal*, 1, 77.

3 P.L. Davies 'The Emergence of European Labour Law', in W McCarthy (ed) *Legal Interventions in industrial Relations: Gains and Losses*, Blackwell, Oxford, 1992, at p.324-5.

4 M.E. Streit and W. Mussler, The Economic Constitution of the European Community: From 'Rome' to 'Maastricht', (1995) 1 *European Law Journal* 5.

regulations affect the choices open to economic actors, the Common Market also offers opportunities to choose between institutional systems, thus allowing what can be termed as 'institutional competition'. On this view the creation of a common market may bring about the harmonisation not only of employment rules determined at enterprise or sectoral levels, but also national legislative rules. Any comparative advantage conferred by national social legislation is an element in the overall process of competition across Europe. This can lead to improvements in the functioning of the national labour market systems in so far as national legislators are able to correct any harmful economic effects of institutional competition between the different national labour market systems. This type of argument prevailed amongst the ILO Committee of Experts commissioned in 1956 to address the question of whether there was a need for the harmonisation of labour law in order to ensure fair competition across the Community.[5] The conclusion was that harmonisation was only necessary to the extent that special factors brought about lower costs in particular situations, differences which would not be reflected in the exchange rate. Davies argues that two exceptions emerged to this general rule, one where there were specially low costs in some areas of production. Such an advantage might be created where women workers did not receive equal pay, thus giving rise to the principle of equal pay in Article 119. The other special circumstance in which Davies argues that harmonisation occurs is in the need to ameliorate the effects upon workers of economic integration, which is the logic underlying the Economic and Social Fund and, subsequently, the Collective Dismissals and Acquired Rights Directives.

In the face of this predominantly economic logic, and in view of the economic progress being made by the Member States, legislative harmonisation of social and labour standards did not play a significant role until the communiqué at the close of the Paris summit in 1972, which declared that the Member States

> 'attached as much importance to energetic proceedings in the field of social policy as to the realisation of economic and financial union.'

The Commission subsequently prepared a Social Action Programme,[6] which was approved by the Council in January 1974. Michael Shanks, himself a

[5] See P.L. Davies, The Emergence of European Labour Law, in *Legal Interventions in Industrial Relations, Gains and Losses* (ed) McCarthy, Blackwell, 1992, (at pp. 318-322).

[6] Council Resolution of 21st January 1974, 74/C13/1. Amongst its aims were 'the attainment of full and better employment within the Community', 'the improvement of living and working conditions so as to make possible their harmonisation while the improvement is being maintained' and 'the increased involvement of management and labour in the economic and social decisions of the Community and of workers in the life of their undertaking'.

former Social Affairs Commissioner, wrote in 1977[7] that the specifically social aims of the Treaty had been confined firstly to ensuring the free movement of labour in order to bring about an optimum distribution of manpower resources which would enhance economic and social welfare, and, secondly, to eliminating distortions of competition arising from unequal social costs. This latter aim was to be approached by means not so much of harmonising the social systems of the Member States, as providing a minimum below which standards may not fall. However, Shanks asserted that it was the fear of a political backlash arising from the effects of economic integration, which drove the leaders of the Community to propose a broader social programme 'to persuade the peoples of the Community to continue to accept the disciplines of the market.' In Shanks's view 'the task of the Community in the social field is not to equalise but to establish minimum standards, below which nobody should be allowed to fall, but on the basis of which those who can afford to do so should build their own more ambitious systems.' As a part of that process, the Council took note of the intention of the Commission to submit to it a directive on the harmonisation of laws with regard to the retention of rights and advantages in the event of changes in the ownership of undertakings, in particular in the event of mergers.

THE AIMS OF THE ACQUIRED RIGHTS DIRECTIVE

The proposal for a Directive on the harmonisation of the legislation of Member states on the retention of the rights and advantages of employees in the case of mergers, take-overs and amalgamations[8] arose from the increased number of mergers and acquisitions which occurred in the 1960's and early 1970's and from the 'far reaching consequences on the social position of the workers employed by the undertakings concerned'[9] which the Commission asserted were inadequately regulated by the laws of the Member States. The preamble to the original proposal for a directive recited that establishment of a single market had resulted not merely in an enlarged market for European undertakings and keener competition in the Member States,

> 'but the economic union thus established has compelled undertakings to alter their structures and methods and size in order to adjust to the new demands of the common market, more particularly by way of merger, concentration and rationalisation.'

7 Michael Shanks, The Social Policy of the European Communities, (1977) 14 CMLR 375.

8 OJ No C104/1, 1974.

9 Proposal for a Directive on the harmonisation of the legislation of Member states on the retention of the rights and advantages of employees in the case of mergers, take-overs and amalgamations, (1974) V/631/74-E.

The directive, based on Article 100, was to achieve four objectives, namely:-

- the automatic transfer of the employment relationship from the old to the new employer,
- the protection of employees against dismissal due exclusively to a change in the structure of the undertakings,
- the prolongation of the terms of applicable collective agreements, and
- information, consultation and negotiation with the representatives of employees.

The original 1974 proposal was much more far reaching than that approved by the Council, extending not only to the transfer of undertakings, but to share transfers and mergers which have the result that one company replaces another as employer. The protected rights included 'obligations arising from customary industrial practice'.[10] Plant and company agreements concluded by the transferor were to be automatically transferred to the transferee.[11] Dismissals were to be permissible only for 'pressing business reasons'. The right to acquire future pension entitlements was not excluded from the directive according to the Commission's explanatory memorandum, although the treatment of existing pension rights distinguished between situations where the capital fund was transferred and those where it remained with the transferor.[12] The provisions on consultation were far stronger than those embedded in the final text of the Directive, resulting in binding arbitration at the request of one party in cases of disagreement.[13] The text approved by the Council was described by Elias as 'but a pale shadow of what might once have been anticipated',[14] with, amongst other changes, share transfers being excluded, dismissals permitted for 'economic, technical or organisational reasons', and no provision for arbitration.

Although a single market measure introduced under Article 100, designed to prevent distortions of competition by reducing differences in the levels of protection afforded to employees in the various Member States,[15] the preamble to the Directive also makes reference to the need to promote the approximation of laws in this field while maintaining the improvement

10 Article 3(1).

11 Article 3(2).

12 Articles 6 and 9 and pages 11-12 of the Commissions explanatory memorandum V/631/74-E.

13 Article 8(2).

14 P. Elias (1982) *Company Lawyer* 147 at 156.

15 The preamble to the Directive provides that remaining differences in the extent of the protection afforded to workers affected by such situations should be reduced, as these differences can have a direct effect on the functioning of the common market.

described in Article 117. The substantive purpose of the Directive is expressed to be 'to provide for the protection of employees in the event of change of employer, in particular, to ensure their rights are safeguarded'. The need for this protection is said to arise from economic trends bringing about changes in the structure of undertakings, though transfers of undertakings, businesses or parts of businesses to other employers as a result of legal transfers or mergers.

Thus the Directive is intended to function as a counterweight to the economic forces unleashed by the common market, which might have a deleterious effect on the livelihood of workers, and possibly engender the type of popular backlash envisaged by Shanks.[16] It is an example of a policy intended to facilitate mutual adjustment of market structures,[17] in this case adjustment of the impact of product market changes upon the labour market. The primary economic logic of the integration of product markets, with the consequent restructuring and rationalisation of enterprises, leads to disruption of the labour market, which the Directive attempts to address.

Freedland[18] argues that in this area of law one can distinguish a realm of economic policy discourse, concerned with the functioning of the common market as such, and a realm of social policy discourse, concerning itself with societal concerns such as health and safety or the environment. Labour market policy lies in a contested area between these two views, neither wholly explicable in terms of free-market economics,[19] not yet entirely divorced from them and purely concerned with social justice. In Freedland's sense, the Acquired Rights Directive is as a labour market policy measure,[20] intended to soften the impact of economic change upon the legitimate expectations of affected workers. Therefore there is both

16 *Supra.*

17 Francis Snyder, *New Directions in European Community Law*, Weidenfeld and Nicolson, 1990, pp. 72-78.

18 Drawing upon Ogus, *Regulation - Legal Form and Economic Theory*, Clarendon Press, 1994.

19 As the Directive is a measure of minimum harmonisation, it cannot be entirely concerned with economic arguments about the possibility of social dumping whilst differing levels of implementation can still remain. Yet G.F. Mancini, in discussing the Collective Redundacies Directive 75/129, stated 'Admittedly, reductions in staff are a terrible thing, and to stand idly by in the face of unemployment...would be unworthy of our Europe, which is heir to the enlightenment and suffused with the notion of welfare. Yet, like it or not, upstream from enlightenment and welfare there is no getting away from the conditions of competition. If a country can authorise redundancies on less stringent conditions than other countries, its industry will be given an incalculable advantage. And it is against that advantage that war is being declared.' (Labour Law and Community Law, (1985) *Irish Jurist* 1, 12, quoted by Wedderburn in The Social Charter in Britain: Labour Law and Labour Courts?, (1991) 54 *Modern Law Review* 1.

20 Mark Freedland, Employment Policy, in *European Community Labour Law, Principles and Perspectives*, (Ed) Davis, Lyon-Caen, Sciara and Simitis, Clarendon Press, 1996, p.285.

an economic and a social logic to the Directive, and both strands of reasoning seem present in the decisions of the Court of Justice. Indeed, one can see a shift over time from the early definition of a transfer in economic terms, to the upholding of the social aims of worker protection in later cases, before a seeming return to the primacy of economic considerations in cases such as *Suzen*.

Harmonisation of Acquired Rights

One can distinguish between several types of legislative harmonisation,[21] ranging from total harmonisation, where the standards adopted are mandatory and from which no derogations or upward revisions are possible, to minimum harmonisation. This latter type, sometimes termed partial harmonisation ,[22] is said to exist where Member states may impose more stringent rules. In its decision on the Working Time Directive, the Court of Justice emphasised that minimum standards did not mean the least possible or lowest standards, but standards which could be improved upon by the Member States. Such harmonisation may be 'exhaustive', under which the Community excludes the competence of the Member States within a given area or 'partial', leaving certain matters to be regulated by national law, as, for example, where reliance might be placed upon a national definition of the contract of employment.

The Acquired Rights Directive is an example of minimum harmonisation, where States may opt for higher standards of worker protection than that provided by the Directive, which extends only to the partial regulation of the field, some matters being left to be defined according to the national systems. The Court of Justice in the *Daddy's Dance Hall* case[23] held that the Acquired Rights Directive

> 'only aims at partial harmonisation in the field concerned, extending in substance the protection for workers guaranteed autonomously by the law of the different Member States also in the event of a transfer of the undertaking. The Directive does not aim at setting up a uniform level of protection for the whole of the Community based on common criteria.'

Therefore, in the *Rask*[24] case the ECJ also held that

[21] P.J. Slot, Harmonisation, (1996) 21 *European Law Review* 378-397.

[22] McGee and Weatherill, The Evolution of the Single Market - Harmonisation or Liberalisation, (1990) 53 *MLR* 578.

[23] [1988] IRLR 315.

[24] [1993] IRLR 136.

'the Directive can be relied on only to ensure that the employee concerned is protected in his relations with the transferee to the same extent as he was in his relations with the transferor under the legal rules of the Member State concerned. Consequently, in so far as national law allows the employment relationship to be altered in a manner unfavourable to employees in situations other than transfers, in particular as regards their conditions of pay, such an alternative is not precluded merely because the undertaking has been transferred in the meantime and the agreement has therefore been made with the new employer.'

However, reliance on a national definition of key terms may not result in the undermining of the objectives of the directive, as was demonstrated by the treatment of 'employee representatives' in the enforcement proceedings on the Collective Dismissals and Acquired Rights Directives C-382/92 and 383/92. Although Article 1(1)(b) of the Directive 75/129 and 2(c) of 77/187 provide that the 'representatives of employees' are to be understood as meaning representatives of employees 'provided for by the laws or practice of the Member State' the ECJ went on to hold in the Acquired Rights decision that

'Admittedly, the Directive achieves only partial harmonisation of the rules for the protection of employees in the event of a change of employer and is for that reason not designed to bring about full harmonisation of national systems for the representation of employees in an undertaking. However, the limited character of such harmonisation cannot deprive the provisions of the Directive, and especially Article 6, of their effectiveness. In particular, it cannot prevent Member States from being required to take all appropriate measures to ensure that employee representatives are designated with a view to the provision of information and consultation provided for by article 6.'

Implementation of the Directive in the UK

The Directive was watered down in the process of negotiation, so that the final 1977 version accepted by the Council was less threatening to managerial freedom than the original 1974 version. Although the 1970's have been perceived as the decade of corporatism, the Labour administration had been cool towards the proposals, according to Davies and Freedland.[25] The

[25] P. Davies and M. Freedland, *Labour Legislation and Public Policy*, Clarendon Press, 1993, at p. 578.

difficulties experienced by the UK in accepting the Acquired Rights Directive as part of the domestic legal system were in part due to the rule in *Noakes v Doncaster Amalgamated Collieries* that the contract of employment is a personal one. The modification of this position by the 1964 Redundancy Payments Act to provide for continuity where a changed employer made an offer of re-engagement before the expiry of the previous contract, or for the payment of a redundancy payment on termination of the contract, constituted a set of arrangements which enjoyed widespread support, not only amongst employers,[26] but trade union members likewise. However, attitudes towards the Directive have changed as unemployment has worsened, and in face of the threat posed to established terms and conditions by the process of contracting out. The broader reason for the difficulty is the legacy of collective laissez-faire in British industrial relations, with no tradition of statutory consultation, which does not offer a wholly natural place for the statutory provision of information and consultation.

However, the social contract period might have provided more fertile soil for the implementation of the Acquired Rights Directive[27] than was afforded by the incoming Conservative government, of which it could be said that the *leit motifs* were deregulation of the labour market and the diminution or marginalisation of trade union power. When introducing the Transfer of Undertakings Regulations to the House of Commons the Conservative minister responsible, Mr David Waddington, made the by now notorious observation that the Regulations were introduced 'with a remarkable lack of enthusiasm'[28] and only then in face of the threat of enforcement proceedings by the European Commission.

Perhaps the most distinctive of the policies pursued by the Conservative government in its quest to create an 'enterprise culture' was that of the privatisation of state enterprises and the imposition of compulsory competitive tendering on the public sector, although neither policy has been wholly rejected by the incoming New Labour administration. At first the Conservative government acted in the belief that these policies were not affected by the Directive, the Transfer of Undertakings Regulations having excluded from their scope, undertakings 'not in the nature of a commercial venture'. The government chose to interpret the Directive in a restrictive manner, excluding non-commercial ventures which could be said not to affect the functioning of

26 W.W. Daniels, The Impact of the Employment Protection Laws, PSI.

27 The Collective Dismissals Directive had been implemented in the Employment Protection Act 1975 and seemed to form a natural and unexceptional part of that piece of legislation. However, Hepple in (1976) ILJ, 5, 4 at p.197 quotes Mr Albert Booth, the then Labour secretary of state for employment as saying that the EC proposals were of 'very little value'.

28 Quoted in Hepple (1982) *Industrial Law Journal*, 11, 1, p.29.

the market.[29] After the *Sophie Redmond Stichting v Bartol*[30] case, in which the ECJ held that the Directive could apply to the transfer of the activities of a non-profit body, the Government attempted for a considerable time to maintain its original policy,[31] but in 1993 the Chancellor of the Duchy of Lancaster in a statement to the House of Commons had to concede that the Regulations could apply to many forms of market testing and contracting out, except where the identity of the undertaking is substantially changed or the employer conducts the operation substantially differently.[32] Subsequently the Trade Union Reform and Employment Rights Act 1993 repealed the non-commercial venture exemption, correctly anticipating the outcome of this aspect of the enforcement proceedings brought against the UK by the European Commission.[33]

Acquired Rights in the Public Sector

The policy of the Government in pursuing market testing and compulsory competitive tendering has no doubt several bases, amongst which must be included the 'rolling-back' of the state, the control of public expenditure, the reduction of bureaucracy, the encouragement of competition, efficiency, cost savings and innovation and the diminution of the influence of public sector unions. It can be argued that these developments have an adverse effect on the rights of employees, in so far as the legitimate expectations of employees are disrupted. The traditional model of public sector employment has been subject to a process of erosion during the past two decades. Hepple[34] posits a 'model' of traditional public sector employment as being characterised by an ideology of the sovereign employer tending to act as a 'model employer', a high degree of centralised rule making, extensive use of consultation and bargaining and considerable extra-legal advantages for employees (e.g. *de facto* job security, machinery for promotions and re-grading etc.). He notes

29 The legal basis of the Directive was Article 100, which gives authority for the approximation of laws and regulations which 'directly affect the establishment or functioning of the common market'. Indeed, in its 1974 memorandum on the proposed Directive, the Commission did not envisage the inclusion of non-profit-making bodies.

30 *Dr Sophie Redmond Stichting v Bartol* [1992] IRLR 336, ECJ.

31 See Acquiring rights - Losing Power: A Case Study in Ministerial Resistance to the Impact of European Community Law, Radford and Kerr, *Modern Law Review*, (1996) 60, 1, pp 23-43, for an ironical account of the tortuous evolution of Government policy on this issue.

32 The DoE conceded as much in a circular issued early in 1994. See chapter 4 for an account of these processes.

33 Case C-382/92 [1994] IRLR 394, ECJ.

34 R. Hepple, Labour Law and public employees in Britain, in *Labour Law and the Community: Perspectives for the 1980's*, (Eds.) Lord Wedderburn and W.T. Murphy, chapter VII, pp. 1-20.

that this model was under attack by the date of publication of that article in 1982, but the policy of contracting out has, for the affected employees, largely displaced it. The internal labour market[35] described by Hepple in his 1982 article could be characterised as being a system of 'bureaucratic' rather than 'market' relations, with relatively settled expectations on each side of the employment relationship. Collins[36] makes the point that in such a system market considerations are confined to the process of entry into the system from the wider labour market. Inside such a system wage and other expectations enjoy substantial isolation from market pressures, which are only brought to bear through comparability exercises and review bodies. Market testing and contracting out bring market considerations far more to the fore, as contractors compete for the available work. Price competition between contractors would, other things being equal, tend to depress wages, worsen working conditions and reduce job security, if only because labour costs are a very large proportion of total costs in a typical market testing or CCT situation. The very process of bundling up service activities for the purpose of contracting out makes these activities constitute a periphery around the core functions of the authority, an arrangement which is consonant with Atkinson's core-periphery model of the flexible firm.[37] Commercial contracts thereby replace contracts of employment and employment decisions are removed from the sphere of direct public service. Collins[38] argues that contractors can save on labour costs by effecting savings in hiring and training, paying lower wage rates and avoiding the cost of compliance with employment protection law, in part by employing a higher proportion of labour on short term contracts. All this can be achieved within a context not characterised by the give and take necessary for any long term employment relationship, but by objective monitoring.

The increased scope of managerial discretion facilitated by the practice of contracting out of labour is limited by the application of the Directive. The

35 See Cappelli P., Rethinking Employment, (1995) *British Journal of Industrial Relations*, 33, 4, pp. 563-601 for a discussion of the impact of modern management practices, including contracting out, upon the internal labour market as a system of relatively settled career expectations and earnings relativities within large corporations.

36 Collins H., Market Power and Bureaucratic Power, *ILJ*, (1986) 15,1, pp. 1-15.

37 Atkinson J. (1984) Manpower strategies for flexible organisation, *Personnel Management*, 16: 28-31. Atkinson asserts that in order to achieve numerical, functional and financial flexibility firms tend to distinguish between a stable core and an unstable and changing periphery. Atkinson's model has been influential, even though it has been criticised as being uncertain whether he is describing or prescribing the development of a core periphery approach to flexibility by Pollert, *Warwick Papers in Industrial Relations*, no 19.

38 Collins H., Independent Contractors and the Challenge of Vertical Disintegration for Employment Protection Laws, 10 *Oxford Journal of Legal Studies*, 353-380.

Directive limits price competition amongst contractors, by maintaining employment relationships on their existing terms, excluding dismissals except on economic, technical or organisational grounds, extending collective agreements and providing for information and consultation. In so far as the Directive maintains a floor of minimum standards for employees, it limits price competition, and frustrates some of the aims of the process of contracting out in the public sector.[39] More argues that it is justifiable to apply the directive to contracting out because this process would otherwise lead to the erosion of labour standards and the diminution of training. The UK Conservative government, amongst others, supported proposed amendments to the Directive made by the EU Commission in 1994 that would have excluded contracting out from its scope, but which were withdrawn in 1977.[40] However, the Court of Justice in *Suzen*[41] has, at the least, excluded from the scope of the directive second-generation contracts in which there is no substantial transfer of assets or any agreement between the two contractors.[42]

The Amended Directive

In 1998 the Council reached a common position on a Directive[43] to amend Directive 77/187/EEC. This Directive came at the end of a four year long process, which began with the Commission's 1994 proposal to replace the 1977 text with a new version.[44] That proposal met with opposition in the European Parliament and amongst the Member States and was withdrawn in 1997, on publication of a set of further proposals to amend the Directive.[45] Although the three proposals for the replacement or amendment of the Directive each make reference in their respective preambles to the relevant provisions of the Social Charter of 1989, they omit the reference in the 1977 preamble to economic trends leading to restructuring at national and Community levels. Nonetheless, the legal base in Article 100 remained the same in each case.

Whilst the preamble to each version provides that considerations of legal certainty and transparency require that the concept of a transfer be clarified,

39 More G., The Acquired Rights Directive; Frustrating or Facilitating Labour Market Flexibility, in *New Legal Dynamics of the European Union*, OUP, 1995, pp 129-145.

40 Discussed in chapter 10.

41 *Suzen v Gebaudereinigung GmbH Krankenhausserice, Lefarth GmbH*, Case C-13/95.

42 The scope of transfers under the Directive is discussed in chapter 3.

43 Directive 98/50/EC.

44 COM(94) 300 Final.

45 COM(97) 60 Final. The original Directive and the 1994 and 1997 proposals are set out in a tabular form in the Report of the House of Lords Select Committee on the European Communities, Acquired Rights Revisited.

the manner of that clarification has been different on each occasion. The 1994 version distinguished between the transfer of an economic entity and an economic activity, which, it was argued, may have had the effect of excluding contracting-out. It was widely argued[46] that that particular proposal would not have led to greater legal certainty but to uncertainty and increased litigation and it was withdrawn by the Commission. Although the 1997 text for an amended Directive omitted that distinction, the effect of that distinction was largely realised by the Court of Justice in the *Suzen* case. The kernel of the *Suzen* judgment has been incorporated as the basis of the 1998 text of the amended Directive. Thus the Council members have accepted the balance between the economic and social effects of the Directive which was struck in the *Suzen* case, as regards the nature of the entity which must be transferred.

That striking of a balance between the economic and social effects of the Directive can be seen in other aspects of the revision of the Directive. All versions of the amended Directive have included a proviso in the preamble and in the text that it applies to private or public undertakings, whether or not they operate for gain. Where the 1998 text differs is that it excludes from the operation of the Directive the reorganisation of public administrative functions or structures, as the Court had held in the *Henke* case. Thus the market is defined as including all other forms of economic structures except those concerned purely with public administration. The drawing of the boundary at this point can be understood as confining the Directive to market matters, although not necessarily strictly commercial matters, whilst leaving to the Member States themselves the freedom to manage their own affairs as regards public administration and any defined categories of public servants within that sphere who enjoy a special legal status. Thus the integrity of Article 100 as a legal base is respected at the same time as respect is accorded to the principle of subsidiarity.

The principle of subsidiarity is also respected in the several options that the amended directive provides for the Member States. The inclusion of an option for Member States to allow variations to employee terms and conditions in the context of insolvency proceedings, to include occupational pension rights in the bundle of transferred rights, not to transfer outstanding debts in insolvency situations and to notify transferees of all rights and obligations known to the transferor all reflect the varying concerns and priorities of the Member States. In the context of the need for unanimity under Article 100, the Directive is not simply providing a floor of rights, with specific options for the Member States either to provide more generously for employees, as, for

[46] See the evidence submitted to the House of Lords Select Committee on the EC report on Transfer of Undertakings: Acquired rights, HL Paper 38, Session 1995-96, 5th Report and the debates in the European Parliament and in the Economic and Social Committee CES 317/95 – SOC/256, 29-30 March 1995.

example, in respect of pensions, but it also allows Member States to strike their own balance between employee rights and economic imperatives in insolvency situations. The option to allow negotiated variations to terms and conditions in such circumstances can be seen as a double exercise of the principle of subsidiarity, first to the Member States, and, if permitted, to the social partners within the enterprise. It can also be seen as the striking of a balance between labour market flexibility and labour market regulation in protecting the future employment and living and working conditions of workers. The balance is quite carefully struck, for flexibility is limited only to insolvency situations, and the determination of terms and conditions is made a matter of consultation with independent workers' representatives. There is neither an unfettered managerial prerogative here, nor a statutorily enforced right to collective bargaining, but information and consultation provisions limited to a situation of *extremis*. Such information and consultation provisions are of a piece with the current proposals for national works councils, should they gain acceptance.

Thus the 1998 text can be seen as a refinement of the balance inherent in the Directive between the recognition that in a free and competitive market restructuring is inevitable and the need to protect workers from the consequences of that restructuring. The inclusion of contracting-out, at the same time as the distinction is firmly drawn between the transfers of an economic entity and activity *simpliciter*, can be seen as another species of the same balancing technique. The transferee employer is left in many, though not all, contracting-out situations with an option as to whether it takes on the workforce with its acquired rights, or seeks a fresh workforce and fresh capital assets. If the transferee wants and needs the asset base of the transferor, it must respect the rights of the workforce; otherwise the workforce is redundant and fresh employees are engaged on (probably) inferior terms. What may not be done is to strike a different balance by changing terms, when the transfer itself is the reason for the change. Whether subsequent case law will allow any refinement of that balance in the light of the compromises struck in negotiating a new Directive, remains to be seen, the decision of the House of Lords in the *Wilson* and *Meade and Baxendale* cases leaving the boundary between transfer-related and other changes in terms and conditions of employment open for later clarification.

Conclusions

The Directive on Acquired Rights was intended to limit the impact on workers of restructuring and rationalisation consequent upon the realisation of the common market. The broad interpretation placed by the ECJ upon the scope of a relevant transfer was thought until recently to have brought within the scope of the Directive the process of sub-contracting in both the public and private sectors. The inclusion of sub-contracting limits the scope of a 'race to the bottom' as regards wages and other terms and conditions as contractors compete to undertake public sector services. The capacity of the Directive to limit such competition can be viewed either as an undesirable brake upon free competition and labour market flexibility, or as a valuable protection of labour standards which limits unfair competition. The twin economic and social logic of the Directive and the ambiguous nature of 'minimum' legislative harmonisation, means that the Court of Justice, whilst still adopting a teleological approach to the interpretation of the Directive, can change the emphasis in its case law as between the protection of workers' interests in a changing labour market and the economic need of both public and private undertakings to pursue cost-efficient forms of organisation.

The case law of the Court has evolved against a changing economic background. The emergence of unemployment as being a major threat to the stability of Europe has led to a new policy emphasis on competitivity.[47] The other new factor is the convergence criteria for economic and monetary union, under which the Member States must reduce public sector deficits, control inflation and keep interest rates low. Thus the employment protection thrust of the case law of the Court of Justice, which found its clearest expression in the *Schmidt* judgment, has given place to a greater recognition of conflicting pressures towards flexibility and efficiency in a market economy.

The Council has finally addressed the conflicting pressures bearing on the protection of workers in transfer situations and an amended Directive been agreed[48]. The amended Directive increases the capacity of the Member States to adopt or maintain diverse practices and confirms the transfer of undertakings as being a sensitive borderland between market forces and social regulation. In each of the key points of the new text, such as the definition of a transfer, the inclusion of pensions and the capacity to vary terms of employment post-transfer, a fine line is trodden between politically acceptable regulation and the economic imperatives of the market. The resolution of these opposing forces has in part been achieved by devolving to the Member States a series of options. These respect the principle of subsidiarity, preserve some national differences and allow the balance of political and economic forces in each country to find some expression. Perhaps the text of the amended Directive demonstrates the limits of the extent of substantive labour market regulation that is politically possible in Europe, at least in so far as it concerns matters perceived as being central to the interests of both employers and employees.

47 *Growth, Competitiveness and Employment, the Challenges and Ways Forward into the 21st Century*, Bulletin of the EC, Supplement 6/93.

48 Directive 98/50/EC.

3. What is a Relevant Transfer?

Colin Bourn

The Acquired Rights Directive continues to be a source of controversy and difficulty, because it embodies the implicit conflict between the economic and social dimensions of the European Union. The realisation of a single market, in which persons, goods and services can circulate freely on a level playing field places liberal market ideas at the core of the development of the EC. The economic wellbeing resulting from the operation of a single market would, in the view of the founding fathers,[1] bring social benefits in its train, but nonetheless Article 117 committed the Community to improve working conditions so as to make possible their harmonisation whilst the improvement was being maintained. These ambiguities and difficulties are manifested in the evolution of the case law of the Court of Justice with regard to the scope of a relevant transfer, the existence of which brings the protections provided by the Directive into play.

The Scope of a Relevant Transfer

The Directive applies to the transfer of an undertaking, business or part of a business to another as a result of a legal transfer or merger, although not to a change in the control of a company by acquisition of the share capital, where the legal identity of the employer does not change.[2] The Explanatory Memorandum of the Commission[3] asserts that the common criterion in this definition is that there is a change of employer with its possible repercussions

1 See the Resolution adopted by the Foreign Ministers of the Member States of the European Coal and Steel Community at the Messina Conference in June 1995 and the Spaak Report of 1956.

2 Article 1(1).

3 See the Explanatory Memorandum of the Commission proposing the Directive, (COM 74) 351 final, which posits a need for a legal framework for such concentrations and rationalisations including company law and competition aspects, as well as giving rise to the need for an instrument to protect the interests of workers in such contexts.

for existing employment relationships. The Memorandum provides no guidance as to what is meant in a factual sense by a transfer, an undertaking, a business or part of a business, or what the constitutive elements are of a legal transfer of the above entities.

The most controversial area of application for the Directive has been to contracted out services. An important part of the Government's policy to liberalise and deregulate economic life in the UK has been the policy of 'outsourcing' and competitive tendering for services generally.[4] Such practices are associated with what has been termed 'post-Fordist' management[5] and the quest for increased labour force flexibility.[6] It is clear that the aim of flexibility is not confined to the United Kingdom, but extends across the European Union, as witnessed by the Commission's Growth White Paper[7] and the strategy adopted to counter unemployment at the Essen summit.[8] In that context the notion of contracting-out work and services in order to increase numerical and functional flexibility is an important aspect of increased labour flexibility and cost reduction. The Acquired Rights Directive limits price competition based on differential labour costs between in-house providers and contractors and between contractors themselves. In so far as it applies to contracting out situations, it provides an effective floor of rights, but increases business costs. Competition is limited initially at least to issues of quality and efficiency in the utilisation of labour, and a 'race to the bottom' as regards employee terms and conditions is precluded or, at a minimum, substantially retarded. Employers in the service industries have in general expressed their hostility to the application of TUPE to public sector contracting out.[9]

4 See chapter 4 for an account of this policy and practice.

5 Post-Fordist Management, A. Amin, *Blackwell*, 1994.

6 Atkinson J., Manpower Strategies for Flexible Organisations, *Personnel Management*, 16, pp. 28-31. See Pollert A. *The Flexible Firm, A Model in Search of Reality*, Warwick Papers in Industrial Relations, December 1987, No 19 for a critique of Atkinsons 'core-periphery' model.

7 White Paper on Growth, Competitiveness and Employment, European Commission, 1994. This is a world-wide tendency as witnessed by the attempts of the South Korean Government to increase labour market flexibility. The Observer, Dec 28th, 1996.

8 Employment and Unemployment in the European Union, Social Europe 3/94 pp 14-23, and From Essen to Cannes: A Re-employment Strategy for the European union Essen Strategy, Social Europe 3/94 pp 24-31, Commission Communication on a European Pact of Confidence for Employment, CSE (96) 1 final of 5.6.96.

9 See the evidence presented to the House of Lords Select Committee on the European Communities, *Transfer of Undertakings: Acquired Rights*, Session 1995-96, 5th Report, HL Paper 38 by the Business Services Association, the Building Employers Confederation, the Constructors Liaison Group and others.

The controversy over the application of the Acquired Rights Directive to contracting-out was addressed in the amendments proposed to the Directive by the Commission in 1994.[10] The Commission proposed to amend the definition of a relevant transfer under the Directive as follows.

> 'The transfer of an activity which is accompanied by the transfer of an economic entity which retains its identity shall be deemed to be a transfer within the meaning of this directive. The transfer of only an activity of an undertaking, business or part of a business, whether or not it was carried out directly, does not in itself constitute a transfer within the meaning of the Directive.'

In the explanatory memorandum produced by the Commission for an amended directive in 1994, it is argued that the above wording reflects the case law of the Court of Justice and 'introduces certain clarifying and other elements to help in interpreting and implementing the directive, more particularly, when only when only one business activity is transferred.' Yet the Commission has not persisted with this distinction between activities and entities after opposition in the Parliament and it was deleted from the 1997 amended proposals for a Directive amending Directive 77/187[11] and does not appear in Directive 98/50. Yet this controversial distinction between activities and entities seems to have entered the jurisprudence of the Court of Justice through the decision in *Suzen*,[12] almost at the moment that it disappeared from the legislative proposals. Perhaps in consequence of this case law development in June 1998 the Council reached a common position on an amended Directive[13], which is based upon the judgments in *Suzen* and *Henke*,[14] the latter case having the effect of excluding the purely administrative reorganisation of public authorities. Whilst there has been pressure in the UK to restore the pre-*Suzen* position, if only as a matter of legal certainty, the Suzen decision was more consonant with the prior national law in France

[10] In particular the preamble to the revised Directive declared that such considerations demanded a 'clear distinction to be made between transfers of undertakings, businesses or parts of businesses and the transfer only of an activity of an undertaking; whereas cases where the transfer of only an activity is not accompanied by the transfer of an economic entity which retains its identity after the said transfer should be excluded from the scope of the directive.' OJ 1994 C279/10, 1/10/94.

[11] COM (97) 60 final.

[12] Case c-13/95.

[13] Directive 98/50/EC amending Directive 77/187/EEC.

[14] *Infra.*

and Germany and was in line with the Commission's 1977 proposals. If the distinction between the transfer of an activity and entity proposed by the European Commission in 1994 for inclusion in a revised Directive had been applied, it would have been in the context of contracting-out.[15]

In *Abels*[16] the Court held that the intepretation of the Directive follows necessarily from a consideration of its purposes, which in this context were held to be to ensure that 'the restructuring of undertakings within the Common Market does not adversely affect workers in the undertakings concerned'.[17] The argument that this aim would restrict free enterprise was rejected by the Court in *D'Urso v Ercole Marelli Electromeccanica Generale*,[18] thus enabling Advocate General Van Gerven in *Dr Sophie Redmond Stichting v Bartol* to conclude that the 'the primary purpose of the Directive is to prevent the process of restructuring within the comon market being carried out to the detriment of the employees of the undertakings concerned'.[19] The social policy emphasis of the Directive leads the Advocate General to the conclusion that the concept of an undertaking should be given a scope appropriate to to the purposes of the Directive, which according to the Court in *Berg*[20] is 'intended to safeguard, in the interests of the employees, the existing employment relationships which are part of the economic entity transferred.'

[15] The House of Lords Select Committee reported that there was general agreement amongst the witnesses who had testified to it that the proposed amendment to the wording was not helpful. The burden of the evidence presented was to the effect that any such wording would be confusing, would tend to produce irrational distinctions between essentially similar situations and discriminatorily disadvantage lower paid public service workers, many of whom are women. The Select Committee recommended that only the first sentence of the amendment should be retained, suggesting that it should perhaps be elaborated by the inclusion of a non-exhaustive list of factors such as was set out in *Spijkers*.

[16] *Abels v Bedrijfsvereniging voor de Metaalindustrieen de Electrotechnische Industrie*, (Professional and Trade Association for the Metal and Electrical Industries) Case 135/83, [1987] 2 CMLR 405.

[17] At point 18.

[18] Case C-362/89, [1992] IRLR 136 at points 14-15.

[19] Case c-29/91, [1992] IRLR 366 at point 7, a conclusion compatible with the interpretation of the term 'undertaking' in other spheres of community law, as where the Court concluded in a case (C-7/90 at point 6) arising from the use of tachometers in road transport, that 'the definition of an undertaking, within the meaning of Art. 15 of Regulation 3820/85, must be governed by the system set up by the Regulations and by its aims'.

[20] Joined cases 144/87 & 145/87, [1989] IRLR 447 at point 13, and *Ny Moll Kro* 287/86, [19889] IRLR 37 at point 12.

What is a Transfer within the Scope of the Directive

In analysing these issues Advocate General Van Gerven in *Dr Sophie Redmond Stichting v Bartol*[21] and Advocate General Lenz in *Henke v Gemeinde Schierke and Verwaltungsgemeinschaft 'Brocken'*[22] fruitfully distinguish *between* the concept of an undertaking, the transfer of an undertaking and the concept of a legal transfer.

The Concept of an Undertaking

The test for the existence of an undertaking was first laid down in the *Spijkers* case[23], in which an abattoir closed down and the premises and equipment sold to new owner, who reopened the slaughterhouse under its own name on the same site two months later. The Court of Justice held that 'the decisive criterion for establishing the existence of a transfer within the meaning of the directive is whether the entity in question retains its identity' which 'will be apparent from the fact that its operation is actually being continued or has been taken over by the new employer, with the same or similar economic activities[24]'.

The Court in *Dr Sophie Redmond Stichting v Bartol*[25] relied on *Spijkers* to hold that 'it is necessary to determine, having regard to all the circumstances of fact surrounding the transaction in question, whether the functions performed are in fact carried out by the new legal person with the same or similar activities, it being understood that activities of a special nature which pursue independent aims may, if necessary, be treated as a business or part of a business within the meaning of the Directive'. The latter qualification suggests that minor or ancillary activities may still fall within the definition of an 'undertaking' provided that the *Spijkers* test is met.[26] Neither is it an obstacle to the application of the Directive that the undertaking in question is a charitable foundation, not run on a commercial basis.

The Court confirmed in *Rask v ISS Kantinservice*[27] that ancillary activities fell within the scope of the Directive. In *Rask,* Phillips, the electrical

21 Case c-29/91, [1992] IRLR 366.

22 Case 298/94, [1996] IRLR 701.

23 Spijkers v Gebr. Benedik Abattoir CV, case 24/85, [1986] CMLR 486.

24 At point 12.

25 Case c-29/91, [1992] IRLR 366 at point 31.

26 Advocate General Van Gerven argues for a broad interpretation of the concept of undertaking to include non-commercial undertakings, as the basis of the Directive lies in the social policy of the Community.

27 *C-209/91* [1993] IRLR 133.

manufacturer, contracted out the management of the canteen service at one of its establishments to a catering firm for a fixed fee. Nonetheless, the Court of Justice held that

> 'Where the responsibility for providing a service is, by agreement, entrusted by the owner of an undertaking to another who assumes the obligations of an employer in respect of the employees who are engaged in the provision of that service, that transaction is capable of falling within the scope of Art. 1(1). Neither the fact that the activity transferred is only an ancillary activity, nor the fact that the agreement relates exclusively to the provision of services for the benefit of the transferor for a fee, prevents the Directive from applying.'

The 1998 text of the amended Directive incorporates this aspect of the case law of the Court, by providing in Article 1(b) that an economic entity is 'an organised grouping of resources which has the objective of pursuing an economic activity, *whether or not that activity is central or ancillary*'. (emphasis added)

In *Christel Schmidt v Spar-und Leihkasse der Fruheren Amter Bordesholm, Kiel und Croneshagen*,[28] the question at issue was whether the contracting out of the work of a single cleaner at a branch bank could constitute the transfer of an undertaking. The Court held that 'when an undertaking entrusts by contract the responsibility for operating one of its service, such as cleaning, to another undertaking which assumes the obligations of employer towards employees assigned to those duties, that operation may come within the scope of the directive'. The similarity of the cleaning activity before and after the transfer was held to be typical of an operation which comes within the scope of the Directive. Neither, the Court maintained, is the Directive excluded by the fact that only one employee is affected.

In *Schmidt* the Court[29] relies on *Rask and another v ISS Kantinservice A/S,*[30] to hold that 'the Directive is applicable where, following a legal transfer or merger, there is a change in the legal or natural person who is responsible for carrying on the business and who by virtue of that fact incurs the obligations of an employer vis a vis the employees of the undertaking, regardless of whether the ownership of the undertaking is transferred'. The Court also relies on *Redmond Stichting*[31] to hold that 'the retention of that identity is

[28] Case 392/92, [1994] IRLR 302 at points 14-15 & 17.

[29] At paragraph 12.

[30] [1993] IRLR 133.

[31] *Dr Sophie Redmond Stichting v Bartol and others,* C 29/81, [1982] IRLR 366 at 17.

indicated *inter alia* by the actual continuation or resumption by the new employer of the same or similar activities' so that the similarity of the cleaning work is sufficient to include it within the scope of the Directive.

Advocate General Van Gerven in *Schmidt* considered that in a case like this the general test in *Spijkers* requires additional clarification. In *Spijkers* the Court had held that to retain its identity the business has to be disposed of as a going concern, rather than simply disposing of its assets, 'as would be indicated, *inter alia*, by the fact that its operation was continued or resumed by the new employer, with the same or similar activities'.[32] A G Van Gerven considered that this presupposes 'a unit with a minimum level of organisational independence, which can exist by itself, or as part of a larger undertaking'. In this context he considers it significant that in its earlier judgment in *Botzen*,[33] which concerned the determination as to which employees were transferred to the new employer, the Court employed the test as to whether a worker was assigned to a department 'which formed the organisational framework within which their employment relationship took effect'. The Advocate General's analysis in *Schmidt* concludes[34] that the phrase undertaking, business or part of a business is 'underpinned by the concept of an economic unit which refers to an organised whole consisting of persons and (tangible and/or intangible) assets by means of which an economic activity is carried on having an objective of its own, albeit one that is ancillary to the objects of the undertaking; a whole which, moreover, can be part of a larger corporate whole'.

The Advocate General in *Merckx v Ford Motors* [35] adopted the concept of a unit with 'a minimum level of organisational independence' to assist in reaching a conclusion that the transfer of a vehicle concession from one dealer to another in a different district of the same town, could fall within the Directive. In spite of the fact that no tangible assets transferred between the dealers, the Court concluded that

> 'The purpose of an exclusive dealership for the sale of motor vehicles of a particular make in a certain sector remains the same even if it carried on under a different name, from different premises and with different facilities. It is also irrelevant that the principal place of business is situated in a different area of the same conurbation, provided that the contract territory remains the same.'

32 *Spijkers* at para 12.

33 *Botzen and others v Rotterdamsche Droogdok Maatschappi BV* C-186/83 [1985] ECR 519 ECJ.

34 At para 16.

35 [1996] IRLR 467, ECJ.

Yet the economic entity transferred must be more than a temporary extension of the work of the transferor, for in *Rygaard,* where a contractor took on the residue of a specific works contract, the Court held that

> 'The authorities ... presuppose that the transfer relates to a stable economic entity whose activity is not limited to performing one specific works contract. That is not the case of an undertaking which transfers to another undertaking one of its building works with a view to the completion of that work.'[36]

It is now clear that the approach in *Rygaard* was not simply a deviation from the path of the previous case law which was confined to a limited range of factual situations where the activity in question was essentially temporary, but that it foreshadowed the approach to be adopted in *Suzen (infra)* with regard to contracting out, where the Court again insisted on the need for 'a stable economic entity whose activities are not confined to one specific works contract'.

The Court of Justice in *Suzen v Zehnacker Gebaudereinigung GmbH Krankenhausservice & LeFarth GmbH*[37] held that an 'entity' is an 'organised grouping of persons and assets facilitating the exercise of an economic activity which pursues a specific objective'. [38] In *Suzen* the Court thus explicitly distinguishes between an 'economic activity' and the 'organised grouping of persons and assets' (i.e. the 'entity') which facilitates the performance of the activity in question. In this case the cleaning contract for a school was re-let to a different contractor, who did not take on the cleaners employed by the former company, including the plaintiff Mrs Suzen. Whilst the Court does not make explicit reference to its previous case law in *Botzen* the definition of an economic entity formulated by the Court is consonant with that decision and with the analysis advanced by Advocate General Van Gerven in *Schmidt,* which emphasised the organisational integrity and functional autonomy of the activity in question.

The Court in *Suzen* recognises that in certain sectors, such as cleaning, it is possible for an economic entity to function without significant assets, and that where this is the case, 'the maintenance of the identity of such an entity beyond the operations which are its object, cannot, on this hypothesis, depend on the transfer of such assets'.[39] Even though a service provider may employ few tangible or intangible assets, the Court nonetheless held that 'an entity cannot be reduced to the activity entrusted to it. Its identity emerges equally

[36] [1996] IRLR 51 at point 20-21.

[37] Case C-13/95, *The Times*, 26th March, 1997.

[38] Case C-13/95 at point 13.

[39] At point 18.

from other factors such as its workforce, its management staff, the way in which it is organised, its operating methods or, indeed, in the case arising, the operational resources available to it.'[40] Thus an undertaking, business or part of a business cannot consist only in the contract and the work in hand, but embraces the surrounding organisational framework, the physical and human assets employed and the operational methods adopted.[41] The Court holds that unless some significant part of those physical or human assets are transferred, there has been no transfer of an entity but only of an activity. In

[40] At point 15.

[41] In *Eidesund v Stavanger Catering A/S*, Case E-2/95, [1996] IRLR 684 a decision of the EFTA Court which can only be of persuasive authority, one catering contractor on an oil rig was succeeded by another, who employed 14 of the 19 catering workers employed by the transferor. The EFTA Court considered firstly that the activities carried out by the transferee catering services provider were not part of the recipient's oil rig operator's business and could not be seen as the transfer of a part of that business. This sets the situation apart from that considered by the ECJ in *Rask* or *Schmidt* where an internal service activity was entrusted to an outside contractor. The EFTA Court held that for the service provider's activities to be considered as an economic entity such activities must be distinguishable from its other activities and have employees assigned to them. If the service provider supplied to several customers from the same facilities, no one customer contract would constitute an economic entity in itself and neither would the loss of one such customer constitute a transfer. There must, echoing *Rygaard*, be a minimum of 'activity and continuity' to give rise to an economic entity capable of being transferred, such as the round the clock services provided in the instant case.

The ECJ in *Suzen* cited the decision of the EFTA Court in *Ulstein v Asbjorn Moller*, in which the Court stated

'As held by the Court in *Eidesund*, in cases where a high percentage of the personnel is taken over, and where the business of the first service provider is characterised by a high degree of expertise of its personnel the employment of that personnel by the second provider may support a finding of identity and continuity of the business. If the work to be performed does not require any particular knowledge or expertise, the taking over of the personnel becomes less indicative of the undertaking. It may also be a matter of consideration whether the taking over of personnel is caused by a desire to carry on the same business as before or merely represents a convenient way for a new service provider to fill its increased need for employees to service the new contract. It may be an indication of the former if the taking over of employees is a condition for the transfer while a filling of vacancies based on individual applications and free competition may be an indication of the latter. For this reason, the procedure and basis for employment may be of significance for the total assessment to be made.'

The foundation of the EFTA Court can be found in EFTA Surveillance Authority-Court Agreement, including Protocol 5 on the statute of the EFTA Court and Protocol 7 on its legal capacities, privileges and immunities. Amongst its functions are the giving of advisory opinions to the national courts, in a procedure modelled on Article 177 of the EC Treaty. Under Article 34 of the ESA-Court agreement, the EFTA Court may give advisory opinions on the interpretation of the EEA Agreement, but there is no obligation on national courts to seek such an opinion, which is not binding on the requesting court. However, in the view of Lief Sevon, The EEA Judicial system and the Supreme Courts of the EFTA States, in *Accord EEE; Commentaires et Reflexions*, (ed) Olivier Jacot-Guillarmot, Schulthess Polygraphischer Verlag AG, Zurich, 1992 , the combination of Article 3 and Protocol 35 of the EEA Agreement has an effect parallel to that of Article 5 of the EC Treaty, i.e. there is an obligation on national authorities to ensure the fulfilment of the obligations of the EEA Agreement.

this way the Commission's original proposals for a revised directive, in which a distinction was drawn between the transfer of an activity and an entity, appear to have been realised in the case law. *Rygaard* is cited as authority for the proposition that an 'entity' must have some degree of permanence, in that an undertaking within the terms of the directive must be a 'stable economic entity whose activity is not limited to performing one specific contract'.[42]

Whilst the Court in *Suzen* held that in the absence of the transfer of the assets employed or the key personnel, the transfer of an entity could not be said to have occurred, it is not necessarily the case that even had those elements been transferred, a transfer of an 'entity' could be said to have taken place, if it was limited to the performance of one specific works contract, as in *Rygaard*.[43]

The decision in *Suzen* was applied by the Court of Appeal within a very short time in *Betts v (1) Brintel and (2) KLM*[44], a case in which KLM won a contract from Brintel to provide helicopter services to Shell oil rigs in the North Sea. KLM provided the service from a new base, utilised its own helicopters and took on no staff formerly employed by Brintel. Whilst it was argued on behalf of the employees concerned that the transfer of the activity was sufficient to constitute an undertaking, at least when combined with the transfer of landing rights at Shell rigs, Kennedy L J giving the judgment of the Court of Appeal held that the entity concerned included not only the activity in question, but the helicopters and infrastructure - the landing strip, premises and buildings - necessary to deliver the service, as well as the staff. The decision of the Court of Appeal in *Dines v Initial Health Care Services Ltd*,[45] in which the succession of a first to a second generation cleaning contractor was held to fall within the scope of TUPE, was distinguished. Kennedy J drew a distinction between labour-intensive undertakings, of which *Dines* was an example, where, if the activity is continued or resumed with substantially the same staff, the transfer of an undertaking may well be held to have taken place and 'other types of undertaking in relation to which the application of the *Spijkers* test involves a more wide-ranging enquiry'.

[42] At point 13. This analysis is consonant with the EFTA Court's notion in *Eidesund v Stavanger* that there must be 'a minimum of activity and continuity' before an 'entity' can be said to exist. The decision in *Rygaard* was distinguished by the EAT in *Highland Council v Walker*, EAT/817/97which upheld a decision by the Industrial Tribunal that there was a relevant transfer when a dog warden service was contracted back in by the Council. The exercise of identifying a relevant transfer was held to be one of fact.

[43] However, the European Court in *Ny Moll Kro* Case 287/86 [1989] IRLR 37, held that a transfer occurred when the lease of a tavern was taken back and the tavern operated by the owner, whilst in *Daddy's Dance Hall* C-324/86 [1988] IRLR 315a transfer was held to have occurred when the lease of a theatre restaurant expired and a new lease was given to a different operator.

[44] *The Times*, April 1st, 1997.

[45] [1994] IRLR 336 CA.

The amended Directive

The Council of Ministers meeting in June 1998 in Cardiff adopted a common position on an amended Directive,[46] which in Article 1(b) draws directly upon the judgment in *Suzen* and provides that

> '(T)here is a transfer within the meaning of this directive where there is a transfer of an economic entity which retains its identity, meaning *an organised grouping of resources which has the objective of pursuing an economic activity*, whether or not that activity is central or ancillary.' (emphasis added)

This definition relies upon the distinction established in *Suzen* between the transfer only of an activity and the transfer of an entity, but does not adopt that wording, which was the subject of criticism in the European Parliament and in other quarters. The distinction is drawn in positive terms, setting out what is meant by an 'economic entity', rather than in the negative terms of the 1997 proposal. The House of Lords Select Committee's second report on acquired rights entitled Acquired Rights Revisited[47] argued for the definition of a transfer to be elaborated by the inclusion of a non-exhaustive list of the relevant factors, in order to avoid the uncertainty present after *Suzen*, but preserving sufficient flexibility for Member States to tailor their implementation to their particular circumstances. The preamble to the 1998 text states that 'considerations of legal certainty require that the legal concept of transfer be clarified in the light of the case law of the Court of Justice' but that 'such clarification does not alter the scope of Directive 77/187 as interpreted by the Court of Justice.' Thus the amendment incorporates the present interpretation of the directive by the Court and is not intended to limit that further or reduce currently available employee protection. This must in practice limit the scope of the Court to interpret Directive 77/187 in a manner unfavourable to employee protection in the period before the revised Directive comes into force.

UK case law on the concept of an 'undertaking'

In *Kenny v South Manchester College*,[48] the education service at a Young Offenders Centre was transferred from a local education authority to a college, at the time when such further education colleges became legally separate corporations. The High Court concluded, following a review of the authorities, that the absence of the transfer of assets, clients or goodwill was not fatal to there being a transfer where there was clear continuity in the activities being undertaken, the control of which moved from one corporate body to another. In the light of *Suzen*, the simple continuity of activities is not sufficient to

46 98/50/EC.

47 HL 98, April 1998.

48 [1993] IRLR 265.

constitute the subject of a transfer within the terms of the Directive. Similarly, Mummery J. (as he then was) held in the EAT[49] that 'the emphasis must be on a comparison of the actual activities of an actual employment situation in an undertaking before and after the transfer'. Even though there is no transfer of the management structure, stocks or equipment, Mummery J. held that the identity of the entity in question may be preserved. In his view the theme running through the case law of the Court of Justice 'is the necessity of viewing the situation from an employment perspective, not from a perspective conditioned by principles of property, company or insolvency law'.[50] In *Suzen* the Court of Justice took a less employment oriented view, implicitly accepting a managerial logic under which the transferee may preserve a discretion as to whether to accept the transfer of an entity or content itself solely with taking on an activity. In an analysis which was derived from the earlier jurisprudence of the Court of Justice, Morrison J in *Council of the Isles of Scilly v Brintel Helicopters Ltd.*[51] held that an economic entity included assets, employees and activities but might comprise only activities and employees, especially in the service sector, reasoning which substantially accords with the conclusions of the ECJ in *Suzen*. According to Morrison J. it was for the employment tribunal to identify the assets, activities and employees in question and to examine their disposition after the alleged transfer, in order to answer the question whether the economic entity has retained its identity.

In the *Betts v Brintel and KLM* case in the High Court[52] Scott-Baker J. held not only that the manner in which the transferee chooses to provide the services (as opposed to the service he is required to perform) carries little weight, but that '(i)t seems to me to put the cart before the horse to conclude that the fact that no employees were transferred helps KLM's case that no undertaking was transferred'. However, the argument by the appellants that KLM should not benefit from its deliberate refusal to take on any Brintel employees was rejected by the Court of Appeal, Kennedy LJ. holding that were a modest number of such employees to have been taken on, that that would not have led to a different conclusion. Nonetheless, in *ECM (Vehicle Delivery Services) Ltd v Cox and Others*,[53] where the transferee declined to take on the dedicated drivers who had serviced the particular car delivery contract which was lost by the original contractor to ECM, Mr Justice Morrison held in the EAT that, having regard to the purpose of the Directive, '(i)t would not

49 *Kelman v Care Services Ltd* [1995] ICR 260 (regrant of school cleaning contract).

50 A view espoused by Professor Hepple in his evidence to the House of Lords Select Committee on the proposal for a revised Directive, evidence p.11.

51 [1995] IRLR 6, in which the fire fighting and baggage handling functions at St Mary's Airport were taken back into the management of the County Council.

52 [1996] IRLR 45, HC.

53 *The Times*, June 14th, 1998.

be proper for a transferee to be able to control the extent of his obligations by refusing to comply with them in the first place'. In the circumstance, the EAT held that the continued employment of the drivers was contingent on the existence of the particular delivery contract and, as such, there was an economic entity which retained its identity after the transfer, as the customers and the work done were essentially the same. Here, the loss of a customer implied the loss of that part of the business, a distinction recognised in *Suzen* according to the analysis of the EAT. The purposive approach of the EAT to the refusal of the transferee to accept any obligation for the employees could seem consistent with the analysis of the Court of Justice in *Rotsart de Hertaing* in which the Court held that contracts existing on the date of the transfer are automatically transferred by the mere fact of the transfer of the undertaking, 'despite the contrary intentions of the transferor or transferee and despite the latter's refusal to fulfil his obligations'.[54] However, the analysis of the Court of Appeal in *Betts* would make the refusal of the transferee fatal to the existence of a transfer and, if there were no transfer, there would be no obligation on the transferee to accept the workforce.

The High Court in *Porter and Nannayakkara v Queens Medical Centre (Nottingham University Hospital)*[55] held that where a new employer provides the same service but by different methods which involve the use of staff who can undertake a different type of work, there will be the transfer of an undertaking, although any dismissal or non-reengagement may be for an economic, technical or organisational reason. *Suzen* does not necessarily imply that in such circumstances the economic entity, including the necessary assets to facilitate the delivery of the service, has not been transferred, even if different methods and a different framework of organisation are used. Nonetheless, if the changes are so great that the identity of the original undertaking is lost, there will not be transfer, as in *Mathieson v United News Shops Ltd.*[56] where a hospital shop was taken over by chain store operator selling a much wider range of items.

The Transfer of an Undertaking

The test as to whether there has been a relevant transfer of an undertaking within the terms of the directive was set out by the Court of Justice in the *Spijkers* case, in which the Court of Justice held that, in order to determine that question, it is necessary

[54] C-305/94 [1997] IRLR 132, ECJ at point 27.

[55] [1993] IRLR 486 Following a scandal, the paediatric services of a hospital were reorganised on a more community oriented basis and responsibility for their provision transferred to the local university hospital.

[56] [1993] IRLR 486.

> 'to consider all the facts characterising the transaction in question, including the type of undertaking or business, whether or not the business's tangible assets such as buildings and moveable property, are transferred, the value of the intangible assets at the time of transfer, whether or not a majority of its employees are taken over by the new employer, whether or not its customers are transferred and the degree of similarity between the activities carried on before and after the transfer period, if any, for which those activities were suspended. It should be noted, however, that all those circumstances are merely single factors in the overall assessment which must be made and cannot therefore be considered in isolation.'[57]

Thus *Spijkers* stands for the proposition that the Directive applies wherever an economic entity retains its identity after the transfer and sets out a multi-factorial test to enable national courts to arrive at a conclusion on any given set of facts.

In *Suzen v Zehnacker*[58] Advocate General La Pergola reviewed the existing case law as regards the application of the *Spijkers* test to 'second generation' contracting-out. In this case a cleaning contract expired and was subsequently awarded to a different and wholly independent contractor. The Advocate General argued that whilst it would be possible to conclude on the basis of the existing jurisprudence (citing, in particular, *Schmidt*) that a transfer such as was in question fell within the scope of Article 1(1) of the Directive, he rejected that option because he contended that contracting out of 'services, of whatever nature, which the enterprise needs to another entity is a choice made in a market economy, which ensures competition between several candidates'. In those circumstances the Advocate General found it difficult to justify why the successful bidder should be obliged to retain the personnel formerly employed by the previous service provider who had not been awarded the contract. Advocate General La Pergola contended that the Court of Justice had approached these matters in an informal way, delimiting the concept of a transfer progressively by confronting the concrete circumstances of different actual cases, but without identifying the essential elements of the transfer of an undertaking, which he identified as being the transfer of tangible or intangible assets, albeit that the extent of those assets will be smaller in some areas of activity than others.

The Advocate General thus sought to give to the concept of the transfer of an undertaking a more precise technical meaning, even though he admitted

[57] *Spijkers v Benedik* Case 24/85 [1986] ECR 1119.

[58] *Suzen v Zehnacker Gebaudereinigung GmbH Krankenhausservice* Case C-13/95.

that it is interpreted differently in the laws of the Member States, as the Court acknowledges in *Sophie Redmond Stichting v Bartol*.[59] The Court in *Suzen* based itself on the multiple test in *Spijkers*, but further refined and delimited the application of the concept of a transfer. The decision proceeded from the premise that 'the mere fact that the service provided by the old and new awardees of a contract is similar does not support the conclusion that an economic entity has been transferred.' This premise is further expressed where the Court holds that

> 'the mere loss of a service contract to a competitor cannot by itself indicate the existence of a transfer within the meaning of the directive. In those circumstances, the service undertaking previously entrusted with the contract does not, on losing a customer, thereby fully cease to exist, and a business or part of a business belonging to it cannot be considered to have been transferred to the new awardee of a contract.'

The Court thereby acknowledges that more is needed than the transfer of an activity, although the Court does not place the same emphasis as the Advocate General on the transfer of assets, that being only one of the criteria to be taken into account by the national court. The decision in *Suzen* is firmly based in the jurisprudence springing from the *Spijkers* case, but it enables several further negative and positive factors to be spelled out. First, the Court states that the absence of a contractual link does not mean that there is not a transfer, but it cannot safely be concluded that the existence of a contractual link means that there is in all cases a transfer. Second, the transfer must relate to a stable economic entity, not limited to the performance of a specific works contract. Third, there must be a transfer of assets, whether tangible physical assets, intangibles, such as goodwill or customer connections, or human assets in the form of the skills and organisation of the workforce. The effect of these last two criteria is to place the existence of a transfer substantially within the control of the transferee, at least where there is no contractual link between the transferor and the transferee. Where a transferee could manage without taking on the skills of the existing workforce, as will often be the case with essentially unskilled service work, and where the physical assets are of little consequence and easily replicated, the transferee will have the option to exclude the operation of the Directive. Whilst the Court of Appeal accepted this conclusion in *Betts v Brintel*[60] the EAT has shown some resistance to it in *Highland Council v Walker* and in *ECM (Vehicle Delivery services) Ltd. v Cox and*

59 And see para 17 of the European Commission's Explanatory Memorandum for an amended directive.

60 *Supra*

Others,[61] leading as it does to great uncertainty and to a weakening of employee rights.[62]

At the time of *Suzen* a further five cases had been referred to the ECJ on the application of the Directive to second generation contracting out. The first group of joined cases included two concerning the taking back in-house of a service contract, whereas the other was concerned with a second generation contractor and the two other joined cases concerned second generation contractors.[63] These cases reiterate the tests set out in *Suzen*, but the ECJ holds that the national court must initially identify whether the activity concerned was organised by the transferor contractor in the form of an economic entity which is sufficiently structured and autonomous to qualify as such, before going to consider whether that entity has been transferred. The Court reiterates that the transfer simply of an activity will not suffice. The slight change in emphasis leaves the national courts to decide, in the light of the *Spijkers* criteria, as interpreted in *Suzen*, whether a transfer of the entity could be said to have taken place.[64] Sometimes, however, the Court has itself decided whether a transfer existed, rather than limiting itself to clarifying

61 *The Times,* June 14th, 1998.

62 Davies argues that *Betts* goes contrary to a policy of employment protection, in that the transferee is given a legal incentive not to take on the staff formerly employed by the transferor. Taken to the Cleaners? Contracting Out services Yet Again, Paul Davies, (1997) *Industrial Law Journal,* 26, 2, pp 193-197.

63 *Francisco Hernadez Vidal SA v Gomez Perez, Santer v Hoecsht, Gomez Montana v Clara sol SA and Red Nacional de Ferrocarriles Espanoles,* joined cases C-127/96, C-222/96 & C-74/97, [1999] IRLR 132 ECJ, *Sanchez Hidalgo v Asociacion de Servicios Aser & Sociedad Cooperaitiva Minerva, Ziemann v Ziemann Sicherheit GmbH & Horst Bohn Sicherheitsdienst,* joined cases C-173/96 & C-247/96, [1999] IRLR 136, ECJ.

64 The European Free Trade Association Court in *Eidesund v Stavanger,* (note 41) considered that services rendered on the same premises with same equipment, which belonged to the recipient oil rig operator, were supportive of the transfer of an entity. The taking over of stores and stocks of provisions was relevant but of 'little significance' overall.

The retention of a high percentage of personnel was considered by the Court to be relevant, but the Court raised the question whether the take over of the personnel represented a desire to carry on the business or was merely a convenient way to carry it on. The retention of staff which possess a high degree of specialised expertise was considered more important than less specialised workers, particularly if the take over of personnel is a condition of the transfer, whilst the free advertisement of vacancies on the contractors terms is to the contrary. The overall conclusion that the termination of a catering contract with one company and the signing of a contract with another does not fall outside the Directive, nor is it excluded by absence of terms requiring the taking over of equipment or employees, is consonant with the emphasis in *Suzen* on the taking over of the effective assets assigned to the activity. An overall assessment remains to be made by the national court, however, on the basis of the above criteria.

the criteria as they apply in a given situation.[65] In this context it is worth noting that TUPE regulation 3(4)(b) provides that a transfer 'may take place whether or not any property is transferred to the transferee by the transferor'. This provision was introduced into TUPE by the 1993 Trade Union Reform and Employment Rights Act, in anticipation of enforcement proceedings intended to be brought by the Commission.[66] Although the Commission was then concerned that TUPE did not on its face cover leases and other such transfers where no property was exchanged, the amendment would certainly seem to permit the UK courts to find a transfer of an undertaking where no tangible assets are transferred, as in *Highland Council v Walker*,[67] in which a dog warden service was held by the EAT to constitute an undertaking

The then current ECJ case law was considered by the Court of Appeal in *Dines v Initial Health Care Services Ltd and Pall Mall Services Group Ltd.*[68] in which a cleaning contract at a hospital came to an end and the contract to provide cleaning services was awarded to a different contractor. The Industrial Tribunal had held that the business of the first contractor ceased when the contract came to an end and the second contractors commenced a new business. The Court of Appeal in *Dines* held, however, that 'the fact that another company takes over the provision of certain services as a result of competitive tendering does not mean that the first business or activity comes to an end'. Neil L J held that as the cleaning services were to be carried out by essentially the same labour force on the same premises and for the same health authority, there was a transfer of an undertaking under the Regulations, especially as hospital cleaning is not an activity which lends itself to the employment of many different techniques. In *Betts v Brintel*[69] Kennedy L J observed that a distinction can be drawn between a labour intensive activity such as hospital cleaning, in which if the staff are re-employed a court may conclude that an undertaking has been transferred, and other types of undertaking to which the application of the *Spijkers* test involves a more wide-ranging enquiry. Whilst *Dines* was accepted as correct on its facts, the circumstances in *Betts* led him to a different conclusion *ie* that no transfer had taken place absent the transfer of either assets or staff. Although the observation is clearly *obiter*, Kennedy LJ could see no logical reasoning why such an approach should not apply to first generation contracting out. In

[65] e.g. *Schmidt v Spar und Leihfasse der Fruheren Amster Bordesholm, Kiel und Cronshagen*, Case no C-392/92 [1994] IRLR 302, *Merckx and Neuhuys v Ford Motors Co (Belgium) SA* Cases 171/94 and 172/94, [1994] IRLR 407.

[66] C-382/92 [1994] IRLR 393.

[67] EAT/817/97 (Lexis).

[68] [1994] IRLR 336.

[69] *The Times*, April 1st, 1997.

Highland Council v Walker[70] Lord Johnston, however, was of the opinion that it is much more difficult to determine that a transfer has taken place in second generation situations, but he held that the contracting-in of a dog warden service in the instant case sat easily within the framework of *Schmidt*, although it was, he said, less than clear what effect *Suzen* has on *Schmidt*, the latter case not having been expressly disapproved by the Court of Justice in *Suzen*. The issue of whether there is a transfer was, however, held to be one of fact, subject only to misdirection or misconstruction of the authorities. However, there has to be a change in the identity of the employer for a transfer to occur, so that where a tender for services is won by an in-house bid, there is no transfer from one person to another, as is required by TUPE regulation 3.1. Therefore according to the EAT in *Burke v Royal Liverpool University Hospital NHS Trust*[71] where an in-house bid succeeds, the employees enjoy no special protection against wage and salary adjustments made with a view to winning the tender, as there is no transfer 'to another person' as is required by TUPE regulation 3(1).

Kennedy LJ also held in *Betts v Brintel* that the refusal of KLM to take on any of Brintel's staff was of very little relevance in the wide-ranging enquiry called for in the circumstances, even though Mr Justice Scott Baker had held in the High Court[72] that to say that because employees had not been taken on by the transferee helped establish that there was no transfer of an undertaking was to put the cart before the horse. However, in *Rotsart de Hertaing v J Benoidt SA (in liquidation)*[73] the Court of Justice held that contracts of employment existing on the date of the transfer are automatically transferred by the mere fact of the transfer despite the contrary intentions of the transferor or the transferee and despite the latter's refusal to fulfil his obligations. If it were to be argued that a refusal to take on the workforce in a labour-intensive undertaking determines whether there is a relevant transfer, this would completely turn the logic of *Rotsart de Hertaing* on its head and defeat the purposes of the Directive.

In the Court of Appeal in *Betts v Brintel Helicopters Ltd. and KLM Era Helicopters (UK) Ltd.*[74] Kennedy LJ held that '*Suzen* does represent a shift of emphasis, or at least a clarification of the law, and that some of the reasoning of the earlier decisions, if not the decisions themselves, may have to be reconsidered'.[75] There has, however, been some resistance to the implications

70 *Supra.*

71 [1997] ICR 730, EAT.

72 [1996] IRLR 45.

73 C-305/94 [1997] IRLR 127.

74 [1997] IRLR 361.

75 At para 52.

of the reasoning in *Suzen* and *Betts*, particularly evident in the conclusions drawn by the EAT in *ECM (Vehicle Delivery Service) Ltd. v Cox and Others*,[76] in which the EAT gagged on the proposition that the transferee could, by refusing to take on the workforce, preclude there being a relevant transfer within the scope of TUPE.[76a] With several cases pending before the Court of Justice on the definition of a transfer, especially in contracting-out situations, the opportunity may be taken to attempt a reasoned reconciliation of *Schmidt* and *Suzen*.

The revised Directive agreed in June 1998 incorporates the notion of a transfer of an economic entity as interpreted in *Suzen*, which means 'an organised grouping of resources which has the object of pursuing an economic activity, whether that activity is central or ancillary'. This expanded definition does not incorporate a non-exhaustive list of the factors identified in *Spjikers*, as recommended by the House of Lords Select Committee in April 1998 in its report, Acquired Rights Revisited,[77] but draws upon *Suzen*. The intention set out in the preamble that the revised Directive does not alter the scope of Directive 77/187, as interpreted by the Court, does not resolve the above issues. The reference to ancillary activities clearly includes contracting-out of services within the scope of the Directive, but only where there is the transfer of an economic entity, meaning an organised grouping of resources which has the objective of pursuing an economic activity. Whether the UK Government chooses to limit any 'grey areas' by legislating in a way more favourable to employees, as the Directive permits, remains to be seen in the light of consultations which will no doubt be conducted with interested parties.

Legal Transfer

For the Directive or the Regulations to come into play, the transfer must be accomplished by a 'legal transfer or merger'. In *Abels v Administrative Board*[78] the Court concluded that a sale effected in the context of Dutch receivership law which was not intended to result in the liquidation of the undertaking, constituted a transfer within the Directive. In approaching this issue, the Court held that in view of the fact some of the language version refers only to contractual transfers (*cession conventionelle*) but others, including the English version, are more widely phrased, it was not possible to rely solely on a textual

[76] Note 51.

[76a] Share transfers are covered neither by Directive 77/187 nor 98/50, so that an attempt to draw upon the purposive interpretation of the Directive in *ECM* so as to include a share transfer which had been arranged to preclude the application of TUPE was unsuccessful in *Brookes v BCS & CLS Care Services Ltd.* [1998] IRLR b36.

[77] HL 98 22nd Report.

[78] Case 135/83 [1987] 2 CMLR 406.

interpretation, but that it was necessary to have regard to the protective purposes of the Directive. The purposes of the Directive have therefore been considered by the Court in a number of cases concerned with the nature of a 'legal transfer' , commencing with three Danish cases arising from the transfer of a lease.[79] In *Daddy's Dance Hall* it was held that where, on the termination of a lease of a theatre restaurant, the lessor grants a new lease to a fresh lessee, who continues to run the business, there is a legal transfer under the directive. The Court held that

> 'The Directive applies whenever, as a result of a legal transfer or merger, there is a change in the natural or legal person responsible for the running of the undertaking and who because of this enters into contractual obligations as an employer towards the employees working in the undertaking. It of no importance to know if the ownership of the undertaking has been transferred.'[80]

This is so irrespective of the fact that the transfer takes place in two phases, in the sense that there is a transfer from original lessee to lessor and out to a new lessee. In *Daddy's Dance Hall* the new lessee continued to run the business without interruption, but in *Ny Moll Kro* the same result was reached even though the owner took back the lease and operated the business itself, after a period of temporary closure and in spite of the absence of the staff at the time of the transfer.

This purposeful employment interpretation arises because, in the view of the Court, whenever an employer changes without a change of ownership, the employees are in a comparable situation to that where the business has been sold and need equivalent protection. This approach was clarified in *P. Bork*, in which the Court held that a legal transfer occurs 'whenever within the framework of contractual relations'[81] there is any change in the natural or legal person responsible for operating the undertaking who enters into employment obligations. Thus though there need not be a change of ownership, there must be some form of legal transfer, albeit indirect and involving a third party, which governs the transaction.[82]

[79] *Forenigen Af Arbejdsledere I Danmark v Daddy's Dance Hall a/s* [1988] IRLR 315, LO v Ny Moll Kro [1989] IRLR 37, *P. Bork International A/S v Forenigen Af Arbejdsledere I Danmark* [1989] IRLR 41.

[80] At point 16.

[81] At point 13.

[82] TUPE 3(4) provides that a transfer may be effected by a series of two or more transactions and may take place even though no property is transferred.

The emphasis on the contractual nature of a legal transfer was not sustained in *Redmond Stichting*, where the Advocate General was of the opinion that a consensual agreement would be sufficient to meet the criteria of the Directive, even if the processes in question fail to satisfy the strict national definition in question of a contract. The Advocate General argues from the inclusion of 'gentlemen's agreements' within the competition regime of Article 85, which must be given a Community meaning in order to make it effective, to include even incomplete agreements of the sort which underlay the transfer of functions between charitable bodies in *Redmond Stichting*.[83] The Court had regard to the protective employment purposes of the Directive and held that the unilateral decision to switch funding from one charitable body to another, was to be compared to the unilateral decision of a lessee to terminate and transfer a lease. Furthermore, there was an element of agreement between the two foundations on the process of transfer of functions, which took place within the context of contractual relationship as regards the subsidy gained from the public authorities. Thus the Court adopts a highly purposive interpretation of the requirement that there be a legal transfer before the Directive is operative.

In *Merckx* there was no contract signed between the transferor dealer and the transferee dealer, although both were in a contractual relationship with the manufacturer, Ford Motors, and had reached at least a verbal agreement as to the handling of customers and the transfer of staff. In response to the argument that no legal transfer had taken place, the Court cited the case law discussed above[84] and concluded that

> 'It is clear from the case that, for the Directive to be applicable, it is not necessary for there to be a direct contractual relationship between the transferor and the transferee'

Do Public Administrative Structures Fall Within The Directive?

The question as to whether the exercise of public administrative functions could constitute an economic entity within the Directive was raised in *Henke v Gemeinde Schierke & Verwaltungsgemeinschaft 'Brocken'*[85] in which a number of municipalities created between them a common collective organisation and the original municipalities were dissolved. The mayor's secretary in one of these municipalities, who was not re-engaged by the administrative collectivity, brought an action claiming that her contract of employment had been

[83] At points 21-23.

[84] At points 28-30.

[85] [1996] IRLR 701, ECJ.

transferred to the new structure. In its original Explanatory Memorandum to the first draft of the Directive, the Commission had proposed to include within the definition of a transfer all companies, including co-operative societies and other persons governed by public or private law, save for those which are non-profit making. The definition of a transfer in the version adopted in 1977 was far briefer, simply referring to the transfer of an undertaking, business or part of a business. Once not for profit organisations had been brought within the scope of the Directive in *Redmond Stichting*,[86] where the Court emphasised the change in the legal person of the employer in the context of the continuity of activities of two foundations, it might be considered that the Court would apply the Directive equally to governmental organisations. True to this approach, the Advocate General in *Henke* argued that such a change in the legal person of the employer responsible for public administrative functions should fall within the scope of the Directive. He rejected the argument that if the legislative basis of the Directive is Article 100, public institutions cannot constitute an 'undertaking', since they commonly carry out activities of an economic character, such as waste disposal, providing public transport or the running of day nurseries. However, the Advocate General did not favour drawing a distinction between the economic activities of public bodies and their administrative, regulatory or governmental functions because the boundary between the public and the private sector is fluid and changing with the growth of contracting out and privatisation.[87] Nor, the Advocate General argued, does Article 100 imply that public administrative activity cannot constitute an undertaking. He based his argument on the primary purpose of the Directive being to protect the rights and interests of employees, rather than to secure the functioning of the common market, as did Advocate General Van Gerven in *Redmond Stichting*.[88] As the protective function of the Directive is to be exercised in relation to all employees within the various schemes of national employment protection, wherever workers are employed, including within the public sector, he argued

[86] A view confirmed in the Article 169 proceedings *EC v UK* C-382/92 [1994] ECR 1-2435, [1994] IRLR 392, para 44.

[87] Interestingly, in its submissions the UK cited the Eurocontrol case (Case C-346/92 *SAT Fluggelschaft v Eurocontrol* [1994] ECR 1-43) on air traffic control as one involving the use of public powers which are not of an economic nature, even though in 1997 the proposition has arisen that air traffic control in the UK should be privatised!

[88] '(W)hether a natural or legal person is an undertaking within the meaning of a Directive which...has a distinctly social purpose, it should be of decisive importance whether one or more persons have the status of employees of the said natural or legal person within the context of an employment contract or relationship within the meaning of Article 3(1) of the Directive.'

that they should be brought within the scope of the Directive.[89] Neither is such an approach incompatible with Article 100, in so far as all employment, if carried out for remuneration,[90] constitutes economic activity because it involves participation in the Community labour market.

The Court, however, chose to base itself on the first recital of the preamble to the Directive, holding that

> 'The Directive sets out to protect workers against the potentially unfavourable consequences for them of changes in the structure of undertakings resulting from economic trends at national and community level, through, *inter alia* transfers of undertakings, businesses or parts of businesses to other employers as a result of transfers or mergers.

The Court also emphasised that in its different language versions the Directive refers to businesses and undertakings, not words apt to describe public administrative functions, which '(e)ven if it is assumed that those activities had aspects of an economic nature, they could only be ancillary.' The terse judgment of the Court does not, however, refer to the Advocate General's opinion that the boundaries of the administrative and the economic are fluid and changing, in the sense that what is now considered to be capable of being provided by private contractors for profit is much wider than was previously thought, including even private prisons. The argument that all employment is inherently economic in so far as it is part of the labour market was implicitly rejected, even though the preamble to the Directive makes clear that its purpose is the protection of employees.

The revised Article 1(1)(c) of the 1998 Directive expressly includes 'public or private undertakings engaged in economic activities whether or not they are operated for gain', but goes on to exclude an 'administrative reorganisation of public administrative authorities, or the transfer of administrative functions between public authorities'. This formulation, which draws directly on the decision in *Henke,* excludes from the scope of the Directive the reorganisation of structures of the public administration or the transfer of administrative functions between public administrative authorities. Clearly the impact of *Henke*, and the reformulation of the Directive drawn from it, upon the rights

89 In *EC v UK* (*supra*) Advocate General Van Gerven argued that the distinguishing feature of an economic activity is that it is carried out for remuneration and the sphere in which this occurs is not of decisive importance.

90 The A G cites *Lawrie-Blum v Land Baden-Wurtemburg* Case 66/85 (1986) for the proposition that all gainful or remunerated employment, irrespective of the sector in which it takes place, is an economic activity.

of employees affected by local government or health service reorganisation could be considerable, affecting all those engaged in governmental functions. The Directive clearly recognises that both private and public undertakings can engage in economic activities, whether or not these are operating for gain. There is nonetheless a possible margin of dispute between what can be termed public administration and economic activities. Is housing administration an administrative function or an economic activity, especially as it may be contracted-out. Likewise, is air traffic control a public administrative function or an economic activity, in the light of privatisation proposals? Similarly, *Henke* raises a question over the application of TUPE to the current wave of mergers of NHS Trusts and to the application of private capital to public infrastructure projects via the Public Finance Initiative. Despite the arguments of the Advocate General in *Henke* and any disagreement concealed behind the spare judgment of the Court on this issue, it is this formulation which has been incorporated into the revised Directive.

Whilst the matter was not considered by the Court, which decided the issue on other grounds, the Advocate General in *Henke* was of the opinion that where corporations are governed by public law, the transfer of functions by public law agreement falls within the scope of a legal transfer.

Conclusions

The Court of Justice has interpreted the scope of a transfer by reference to the purposes of the Directive, objectives which are themselves ambiguous, as a labour market measure having both an economic and a social logic. The Directive is concerned with the labour market implications of restructuring and rationalisation in product markets and overtly unconcerned with the internal labour market of large undertakings. Thus *Spjikers* placed its emphasis upon the transfer of an 'economic entity', locating the Directive firmly as dealing with the labour market consequences of rationalisation and mergers which arise from closer economic integration. In later cases from *Rask* to *Schmidt* the Court seemed prepared to contemplate the application of the Directive, without feeling itself circumscribed by a precise application of the test that there be the transfer of an economic entity, so long as there was a change in the legal identity of the employer. In this way the sub-contracting of services and ancillary activities became subject to the Directive, even where there was a transfer of neither tangible nor intangible assets. In this phase of its jurisprudence the Court of Justice gave great weight to the social logic of the Directive, extending its protection to a wider range of employees. These developments paralleled the tendency for contracting out and privatisation to replace the bureaucratic structures that normally characterise the internal labour market of large organisations with external market relations. As the boundary of market and administered labour relations changed, the application of the Directive simply followed suit. In the third phase of its jurisprudence, ushered in by *Henke* and *Suzen*, the Court of Justice once more became seized of the need for the transfer of an economic entity to entail more than the transfer simply of an activity, before the Directive can apply. In this phase the economic logic of the Directive again predominates, withdrawing from what may be seen as internal labour market questions, even though the legal identity of the employer changes. The effect, however, is that employees affected by the tendency to contract-out work, itself most surely the result of what the preamble to the Directive terms 'economic trends bringing in their wake at both national and Community level, changes in the structure of undertakings' may be excluded from the protection of the Directive.

Davies has advanced the 'hidden balancing' hypothesis in another context,[91] where he argues that the impact of social measures has been implicitly weighed by the Court of Justice against the capacity of such measures to limit the principle of free movement. In the context of the globalisation of the economy, where employers need to maintain competitivity and governments need to reduce public expenditure, is it legitimate to infer that the Court of Justice has implicitly weighed the need to maintain competitivity and control public expenditure against the protective purposes of the Directive. Whilst the Court does not engage in an explicit balancing of the protection of employees against the need to ensure the freedom of employers to engage in what the Growth White Paper terms 'farming-out and sub-contracting', the Court, even while reaching decisions on legitimate legal criteria, does not take its decisions insulated from either public opinion or the changing intellectual diagnosis of the problems which confront the construction of Europe.

Can *Suzen* be reconciled with *Schmidt* as regards the definition of an undertaking? Whilst in *Suzen* an 'entity' is characterised as 'an organised grouping of persons and assets' in *Schmidt* it is the transfer of 'the obligations of an employer' which is crucial. Is this the substitution of a commercial for an employment law test, as Davies argues?[92] The decision in *Suzen* is certainly referable to *Spijkers* and foreshadowed in the analysis of the Advocate Generals in *Schmidt* and *Merckx*, but it does seem to represent a change of emphasis by the Court, when compared to its decision in *Schmidt*. Davies makes a telling point that the decision in *Schmidt* was inconsistent with the interpretation of the parallel domestic provisions in both France and Germany, although it

91 Paul Davies, Market Integration and Social Policy, *Industrial Law Journal*, (1995) 24, 1, at pp. 67-68.

92 Taken to the Cleaners? Contracting Out of Services Yet Again. *ILJ*, 26, 2, pp. 193-197 at p. 195.

had the great merit of certainty in the UK. It is indeed the commercial consequences of *Schmidt* that have seemed to have led to a re-evaluation of the balance between the economic and organisational emphasis of *Spjikers* and the employment protection emphasis of *Schmidt*.

With the agreement on a revised directive incorporating a definition of a transfer based upon *Suzen* and *Henke*, the Council has brought a measure of certainty to this vexed question. It is evident, however, that the application of this test will not be entirely straightforward, with the issue as to how far a transferee may act so as to control the application of the Directive, by declining to take on the workforce or the assets of an out-going service provider, remaining an open question. Equally, the transfer of an economic entity, consisting in an organised grouping of resources, will need to be determined ultimately in the light of the *Spjikers* criteria. In implementing the new Directive there is the possibility that the UK, and other Member States, may choose to enact the amended Directive in ways which seek to resolve some of the current issues in favour of the affected workers.

4. The History and Nature of Contracting-Out of Services in the Public Sector: An Overview

Karl Larrad

Introduction

This chapter is concerned with setting 'contracting-out' of services in the public sector in its historical, economic and political context as part of the Conservative government's wider programme of 'privatisation' after 1979. The 'privatisation' process has resulted in a fundamental restructuring of the public sector economy, labour market and the way services are delivered in the public sector.[1]

The term 'privatisation' is a broad concept encompassing not only high profile transfer of public assets into the private sector but also the competitive tendering of public services. It is often used interchangeably with a plethora of terms like, 'contracting-out', 'compulsory competitive tendering' (CCT), 'externalisation of services,' 'out-sourcing', 'market testing,' 'facilities management' and 'management buy-outs'. However, this can be misleading. Professor Brian Napier defines some of the differences.[2] 'Facilities

1 Davies, P.L., *Interim Report : Contracting Out of Services, The Impact of Directive 77/187/EEC in The United Kingdom, Ireland and Denmark,* Oxford University, October 1993, pp 8-9.

2 Napier, B., *CCT, Market Testing and Employment Rights*, London, The Institute of Employment Rights, 1993, p.2.

Management' is a process which has gained acceptance in the National Health Service (NHS) and for certain services in local government. It often involves the contracting-out of an activity such as computer services to a private contractor by mutual agreement, who makes use of its own personnel and resources.[3] 'CCT' consists of the compulsory tendering of certain defined local and public authority (as opposed to central government) services which is governed by an extremely complex statutory framework.[4] The CCT process does not preclude in-house bids and indeed it only applies if an authority wishes to continue to provide certain defined services with its own directly employed workforce. The Conservative government's policy of CCT was predicated upon its view that 'services should be provided in-house only if a local authority can demonstrate that it can provide the service as effectively and efficiently as the private sector'.[5] Thus, CCT is not intended to result in the automatic contracting-out of public services and under this regime they can be retained in-house if the in-house service provider submits a tender which shows it can do so competitively.[6]

'Management buy-outs' involve former in-house managers setting up a private company to tender for services for their own profit formerly performed in-house. This has occurred in the National Health Service, central government and local government.[7] 'Market Testing' is a term which refers to the process of subjecting to voluntary competition public sector services and is particularly linked with the civil service. It is a process carried out as a matter of policy to test the value for money of in-house services against tenders from private contractors rather than enforced by statute.[8] A strategic decision

3 In-house employees are now usually transferred to the contractor on the basis that the Transfer of Undertakings (Protection of Employment) Regulations 1981 (as amended) SI 1981 No. 1794 may apply.

4 Part III of the Local Government, Planning and Land Act 1980; Part 1 of the Local Government Act 1988; and the Local Government Act 1992. The defined activities under the 1988 Act include, *inter alia*, refuse collection, cleaning, catering, grounds maintenance, repair and maintenance of vehicles, sports and leisure management together with certain professional 'white-collar' services such as legal, finance, personnel, housing management, IT/IS construction and property services. The Local Government Bill 1998 proposes the abolition of CCT from 2 January 2000. This will be achieved by the repeal of Part III of the 1980 Act, Part 1, Section 32 and Schedule 6 of the 1998 Act, and Section 8-11 and Schedule 1 of the 1992 Act.

5 *Competing for Quality : Buying Better Public Services*, HMSO, London, November 1991, CM 1730, p.22.

6 See Department of the Environment Circular 5/96, 2nd April 1996; paragraphs 19-20, page 5 for guidance on evaluating quality and price.

7 Napier, *supra*, n.2, p.2, and Sparke, A, *The Compulsory Competitive Tendering Guide*, London, Butterworths, 2nd Edition, 1996, pp. 195-196 and *Better Quality Services: A Handbook on Creating Public/Private Partnerships Through Market Testing and Contracting-Out*, HMSO, 1998, pp.63-64.

8 Napier, *supra*, n.2, p.2.

is taken at the outset when selecting potential activities for market testing whether for policy or management reasons, the service should be contracted-out to the private sector without an in-house bid.[9] However, market testing which involves an in-house bid does not necessarily lead to contracting-out and the service may be retained in-house if it offers value for money.[10] Notwithstanding the differences in the above terminology they are all based on the same liberal economic philosophy which has seen a general development of market mechanisms in the public sector after 1979.[11]

The Public Sector

Any attempt to distinguish between the public sector and the private sector is fraught with imprecision. Perrin[12] argues that an initial distinction can be made in terms of purpose and ownership. Where ownership is by and for the benefit of private sector persons and organisations such as shareholders, it can be categorised as part of the private sector. However, where ownership is in the public domain and exercised for the benefit of society as a whole it forms part of the public sector. Thus, organisations whose main objective is to make profits are within the private sector; whereas those concerned with 'public service' provision are within the public sector.[13] This is of course simplistic. For example, nationalised industries attempted to make profits. Furthermore, as a result of CCT, local authority direct labour organisations (DLO's) and direct service organisations (DSO's) are organised along commercial lines.[14]

9 *The Government's Guide to Market_Testing*, London, HMSO, 1993, paragraph 1.5, page 2. The contracting-out for policy and management reasons has included transfer of training and enterprise schemes to TEC's, contracting out grounds maintenance in Royal Parks, use of contracts with private sector for major IT projects in the DSS, and privatizing PSA Services and contracting out of property, design and project management services. C.f *Competing for Quality*: 1991, Office of Public Service and Science, Efficiency Unit, *supra* n.5, page 10.

10 *The Government's Guide to Market Testing*, *supra*, n.9, paragraphs 1.10 to 1.11 and 1.14, pages 3-4. The Government's Guide to Market Testing has been replaced by a new document entitled, *Better Quality Services: A Handbook on Creating Public/Private Partnerships Through Market Testing and Contracting Out*, HMSO, 1998.

11 Napier, *supra*, n.2, page 3 and Walsh, K, *Competitive Tendering for Local Authority Services: Initial Experiences*, HMSO, London, 1991, paragraph 2.1, page 7.

12 Perrin, J.R. 'Differentiating Financial Accountability and Management in Governments, Public Services and Charities,' *Financial Accountability of Management* Vol.1 No. 1 1985 pp 11-32.

13 Wilson, J, 'Public Services in the UK', Chapter One in John Wilson and Peter Hinton, (eds), *Public Services & The 1990's : Issues in Public Service Finance and Management* 1993, Tudor Business Publishing, page 2.

14 Section 10 of the Local Government Act 1988 empowers the Secretary of State to specify financial objectives for DSO's and for different defined activities. All defined services under the Local Government, Planning and Land Act 1980 and most services under the Local Government Act 1988 must break even after allowing for a six per cent per annum rate of return on capital assets employed by the DSO. The exceptions are building, cleaning and leisure management where costs should not exceed income.

The public sector is a large, complex and diverse collection of organisations and may be divided into three groups. Firstly, central government (the civil service) and other, quasi-governmental, bodies funded through taxation, such as the NHS. Secondly, local government which consists of 467 local authorities throughout the UK[15] which are funded through a combination of central government and local taxation. Thirdly, those dwindling number of public undertakings (nationalised industries) with legal duties for the provision of transport, energy and communications.[16] As we shall see, different market mechanisms have been employed depending on which part of the public sector they were being applied to. Competitive tendering for public services has focused primarily on the civil service, the NHS, and local government.

PRIVATISATION

Prior to 1979, the political debate about public ownership and the provision of public services was conducted within the sterile context of 'nationalisation' and 'denationalisation'. The Thatcher government popularised the more trendy term 'privatisation'.[17] Mrs Thatcher argued that privatisation, 'was one of the central means of reversing the corrosive and corrupting effects of socialism'. It 'is at the centre of any programme of reclaiming territory for freedom'.[18] So what does it mean? It is essentially an umbrella term encompassing various measures designed to reduce the power of the State and enhance private sector provision and ownership by selling off public assets such as British Airways, British Telecom and the National Freight Corporation to promote competition and thereby lead to improved efficiency.

It is possible to detect two broad strands to the policy of privatisation. Firstly, denationalisation which refers to the transfer of state ownership in nationalised industries to the private sector in order to improve efficiency and reduce the cost to the Exchequer. However, privatisation is a wider concept than this. It also encompasses liberalisation measures designed to increase competition in the private sector in the provision of publicly funded goods and services. Generally speaking, this is understood to mean deregulation - that is the removal of monopoly powers of certain industries such as occurred with the opening up of the Telecommunications industry to wider competition; and the subject of this chapter, competitive tendering.[19]

15 *Municipal Year Book*, 1999, Volume 1, Newman Books, page 2.

16 Winchester, D., 'Industrial Relations in the Public Sector' in G S Bain (ed), *Industrial Relations in Britain*. Blackwell, 1983 pages 155-178 at pp.156-157.

17 Geoffrey Howe credits David Howell with the invention of the word 'Privatisation' (See G Howe, *Conflict of Loyalty*, Macmillan, London, 1994, page 253).

18 Thatcher, M., *The Downing Street Years*, 1993, Harper Collins, London, p 676.

19 J. Wilson, 'Privatisation', chapter 5 in J Wilson and Peter Hinton (eds), *Public Services & The 1990's: Issues in Public Service Finance and Management*, Tudor Business Publishing Ltd, 1993, page 82.

Denationalisation

The long term aim had been the product of Opposition, and was alluded to in *The Right Approach to the Economy* in 1977: 'to reduce the preponderance of state ownership in our community'.[20] However, privatisation hardly featured in the 1979 Conservative election manifesto which promised : 'to sell back to private ownership the recently nationalised aerospace and shipbuilding concerns ... and selling shares in the National Freight Corporation to the general public.'[21] Indeed, it was not a major concern in the 1983 election.[22]

From the outset the privatisation policy lacked a coherent set of aims and objectives. It was only with the passage of time that it changed in a pragmatic way into a consistent philosophy of 'rolling back the frontiers of the State'.[23] As Geoffrey Howe argues, the policy of privatisation took time to gain momentum until it was able to secure political and public support.[24] Denationalisation commenced cautiously with special asset sales which included portfolio sales of shares of companies in which the government had an interest but which were not part of the public sector. In 1979, disposals began with a £290 million tranche of BP shares. [25] The early privatisations carried out between 1979-1983 did not involve major public sector monopolies but government-owned industries which competed with the private sector such as British Aerospace, Ferranti, ICL, British Sugar, ICI, National Freight Corporation, Britoil, Sealink, Land Rover, British Telecom, and Enterprise Oil. Between 1986-1989 privatisation affected British Gas, British Steel, British Airports Authority, British Airways, Royal Ordnance factories and the National Bus Company. Between 1989-1991, Regional Water Authorities, and Regional Electricity Companies were added to the list.[26] After 1992, privatisation was applied to British Coal and British Rail's monopoly was ended. It is beyond the scope of this chapter to make an assessment of the merits of privatisation and it is intended to focus on competitive tendering, and contracting-out.

20 Howe, G., *Conflict of Loyalty*, London, Macmillan, 1994, page 253.

21 Thatcher, M., *supra*. n.18, at pages 677-678.

22 Brittan, S., 'The Politics and Economics of Privatisation', *Political Quarterly* 55, 1984, pages 109-128 at p.109.

23 O'Connell-Davidson, J. 'Metamorphosis? Privatisation and the Restructuring of Management and Labour', (chapter for an edited book which may not be published for some time) pages 1-35 at page 1.

24 Howe, G., *supra*, n.20, at p.253.

25 Howe, G., *supra*, n.20, at p.254.

26 Clarke, P., 'The Argument for Privatisation' in J Neuberger (ed), *Privatisation: Fair Shares for All or Selling the Family Silver*? London, Paper Mac, 1987, pages 66-91, at pages 68-69; and Brittan, S., The Politics and Economics of Privatisation, *Political Quarterly*, 55, 1984, pp.109-128 at pp.109-111.

CONTRACTING-OUT

Contracting-out the provision of public services to the private sector is not a new phenomenon. The public sector had long operated before 1979 some form of competitive tendering procedure to enable private sector contractors to bid against one another for contracts to provide goods and services. However, this was done in a pragmatic way to meet specific needs, for example, as a way to handle labour shortages particularly prevalent in the 1950's and to provide expertise which was not cost effective to maintain in-house. During the 1950's a number of contracts were placed with the private sector for refuse collection and waste disposal, albeit mainly in the South-east. There was also a limited amount of contracting-out in the NHS in the 1960's. These contracts do not appear to have been politically contentious. Indeed, public sector trade unions were fully recognised, and staff enjoyed the same rates of pay as their local authority counterparts. Needless to say, contracting-out often proved to be more expensive than in-house provision.[27]

After 1979, the nature of contracting-out in the public sector changed and became increasingly politicised. Competitive tendering was to be mandatory for certain services and imposed in the face of trade union hostility. Generally, where authorities were satisfied with in-house provision, the in-house workforce has been permitted to bid against private contractor tenderers. The in-house team have kept the service where they have submitted the most competitive bid.[28] Thus, even where services are retained in-house it has forced the public sector to monitor its costs and to work to a contract specification in the interest of taxpayers.

Prior to 1992, and developments in European case law, it was widely believed that the Transfer of Undertakings (Protection of Employment) Regulations 1981 (TUPE) did not apply to competitive tendering of services in the public sector. Consequently, if the private sector submitted the most competitive bid, the in-house service was disbanded and public sector employees were made redundant. Given the labour intensive nature of the services subject to competitive tendering, authorities who were bound by national terms and conditions of employment were at a disadvantage compared to the private sector who could submit a lower tender based on inferior terms and conditions and fewer staff.[29]

27 Ascher, K., *The Politics of Privatisation*, London, Macmillan, 1987, pages 23-24.

28 Ibid., page 11.

29 Wilson, J., *supra*, n.19, page 93. Developments in European case law after 1992 have shown that services contracted-out following competitive tendering may involve the transfer of an undertaking: *Watson Rask and Christensen v ISS Kantineservice* [1993] IRLR 133; *Dr Sophie Redmond Stichting v Bartol* [1992] IRLR 366; and *Schmidt* v *Spar* [1994] IRLR 302. However the position is less certain in the light of *Süzen v Zehnacker* [1997] IRLR 255 and *Betts* v *Brintel Helicopters Ltd* [1997] IRLR, 361.

The enforced nature of this type of tendering has proved extremely controversial and bedevilled central government relations with both the NHS and local government under the Thatcher and Major Administrations.

We now turn to the driving forces behind the policy, many of which overlap with the objectives of denationalisation before looking in more detail at competitive tendering in central government, the NHS and local government.

ECONOMIC FACTORS

In 1979 the Conservative government was returned to power determined to reverse a century of relative economic decline which was considered to be exacerbated by excessive state intervention in pursuance of Keynesian economic policies in the post-war years which had led to the economic crisis of the mid 1970's. This manifested itself in terms of slowing economic growth and rising unemployment coupled with rising inflation.[30] This reversal of economic policy was to entail a radical departure from the consensus politics of the post-war years. There was to be no more accommodation with trade unions in terms of incomes policies combined with what were perceived to be failed macro-economic measures designed to maintain full employment.[31]

The instrument of this proposed economic renaissance was to be the control of inflation through the economic philosophy of 'Monetarism', market forces and greater competition, propounded by its leading exponent, Milton Friedman. Basically, this emphasised the importance of controlling two interdependent economic variables - the money supply and the Public Sector Borrowing Requirement (PSBR).[32] A corollary of this was high interest rates to restrain the availability of credit and reduce debt.[33]

This counter-inflationary approach was bolstered by the Medium-Term Financial Strategy (MTFS) announced in the 1980 budget and maintained in various forms throughout the 1980's. This was intended to be the monetary framework for the economy over a period of years, which set targets to reduce inflation by decreasing the money supply and announced the intention of increasing interest rates to achieve this.[34]

30 O'Connell - Davidson, *supra*, n.23, page 1.

31 Crafts, N., Reversing relative economic decline? The 1980's in historical perspective, in Oxford Review of Economic Policy, Vol 7, No. 3, 1991, pages 81-98 at p.81 and Anderman, P., *Labour Law : Management Decisions and Workers' Rights*, London, Butterworths, 2nd Ed, 1993, pages 9-10.

32 Johnson, A., 'The Historical and Legal Context' in M. T. Lyons and A. Johnson, *Preparing the Winning Bid : A Handbook for Competitive Tendering*, Charles Knight Publishing, 1992, page 27.

33 Davies, P. and Freedland, M., *Labour Legislation and Public Policy*, Oxford, Clarendon Press, 1993, pages 430-431.

34 Ibid., p.431 and Thatcher, M., *The Downing Street Years*, London, 1993, pages 96-97 and G. Howe, *Conflict of Loyalty*, London, 1994, pages 161-164.

Another important feature of the MTFS and monetary policy was to restrain public expenditure - to reduce the annual deficit of public expenditure compared with public revenue known as the PSBR.[35]

Thus, the government abandoned Keynesian economic policies which urged demand-led growth in the economy and which regarded public expenditure as a virtue if it meant full employment and which underpinned the mixed economy and the welfare state. The switch to Monetarism and the control of inflation reflected a lower priority for these goals. However, Monetarism had its downside, not least a marked increase in unemployment which doubled between 1979 and 1981 and passed 2 million in 1980 and 3 million in 1981.[36] One commentator has suggested that this created an 'essential pre-condition for the reduction of costs by competitive tendering: the ready availability of low cost labour'.[37]

Government demanded 'good housekeeping' at both the macro-economic and micro-economic level. Thus, the public sector found itself subject to 'cash limits'. This market forces ideology entailed an overhaul of labour legislation and a reduction in trade union power since they found such policies anathema and were seen as an obstacle to the free market. The policy of 'privatisation' in its widest sense was an attempt to restrain counter-inflationary tendencies in the public sector but more importantly represented part of a coherent collection of measures designed to deregulate the labour market economy and allow government to withdraw from a collectivised industrial society.[38]

Restructuring of the Public Sector Labour Economy

Between 1918-1979 successive governments pursued a corporatist approach to industrial relations which encouraged the private sector to emulate the State's example in the public sector as a 'model employer'. Thus, employees were encouraged to join trade unions on the basis that it promoted good industrial relations; and promoted national collective bargaining through which generally good packages of job security, terms and conditions of employment were negotiated.[39]

35 Davies and Freedland, *supra*, n.33, page 431.

36 Ibid, page 432 & Johnson, A., *supra*, n.32, page 28.

37 Johnson, A., *supra*, n.32 page 28.

38 Davies & Freedland, *supra*, n.33, pages 432-435 and page 639.

39 Fredman, S. and Morris, G., 'The State as Employer : Is it unique?' (1990) 19 *Industrial Law Journal* 142 at page 142.

The advent of the Thatcher government in 1979 broke with these ideals, which were anathema to its free market principles, and which regarded public services as 'inefficient, uncompetitive and an obstacle to the market'.[40]

Integral to the government's commitment to reduce inflation and public expenditure was its resolve to cut back the size of the public sector and thereby weaken public sector trade unions. It was seen as important to challenge and undermine collective pay bargaining which pursued comparability of pay and other conditions with the private sector.[41] The lowering of wage expectations would assist in the control of inflation. Thus, the policy of contracting-out public services and privatisation was to be a means whereby the public sector of the economy was to be subject to market forces, freed from its former rigidities which distorted the operation of the labour market. It would place a greater imperative on adopting more flexible working practices including reduced staffing.[42]

It is not possible to say with certainty whether the driving force behind the policy was primarily the covert political objective of weakening public sector trade unions or whether it was the overt economic advantages which supposedly flow from competitive tendering.[43] On balance it is likely to have been a happy coincidence of interest.

Central Government

The need for the Civil Service to reduce the 'headcount' and to achieve 'value for money' began before 1979. Ascher argues that ironically it was as a result of the devaluation crisis of 1967 which led Wilson's Labour government in 1968 to contract-out a substantial amount of cleaning services in central government departments. This arose out of the perceived need to reduce the size of the Civil Service. It resulted in savings of around £500,000, a loss of 35,000 jobs and enabled contract cleaning firms to gain an important foothold.[44]

Consequently, in 1979 the Conservative government found contracting-out commonplace in the Civil Service. It was not just confined to cleaning but extended to 'White Collar' services such as computing and management consultancy. However, the scope of 'contractorisation' was to be extended.

40 Ibid., page 145.

41 Davies and Freedland, *supra*, n.33, page 616.

42 Ibid., pp 615-619.

43 Ascher, K., *supra* n.27, pages 47-49.

44 Ibid., pages 24-25, 52.

In 1980, Mrs Thatcher announced in Parliament that it was the government's policy to transfer work out of the public service where this was 'commensurate with sound management and good value for money for the taxpayer'. Towards the end of 1982 a renewed commitment to contracting-out was made in areas such as cleaning, building and grounds maintenance, printing work, vehicle maintenance, debt collection and training.[45] In March 1985, the government announced plans to extend its programme of competitive tendering and contracting-out.

The Treasury highlighted suitable areas such as: laundry, cleaning, catering, security and maintenance work. Other possible areas included press cutting, postal, messenger and library services. The first round of tendering was to be completed by April 1987, and re-tendered regularly.[46] By 1985 the proportion of contracting-out was already high. An estimated 84 per cent of cleaning; 83 per cent of maintenance work and 73 per cent of laundry work were contracted-out. Whether contracting-out has resulted in savings is a contentious area and Ascher argues that they were only modest.[47] The Ministry of Defence and the Property Services Agency were in the forefront of contracting-out and work transferred to the private sector included warship refitting; transport; aircraft servicing and repair; motor transport repair; ship design; estate management; catering; cleaning; gardening; mail services; security; insurance; warehousing; teaching and so on. In the Property Services Agency, the number of employees reduced from 50,142 in April 1979 to 24,296 by April 1985 and in March 1983 the government claimed that savings of £42m had been made (Hansard 20.4.83). From 1983, civil service catering was opened up to competitive tendering. In the Treasury, security was contracted-out; in the Department of the Environment, cleaning and security; in the then DHSS, cleaning and in the DTI, security; in the Home Office, security, cleaning, catering, transport and building maintenance.[48]

Civil Service reform was a high priority for Margaret Thatcher. Contracting-out of services was closely linked with her commitment to reducing the size of the Civil Service and she imposed an immediate recruitment freeze to reduce the government's pay bill. In 1979, the size of the Civil Service was 732,000. By May 1980 she was able to tell the House of

45 Ibid, pages 42-43.

46 Ibid, page 44.

47 Ibid, pages 44-45.

48 *Competitive Tendering in the Public Sector*, Institute of Personnel Management and Incomes Data Services Public Sector Unit, October 1986, pages 13-14.

Commons that it had fallen to 705,000 with an intention of reducing it further to 630,000 by 1984.[49]

In 1981 the government put what it preached into practice by abandoning collective bargaining for the Civil Service. This precipitated the Civil Service pay strike of 1981-1982, which culminated in a settlement which included an inquiry under the Chairmanship of Sir John Megaw into the future of Civil Service pay determination. This was an attempt to reconcile the twin roles of government, firstly as employer and more importantly its responsibility for the national economy. This represented a conflict between the unions' adherence to pay comparability (with the private sector) and the government's imposition of cash limits to contain public expenditure.[50] In September 1983, the government decided to withdraw the fair wages clauses from all its existing and prospective contracts, which resulted in reduced pay rates.

In 1988 these reforms culminated in the radical 'Next Steps' programme.[51] In order to improve efficiency, the 'administrative work' of government departments (as opposed to 'policy advice') was to be the responsibility of executive agencies staffed by civil servants and headed by a Chief Executive free from day to day control of government departments.[52] This was partial privatisation and its significance lies in reforming the management of the Civil Service. Davies and Freedland consider these reforms to be a 'combination of localisation of pay and other terms and conditions and contractualisation'. Such an approach was designed to separate the policy makers and purchasers of services from the providers of those services.[53]

A substantial expansion of competition during the 1990's under John Major's government was promised in *The Citizen's Charter*[54] which endorsed the subjection of public services to competition to secure quality and value for money. The proposals were published in a Treasury White Paper, *Competing for Quality : Buying Better Public Services.*[55]

49 Thatcher, M., *supra*, n.18, page 32 and page 46, This target was achieved without compulsory redundancies because some 80,000 left the Civil Service annually due to resignation or retirement. In 1990-91 the Civil Service employed 560,000 employees representing a reduction of 24 per cent, c.f. J. Wilson. 'Public sector services in the UK' in J Wilson and Peter Hinton (eds), *Public Services & the 1990's* pp. 3-4.

50 Howe, G, *supra*, n.20, at page 252 and Davies and Freedland, *supra*, n.33, page 547.

51 *See Improving Management in Government: The Next Steps,* Efficiency Unit, London, 1988.

52 Thatcher, M., *supra,* n 18, page 49 and Davies and Freedland, *supra*, n.33, pages 622, 628-630.

53 Davies & Freedland, *supra,* n.33, pages 629-631.

54 Cm. 1599, July 1991. Also see *The Citizen's Charter. First Report* : 1992 (Cm 2101, November 1992) which sets out the aims and target areas for market testing within central government.

55 Cm. 1730, November 1991, pages 10-13.

As the White Paper stated, 'there has always been a wide area of activity where the government has decided to contract out for policy or management reasons'. An example is the transfer of training and enterprise schemes to TEC's. Thus, where a strategic decision is taken in favour of contracting-out, market testing is inappropriate since there will be no in-house bid, although competitive tendering amongst private contractors will generally apply to ensure value for money.[56]

For other services performed in-house, market testing an in-house bid against private contractors was considered necessary to deliver value for money services. The White Paper confirmed that up to the end of 1991, 'the majority of contracts subjected to market testing have been won by the private sector'.[57] It was proposed to speed up the competitive tendering process and from 1992 onwards departments and Executive Agencies were to be set targets for market testing.[58] The government noted that 'promising areas' for market testing/contracting-out were professional and specialist services, executive and clerical operations, office services and estate and construction services.[59]

The Citizen's Charter (November 1992) set out a £1.5billion market testing programme affecting the work of 44,250 civil servants which was to be completed by September 1993. Ministerial statements indicated that they envisaged the work of 130,000 civil servants, which constitutes 25 per cent of the total, being exposed to competition.[60]

THE NHS

The NHS in 1992 accounted for 13.3 per cent of UK public expenditure and employed a little under one million employees.[61] It similarly had a long history of contracting-out non-medical services. For example, building construction and maintenance had always been purchased from external suppliers and subject to market testing.[62] In 1983/84, expenditure on 'ancillary services' such as cleaning, catering, laundry, gardening, building maintenance and engineering, amounted to £1.3billion in England and was responsible for employing around 240,000 workers.[63]

[56] Ibid., pp 10-11.

[57] Ibid., p 11.

[58] Ibid., p 8.

[59] Ibid., pages 12-13 For further guidance on Market Testing and Contracting Out see *Better Quality Services: A Handbook on Creating Public/Private Partnerships Through Market Testing and Contracting-Out*, London HMSO, 1998.

[60] Bennett, J. and Digings, L., *EC Public Procurement: Law and Practice*, 1992, Longman, paragraph C2.3, page C2/3.

[61] Carroll, A and Wilson, J, 'National Health Service' in J. Wilson and P. Hinton (eds), *Public Services & the 1990's*, 1993, pp. 190-209 at p. 190.

[62] Wilson, J., *supra*, n.19 at p.91 and *Competing for Quality*, *supra*, n.5, page 14.

[63] Ascher, K., *supra*, n.27, p 172.

Ascher notes that during the 1960's contractual work in the NHS continued to expand with small but significant numbers of contracts in catering, cleaning and laundry work. Contracting-out was on an ad hoc basis and largely a response to shortages of supervisory staff.[64] Rather than full contracting-out it tended to be on the basis of a 'management contract' where private contractors provided managers and supervisory staff but the ancillary staff remained NHS employees. This was generally more expensive than in-house provision. As late as 1970 wages paid by private firms were generally higher than in the NHS.[65] However, penetration by private firms declined significantly from the mid-1970's in favour of in-house services, largely due to organisational changes in the NHS which occurred under the Heath government.

By 1979, only three private contractors were active in cleaning services, which was the largest of the ancillary services within the NHS, and only around forty contracts were in private hands. These contracts represented 2 per cent of the NHS market for cleaning services and were generally confined to London and the south-east.[66]

The private sector had found it easy to obtain management contracts in the catering market during the 1950's and 1960's when in-house provision was less efficient. However, during the late 1960's and early 1970's the growth of contract catering declined due to improved performance of and significant savings to be had from in-house provision.[67] Indeed, by 1982, only four contractors held contracts in either cleaning or catering services.[68] Thus, contractors in all three ancillary services (cleaning, catering and laundry) were anxious to reverse their decline in market share and lobbied government for mandatory contracting-out.

The 'winter of discontent' in 1978/79 in which ancillary workers in hospitals participated in strike action convinced the Conservative government of the need to reduce the power of trade unions in order to prevent future disruptions to service delivery. Moreover, many health service managers took a renewed interest in contracting-out as a result of the strike.[69] The government wasted no time in extolling the virtues of contracting-out and in 1980 published the first of many circulars on the subject.[70]

64 Ibid., pp 23-24.

65 Ibid., pp 179-180

66 Ibid., p 176.

67 Ibid., pp 178-179.

68 Ibid., p 25.

69 Ibid., p 25-26.

70 *Revised Guidance on Contractual Arrangements and Co-operative Schemes*, May 1980. This advised health authorities to consider contracting out security, catering, laundry, computing, building maintenance and certain forms of transport. This circular largely restated advice dating back to 1972, e.g. Circular 72(56), issued in 1972, stated that contractual arrangements were to be regarded as an integral part of providing hospital services. *British Medical Journal*, 284, 3rd April 1982, p. 1060 c.f. Ibid., pp. 26-27.

In August 1981, the Secretary of State considered progress to be unsatisfactory and recommended that serious consideration be given to contracting-out.[71] Health authorities had not adopted voluntary contracting-out to any significant degree. At the same time, pressure from interest groups such as the CBI, Adam Smith Institute, Institute of Directors and Conservative MP's in favour of contracting-out were becoming increasingly vocal. It was a combination of these factors, together with the government's own commitment to reducing public sector employment and expenditure and thereby reducing the power of public sector trade unions, which led it to take action.[72]

Since 1983 the government has required a compulsory and extensive programme of competitive tendering in the NHS. This policy was embodied in a circular entitled, 'Competitive Tendering in the Provision of Domestic, Catering and Laundry Services'. This obliged District Health Authorities to market test the cost effectiveness of these services and to take appropriate action, 'where these tenders show that savings can be made, a contract should be let'. [73] In September 1983, the Fair Wages Resolution of 1946 was rescinded, and the Secretary of State instructed Regional Health Authorities not to stipulate minimum pay and conditions for contractors in their contracts. TUPE was not thought to apply to contracting-out at this time, and it thus enabled contractors to bid on the basis of inferior rates of pay and conditions to those applicable in the NHS. By 1989 a total of 1515 contracts had been awarded for these services, of which 15 per cent were let to private contractors.[74] By 1990 only 14 per cent of contracts for these support services had been awarded to private contractors.[75]

The government claimed that this policy had resulted in substantial savings. Between 1984 to 1985 and 1989 to 1990 the cost of cleaning and other domestic services in the NHS fell from £514million to £482million, a fall of 29 per cent in real terms. Laundry and catering costs over the same period increased at less than half the rate of growth of revenue expenditure on hospital and community health services.[76] Between 1983 and 1991 the government estimated that market testing of support services in the NHS produced savings in excess

71 Ascher, K., *supra*, n.27 at p 27.

72 Cousins, C., 'The contracting out of ancillary services in the NHS' in G. Jenkins and M. Poole (eds) *New Forms of Ownership*, London: Routledge, 1990 at page 99.

73 DHSS (1983b) Circular HC (83) 18, Competitive Tendering in The Provision of Domestic, Catering and Laundry Services, Department of Health and Social Security, London: HMSO, issued on 8th September 1983. Welsh Office Circular (83) 24. The Scottish Office did not issue a circular at this time.

74 Walsh, K., *supra*, n.11, paragraph 2.9, pages 8-9.

75 *Competing for Quality*, *supra*, n.5, page 15.

76 Ibid., pages 14-15.

of £626million.[77] However, as Cousins notes, the extent of cost savings are debatable. In the first round of tendering, where contracts were awarded to private contractors, some of these were loss-leader bids which, prior to the applicability of TUPE, resulted in redundancies and reductions in quality of service. Moreover, the National Audit Office noted that health authorities adopted different approaches to reporting savings. For example, some included redundancy costs, while others did not. Nor do they take account of the amount of management time required in terms of monitoring and evaluation.[78] Many individual health authorities have market tested a wide range of other support services such as legal services, data processing, grounds maintenance, personnel, and payroll. Indeed, it continues to be government policy to extend contracting-out of most support services in the NHS and encouraging the use of facilities management contracts.[79]

The NHS was restructured by the National Health Service and Community Care Act 1990 which provided a framework within which competition was to be introduced by way of the creation of an 'internal market' in the provision of publicly funded health care. It also enabled hospitals to opt-out and become NHS Trusts with the right to employ their own staff on their own terms and conditions. Again, the primary aim of this was to undermine national collective bargaining in favour of local determination of pay.[80]

Local Government

Local Authorities have traditionally operated some form of competitive tendering procedure to enable private contractors to supply goods and services not available in-house such as laundry, pest control and management consultancy services.[81]

During the late 1970's and early 1980's, Southend, Wandsworth, Merton, Dudley and some other Conservative controlled Councils had resorted to voluntary competitive tendering of a wide range of blue collar services.[82] However, voluntary tendering had failed to capture the imagination of all but a few Conservative controlled local authorities, the majority of whom

77 Ibid., page 17.

78 Cousins, C., *supra*, n.72, page 100.

79 *Competing for Quality*, *supra*, n.5, pages 15-17, 19-20.

80 Davies and Freedland, *supra*, n.33, page 627.

81 Fenwick, J., Foreman, A., McCarthy, A. and Shaw, K., *Compulsory Competitive Tendering in Local Government: An Annotated Bibliography*, Earlsgate Press, 1993, page 1.

82 Johnson, A., *supra*, n.32 at page 32.

remained sceptical about its merits.[83] In 1984 a Local Government Chronicle survey suggested that, 'the impetus appears to have gone from the drive to privatize local authority refuse collection. The number of authorities actively pursuing privatisation of refuse collection and privatisation in general has dwindled and a substantial number have now examined but rejected privatisation'.[84] The survey revealed that only eighteen out of the 318 Councils which had responded had contracted-out their refuse collection - and many of these were very small District Councils. 79 other Councils had considered this option in 1982-1983 and a further 29 in 1983-1984, but had rejected it. In 1983-1984 only three of the Councils contracted-out street sweeping, six toilet cleaning and four, all or part of their school cleaning.[85]

The development of compulsory competitive tendering can only be understood within the overall context of the Conservative government's policy of privatisation. Since 1979, a '... different form of competitive tendering has grown in prominence within British local government. These tendering exercises have involved services previously provided by in-house workers. In most cases, the in-house workforce has been asked to compete against interested private bidders. If it wins the work, then the contract price becomes its budget and it operates as if it were an arm's length organisation serving the local authority. If it loses the service, it is contracted-out to a private company ... This form of competitive tendering has grown up as a central plank of the national government's privatisation programme.'[86]

The purpose of CCT according to recent statutory guidance issued in 1996 was, 'to stimulate greater efficiency and secure better value for money by requiring full and fair competition between local authorities' own in-house teams and private contractors'. [87] However, this is not its only objective. Indeed, the driving forces behind the policy are the same as those which led to an extensive programme of contracting-out in the NHS. Those forces came from several directions. Firstly, certain 'flagship' Conservative Councils were pioneering competitive tendering which was allegedly delivering greater value for money for their ratepayers. Secondly, the policy of CCT was given ideological credibility from the proponents of 'market forces' both within and outside the Conservative Party. Internal pressure came from Conservative politicians such as Christopher Chope (ex-Leader of Wandsworth Council)

83 Davies, P.L., *supra* n.1, p.9.

84 Johnson, A., *supra*, n.32 at page 32.

85 Ibid., pages 32-33.

86 Holgate, G, Competitive Tendering : Judicial Elucidation, in *Local Government Review*, August 31, 1991, pages 682-685 at page 682.

87 Department of the Environment, Circular 5/96 : Guidance on the Conduct of Compulsory Competitive Tendering, 2nd April 1996, paragraph 7, page 2, (Welsh Office Circular 11/96). This was replaced by Department of Environment, Transport and the Regions Circular 16/97; W.O. Circular 62/97.

and Michael Forsyth who, in his *Reservicing Britain* published by the Adam Smith Institute in 1980, called for privatisation on a wide scale.[88] He suggested contracting-out services to the private sector would benefit business and ratepayers alike by way of an injection of private sector skills leading to cheaper services.[89]

External pressure came from bodies such as the Adam Smith Institute, The Aims of Industry, Institute of Economic Affairs, Centre for Policy Studies, and groups representing business such as the CBI and others who stood to make profits from CCT.[90] Indeed, data from the Local Government Management Board shows that £2.5billion worth of work is put out annually to tender.[91]

Thirdly, the government was determined to learn the lessons of the 1974 miners' strike which brought down the Heath government and the 1978/1979 'winter of discontent' which contributed to the demise of the Callaghan Labour government. Ascher has suggested that an important motive for CCT was to weaken public sector trade unions.[92] Her view is given credence by ministerial statements emanating from persons such as Nicholas Ridley [93] who stated:

> 'The root cause of rotten local services lies in the grip which local government unions have over the delivery of those services in many parts of the country ... our compulsory competitive tendering provisions will smash that grip once and for all.'[94]

As Margaret Thatcher has pointed out, 'His [Nicholas Ridley] vision was that local authorities should enable services to be provided but, unless it was truly necessary, local authorities should not provide services themselves'.[95] Furthermore, given that local government accounts for 26 per cent of all public expenditure,[96] the control of central government expenditure is likely to have been an equally important impetus for the policy.

88 Fenwick, J., Foreman, A., McCarthy, A. and Shaw, K., *supra*, n.81, page 1.

89 Johnson, A., *supra*, n.32 at pages 31-32.

90 Ibid., page 31.

91 Sherrington, M. 'A Private Take Over' in the *Municipal Journal*, 29th November 1996, page 20.

92 Ascher, K., *The Politics of Privatisation*, Macmillan, 1987; c.f. Johnson, A., *supra*, n.32 at page 31.

93 Secretary of State for the Environment, May 1986 to July 1989.

94 Ridley, N., quoted in *Local Government Chronicle*, 14th April 1989, page 1, c.f. Fenwick, J, Foreman, A, McCarthy, A. and Shaw, K., *supra*, n.81, page 1 and also see Johnson, A., *supra*, n.32 at pages 30-31.

95 Thatcher, M., *supra*, n.18, page 651.

96 Municipal Year Book 1997, Newman Books, page 246.

Legislative Context

The compulsory nature of competitive tendering for local authority services is unique to Britain.[97] Unlike other parts of the public sector where competitive tendering could be introduced by ministerial dictate, legislation was required forcing local authorities to adopt this policy.[98] Thus, CCT is a statutory requirement imposed on local authorities which provides that they may only undertake certain defined categories of work using their own directly employed workforce, if they have successfully secured that work following a fair competitive procedure. The CCT rules do not apply where a local authority does not intend to permit an in-house bid; or where certain exemptions apply; or it is below certain monetary thresholds which vary for different services where it is considered that there is little cost benefit to be derived from operating the regime.[99]

Local Government, Planning and Land Act 1980

CCT began in local government in 1980 by virtue of Part III of the Local Government, Planning and Land Act 1980 (the 1980 Act). This Act was the first cautious step designed to introduce market discipline into the operation of local authorities' Direct Labour Organisations (DLO's). This was a self-contained piece of legislation and was confined to a narrow range of blue-collar services, namely, general highways work, sewer construction and maintenance works, other new construction work relating to non-highways and non-sewer building works and civil engineering; other works of

[97] Walsh, K., *supra*, n.11, paragraph 2.2, page 7.

[98] Davies, P.L., *supra*, n.1, page 9.

[99] Sparke, A., *supra*, n.7, page 1; Napier, B., *supra*, n2: pages 1-2; Elias, P. and J. Bowers, *Transfer of Undertakings: The Legal Pitfalls*: Longman, 5th Edition, 1994, page 23.

maintenance such as minor renewals and improvements to structures.[100] The 1980 Act required DLO's to make a 5 per cent per annum rate of return on capital employed in order to ensure fair competition with the private sector or risk closure.[101]

The legislation specified a competition requirement in relation to a threshold level. The percentage of the value of the previous year's work varied above and below that threshold figure. The threshold value and percentage of work required to be subjected to CCT was varied by the government from time to time by regulations. Thus, in 1980 all highways work above £100,000 had to be exposed to CCT. This was altered in 1982, so that all highway work above £50,000 had to be tendered. In 1983 the regime was further tightened such that 30 per cent of all work below £50,000 had to be tendered. Subsequently, all projects over £25,000 in value and 60 per cent of all highways work less than £25,000 in value had to be tendered. In other words, 40 per cent of all such work could be carried out in-house as of right. However, from April 1995 all general highways work was subject to CCT irrespective of value and the competition free requirement was removed.

In 1980 all new building work, which mainly related to council housing, above £50,000 in value was subject to CCT. In 1982, the rules were altered so that in addition, 30 per cent of all work below £50,000 was subject to CCT. In 1983, 60 per cent of all such work below £50,000 was substituted, which reduced the competition free allowance for new construction worth less than £50,000 to 40 per cent. The effects of this were limited given that only the largest DLO's had the capacity to do such work and that local authorities were generally not involved in new-build from 1980. In 1989, regulations removed the competition free allowance for new construction of a value less than £50,000.

A similar approach was applied to building maintenance work, which was the core work of DLO's (i.e. mainly council house repairs). In 1980, CCT

100 Sparke, A., *supra* n.7, pages 5-6.

101 Walsh, K., *supra*, n.11, paragraph 2.11, page 9.

The current position is that all services subjected to CCT under both the Local Government, Planning and Land Act 1980 and the Local Government Act 1988 must break even after allowing for a 6 per cent per annum rate of return on capital employed by the DLO/DSO. This 6 per cent rate of return is referred to as a capital financing charge. The purpose of the financial objective is to ensure that DLO's/DSO's prepare viable tenders which they must comply with if successful and continue to provide value for money. The 6 per cent charge on capital employed is intended to ensure DSO's/DLO's make efficient use of local authority capital assets. For further details about the financial objective see DoE Circular 12/94. Local authorities are required to maintain DSO accounts until 1 January 2000 and the abolition of CCT, but should aim to continue with these until 31 March 2000 when new financial and accounting arrangements are expected to come into force. Clause 22 of the Local Government Bill contains provisions which enable the Secretary of State to specify the form of accounts required under Best Value.

applied to all work above £10,000 and in addition from 1982 it also applied to 30 per cent of all work below £10,000. In 1983, 60 per cent was substituted for all work below £10,000. From 1989, all such work had to be competed for.

CCT currently applies to all works for the construction and maintenance of sewers for work in excess of £50,000 in value and to 60 per cent of all work below £50,000. This permits DLO's to undertake as of right without competition, 40 per cent of all such work costing less than £50,000. The 1980 Act originally only applied to DLO's employing more than 30 people. However, this was reduced in 1989 to fifteen people in a particular type of construction and maintenance work. The 1989 regulations also redefined emergency work which was originally exempt from CCT. Henceforth, 'predictable' emergency work, had to be put out for tender, which left only 'unpredictable' emergency work exempt from CCT.[102]

Thus, as Walker notes, 'the trend in the legislation over the last decade has been one of systematically exposing more DLO work to competition, attempting to clarify the rules according to which the competitive process is implemented and, in 1989, extending the legislation to all but the very smallest DLO's'. This process resulted in a fall in the amount of local authorities' building maintenance work undertaken by DLO's nationally in England and Wales, between 1982/83 and 1990/91, from 64 per cent to 51 per cent.[103]

This mixture of cautious legislation and voluntary competitive tendering on the part of certain Conservative-controlled Councils in the south-east of England (mainly small contracts which related to refuse collection and street cleaning) had not resulted in any significant impact by the mid 1980's either in terms of private sector penetration or value of work put out to tender. The reasons for this were basically twofold. Firstly, various exemptions excluded smaller contracts from CCT (such as building maintenance work under £10,000), and secondly, because the majority of the work covered by the 1980 Act was won in-house under the larger Labour-controlled Councils, which were politically opposed to CCT and voluntary tendering in general and regarded it as unwarranted central government interference in local affairs.[104]

In 1993 a study [105] found that the number of workers employed and terms and conditions of service had been affected by the fierce competition faced by DLO's. The number of direct employees in local authority new construction and maintenance fell significantly in 1990/91 by 45 per cent. This was due

[102] Walker, Bruce, *Competing for Building Maintenance - Direct Labour Organisations and CCT*, 1993, London : HMSO, p.14.

[103] Ibid., p.15.

[104] Fenwick, J., Foreman, A., McCarthy, A., and Shaw, K., *supra*, n.81, page 2 and Walsh, K., *supra*, n.11, paragraph 2.12, page 9.

[105] Walker, Bruce, *supra* n.102.

largely to the economic recession rather than the 1980 Act itself. There appears to have been a reluctance on the part of local government to depart from nationally agreed wage rates and increases. The reasons for this were that local pay bargaining had never really gained a foothold in local government, coupled with the 'model employer' concept which was widely prevalent. Nevertheless, the 1980 Act did usher in a more commercially oriented approach to management. Most DLO's have preferred to negotiate changes relating to productivity, absenteeism, tackling sickness levels, tightening up bonus schemes and adopting multi-skilling together with increased flexibility among the workforce in order to remain competitive.[106] Commercial pressures seriously undermined the ability of many DLO's to offer apprenticeships, which clearly had implications for authorities' equal opportunities policies.[107] These pressures also caused changes in the numbers employed in particular trades, especially painters.[108]

A significant finding of the survey was that DLO's did not object to having to compete for work. Furthermore, many DLO's noted that competition had markedly improved the quality of work, productivity, and administrative systems. However, critics of the 1980 Act were concerned at the constraints imposed on local authorities which gave the private sector an unfair and uncompetitive advantage over DLO's, such as the rate of return requirements and their inability to compete for work beyond a restricted part of the public sector.[109]

Throughout the early 1980's, the proponents of the 'free market' had been actively lobbying the government to extend the scope of CCT. By October 1984 Christopher Chope and other supporters of CCT had won a commitment to further CCT following a 10 minute rule motion,[110] notwithstanding the Prime Minister's initial reluctance to legislate because 'it would be a very technical measure to put through the House'.[111] In February 1985, the government's Green Paper, *Competition in the Provision of Local Authority Services*

106 Ibid., paras 8.2 to 8.4 and 8.7 to 8.16.

107 Ibid., paras 8.19 to 8.22. In 1977 local authorities were responsible for 46 per cent of all trainees and apprentices in construction. In 1979, there were 9,522 local authority apprenticeships. Between 1981 and 1984, LACSAB, a local authority employer's body, estimated that there was a 36 per cent fall in the number of employees. This position deteriorated further after 1989, c.f. *Competitive Tendering in the Public Sector* Institute of Personnel Management, October 1986, pp. 19-20.

108 Ibid., paras 8.5 to 8.6.

109 Walker, B., *supra* n.102, para E13, page 3.

110 *Hansard's Parliamentary Debates*, Vol 57, cols 820-827, 3 April 1984, c.f. Johnson, A, *supra*, n. 32, page 33.

111 *Hansard's Parliamentary Debates*, Vol 57, cols 137-138, 27th March 1984, c.f. Johnson, A., *supra*, n.32, page 33.

followed with proposals to legislate. The paper stated that generally speaking, the 1980 Act's objectives had been successfully achieved, but noted that there was an increasing need for councils to consider value for money. It went on to state, 'it is the declared and continuing intention to promote the extension of free competition in the provision of local authority services'. The paper also pointed out, that 'far too many authorities appear to have been unwilling to open services to competition, particularly where traditions of in-house provision remain strong'.[112] This consultation process resulted in the most radical change to local government in recent times when the Local Government Act 1988 (the 1988 Act) received the Royal Assent in April 1988.

The Local Government Act 1988

The 1988 Act applied to 'defined authorities',[113] which are county, district, parish and community Councils in England and Wales and regional, island and district Councils in Scotland. Other public bodies such as police, fire services and waste disposal authorities were also included. This legislation extended CCT to a broad range of 'defined activities',[114] namely, refuse collection, street cleaning, grounds maintenance, schools and welfare catering, other catering, vehicle maintenance, and building cleaning. The Act gave the Secretary of State the power to add other activities by Parliamentary Order, and the management of local authority sports and leisure facilities was added in November 1989.[115]

The advocates of contracting-out often refer to the inherent superiority of private sector provision. However, this is not substantiated. Indeed, the government accepted that, 'the best of public sector management now rank alongside the best private sector management'.[116] Therefore, not surprisingly, 'competition has not necessarily meant that service provision has been contracted-out to private firms. Local authorities' own workforces have won work by demonstrating efficiency savings, often substantial'.[117]

Academic studies are few but there is some support for this view. Domberger, Meadowcroft & Thompson[118] suggested that local authorities

112 *Competitive Tendering in the Public Sector* : Institute of Personnel Management and IDS Public Sector Unit, October 1986, ISBN 0 85292 3783, Gresham Press, pages 20-21.

113 Section 1 of the Local Government Act 1988.

114 Section 2 of the Local Government Act 1988.

115 Section 2(3) of the Local Government Act 1988; Local Government (Competition in Sports and Leisure Facilities) Order 1989. (SI 1989 No. 2488). In 1994, On-street parking, security services, vehicle fleet management were added by order of the Secretary of State.

116 *Competing for Quality*, *supra* n.5, page 1.

117 *Competing for Quality*, *supra* n.5, page 22.

118 Domberger S., Meadowcroft S., Thompson, D. (1986) 'Competitive Tendering and Efficiency: the Case of Refuse Collection *Fiscal Studies* Vol 7, No. 4 pp 69-87 c.f. Wilson, J., *supra*, n.19, page 94.

had reduced the cost of refuse collection services by an average of 20 per cent regardless of whether contracts were awarded in-house or to the private sector. Subsequent research by Cubbin, Domberger and Meadowcroft[119] suggested these were largely efficiency savings due to improved productivity. Hartley and Huby[120] found yearly savings to local authorities averaging 26 per cent. Thompson[121] on the other hand estimated savings of 20 per cent. According to the government, the costs of providing services subject to CCT under the 1988 Act have reduced overall by around 6 per cent.[122]

Walsh and Davis [123] found that competition had led to an average overall reduction in service costs of 6.5 per cent, ranging from an increase in cost of 62.4 per cent to a reduction of 49.7 per cent. They noted that reductions increased over time, as competition became tighter and that reductions in costs were greatest in refuse collection, building cleaning and grounds maintenance, and limited in other cases. They also found that cost reductions were the product of changes in work methods, productivity, and to a lesser extent, the pay and conditions of staff.

The Walsh and Davis study showed that CCT had resulted in staff reductions (56 per cent of cases); and changes to hours (51 per cent of cases). Bonus schemes had been changed or abolished (47 per cent of cases), shift systems altered (25 per cent of cases) and holiday or sick pay arrangements changed (30 per cent). Basic pay had not tended to be reduced. The study highlighted a growing casualisation of the workforce and that overall staffing levels had reduced by approximately 12 per cent, with the highest in building cleaning. Moreover, there had been an increased trend towards local pay bargaining.

A follow up study[124] published in March 1997 examined the experience of authorities during the second round of tendering for blue collar services

[119] Cubbin J., Domberger, S. & Meadowcroft S. (1987) 'Competitive Tendering and Refuse Collection : Identifying the Sources of Efficiency Gains' *Fiscal Studies* Vol 8, No. 3, pp 49-58. c.f. Wilson, J., *supra*, n.19, page 94.

[120] Hartley, K. & Huby, M. (1985) 'Contracting-Out in Health and Local Authorities : prospects, progress and pitfalls', *Public Money*, September 1985, pp 23-26, Public Finance Foundation pp 23-26, c.f. Wilson, J., *supra*, n.19, page 95.

[121] Thompson, D. (1990), *The Tender Traps*, Adam Smith Institute. c.f. Wilson, J., *supra*, n.19, page 95.

[122] *Competing for Quality*, *supra*, n.5, page 23.

[123] Walsh, K., and Davis, H., *Competition and Service: The Impact of the Local Government Act 1988* London: HMSO, 1993, para 14, pages V-VI.

[124] Department of the Environment, Local Government Research Programme, Research Summary, *CCT and Local Authority Blue-collar Services*, Research conducted by Austin Mayhead and Company Limited, March 1997. This study was designed to follow up the earlier INLOGOV (University of Birmingham) work carried out by Walsh and Davis, published in 1993. It looked at the experience of 38 local authorities during the second round of tendering for blue collar services.

required by the 1988 Act. This study found that average annual cost savings under the second round of tendering were approximately 9 per cent compared with 6.5 per cent achieved at the first round of tendering.[125] The costs of tendering were reported as being low.

These savings have not been accompanied by a wholesale substitution of private sector provision for that of the public sector. However, around 40 per cent of all contracts are now in the private sector, which is not insignificant, although 75 per cent of the total value of work has been retained by in-house teams. [126] Nonetheless, the success rate of private contractors has varied depending on the type of service submitted to tender under CCT and where they have tendered. In the main, local government has responded well to the challenges of CCT. In mid-1996 metropolitan district councils awarded 84 per cent of all contracts to their in-house DSO's, but DSO's were only awarded 42 per cent of county council work.[127] DSO's continue to be successful in being awarded contracts for sports & leisure management by winning 79.4 per cent of all work put out to tender, but are less successful in winning building cleaning contracts where they have 41.5 per cent of all contracts but retaining 71.8 per cent of the work by value. In other activity areas DSO's share of contracts awarded is 62.2 per cent in refuse collection, 64.4 per cent of other cleaning, 71.2 per cent of vehicle maintenance, 59.6 per cent of other catering, 69.6 per cent of school and welfare catering, and 53.3 per cent of grounds maintenance work.[128]

However, figures from the Department of the Environment show that the percentage of work undertaken by DSO's by value had fallen from 82 per cent to around 73.5 per cent between June 1994 and June 1996. Similarly, figures for the percentage of the number of contracts awarded indicate that the DSO share fell from 61.8 per cent of the total to 57.3 per cent.[129] The latest results from the Local Government Management Board survey show similar patterns in the award of the £2.5billion of local authority work exposed to CCT annually. An average of 55.5 per cent of contracts and 73 per cent of contracts by value were awarded in-house.[130]

Whether DSO's will continue to lose work to the private sector will depend on a number of factors such as their continuing ability to demonstrate efficiency savings, and the level of competition from the private sector. Recent research

[125] Ibid., Executive Summary, para 1.4.2

[126] *Municipal Year Book* 1997, Newman Books, page 123.

[127] Sherrington, M., 'A Private Takeover' in *Municipal Journal*, 29th November 1996, pages 20-21.

[128] Competition update summer 1997 CIPFA supplement to Local Government Chronicle, pp. 6-7.

[129] Sherrington, M, *supra*, n.127, page 20.

[130] *supra,* n.128, p7.

on behalf of the Department of the Environment has been carried out on why some private contractors do not bid for CCT work. The study concentrated on the vehicle maintenance, catering and building services sectors. The research found that there was low awareness and little knowledge of CCT. Key barriers to tendering for CCT contracts involved financial implications of TUPE, a perceived bias in favour of in-house DSO's, low profit margins, level of performance bonds, and the complexity of the tendering process. The report identified the need for more information about CCT, greater publicity about specific contracts being put out to tender and a simplification of the tendering process.[131] Many of these concerns were addressed by DoE Circular 5/96 and related guidance which required tenders to be tailored to meet 'the market' as well as local authority needs.

In November 1991, the Conservative government of John Major announced its proposals[132] to extend CCT to a range of local authority professional and technical services in which 250,000 to 300,000 employees were engaged at an annual cost of between £5billion and £6billion. These services fell into three main areas, namely direct public services: the management of theatres and art facilities; library support services; parking services; secondly, construction related services: architecture; engineering; property management; and thirdly, corporate services: corporate and administrative; legal services; finance; personnel; and computing. It also suggested the extension of CCT to certain manual services not previously covered, which included cleaning of police buildings and maintenance of police vehicles; the maintenance of fire service vehicles; and provision of home-to-school transport. The government decided not to pursue library support services, management of theatres and arts facilities or corporate and administrative services.[133]

The Local Government Act 1992 (the 1992 Act) followed and gave the government power to extend CCT to white collar services.[134] Unlike blue collar services, professional services CCT required percentages of each service to be tendered. Orders defining the activities were laid covering construction and property services, legal services and housing management. These were followed by orders covering finance services, information technology services

[131] Letter from the Department of the Environment to Local Authority Chief Executives, dated 17th December 1996 enclosing a report summary entitled, 'CCT Non-Bidders' carried out by BMRB International Ltd between October 1995 and May 1996. The full report, 'CCT Non-Bidder' by BMRB International Ltd is available from retail outlets of the Stationery Office (ISBN 0117533424) priced £24.00.

[132] Department of the Environment, *Competing for Quality: Competition in the Provision of Local Services : A Consultation Paper,* November 1991.

[133] Ibid., page 14.

[134] Section 8 of the Local Government Act 1992.

and personnel services. The government also added new blue collar services, parking management, fleet management and security work. The first contracts were let in April 1996. Legal services had the greatest number of contractors bidding, and apart from housing management, the white collar services, have had competition levels comparable with the most developed blue collar services. DSO success rates for current contracts for professional services vary between construction and property services 79.4 per cent, legal services 76.5 per cent and housing management 88.6 per cent. [135] The government was disappointed at the level of private sector penetration. Furthermore, as the Minister noted '... a number of authorities were interpreting the regulations very imaginatively and the amount of work going out to tender was far lower than we expected'. [136] The government's response was to change the regulations in February 1997 to increase the amount of work which had to be subject to competition.[137]

Anti-Competitive Conduct

The 1988 Act introduced the concept of anti-competitive conduct which requires a local authority not to 'act in a manner having the effect or intended or likely to have the effect of restricting, distorting or preventing competition'.[138] The scope of this provision was unclear and while the government had issued guidance,[139] it was concerned that, 'too many authorities have sought to bend the rules laid down by the legislation, to cushion their workforces against the full force of competition.'[140] Thus, the 1992 Act [141] permitted the Secretary of State to 'flesh out' his interpretation of 'anti-competitive' conduct by way of regulations and guidance with a view to clarifying the framework for CCT.[142]

135 Jon Sutcliffe, 'Market Watch', *Local Government Chronicle*, Competition Update, summer 1997,

136 Sir Paul Beresford, Environment Minister, 'Don't listen to the Luddites' in the *Local Government Chronicle* (CCT Focus) 22 November 1996, page 3.

137 The Local Government Act 1988 (Competition) (England) Regulations 1997 (SI No. 175/1997).

138 Section 7(7) of the Local Government Act 1988. A similar provision is included at Section 7(1) A and 9(a)(aaaa) of the Local Government, Planning and Land Act 1980. These Provisions will be repeated by the Local Government Act 1999.

139 Department of the Environment, Circular 1/91, SOED, Circular 6/1991, WO, Circular 10/91.

140 *Competing for Quality*, *supra*, n.132, paragraph 1.6, page 4 and *Competing for Quality*, *supra* n.5, page 25.

141 Section 9 of the Local Government Act 1992.

142 *Competing for Quality*, *supra*, n.132, paragraph 1.29, page 10, *Competing for Quality*, *supra*, n.5, page 25. Also see Johnson, A., *supra*, n.32, pages 47-48. See Local Government (Direct Service Organisations) (Competition) Regulations 1993 (SI 1993 No. 848) and DoE Circular 10/93, superseded by DoE Circular 5/96 which was itself replaced by DETR Circular 16/97, (WO Circular 62/97).

The 1993 Competition Regulations and DoE Circular 10/93 (now Circular 16/97) (which has statutory force) gave further guidance which was designed to ensure a 'level playing field' on which local authorities' in-house teams and private contractors can compete fairly.[143] The purpose of the latest Circular guidance is to place the onus on authorities to show at each of the key stages of the tendering process in a transparent way how their proposals for tendering the work are designed to avoid anti-competitive conduct. For example, it requires authorities to consult the private sector on how contracts are packaged, size, and duration and so on.[144]

Anti-competitive conduct is an elastic concept and may include, amongst other things, packaging contracts in large amounts to limit the number of private contractors capable of performing such work, packaging 'exotic' mixes of unrelated work within a contract, failing to make key assets available, onerous contract conditions, accepting the non-lowest bid of the in-house team, and failing to handle TUPE matters in accordance with Annex A of the Department of the Environment's Issues Paper dated 21st January 1994.

Section 7(7) of the 1988 Act must be seen in the light of Sections 13 and 14 of the 1988 Act (and Sections 19A and 19B of the 1980 Act) which provided statutory powers enabling the Secretary of State to take action against authorities which do not comply with the CCT rules. If a complaint is made against an authority, the Secretary of State may decide to investigate the allegations, and if the grounds for complaint appear well founded, he may initiate statutory action against the authority by serving a Section 13 notice, which requires the authority to explain its action in awarding the contract to the in-house team. It is worth noting that there is no power to issue a Section 13 notice if a contract is awarded to a private contractor. If the Secretary of State, having considered the authority's response, remains of the view that it has behaved 'anti-competitively', a direction may be given under Section 14. The Secretary of State's powers under Section 14 are wide and range commonly from requiring the authority to re-tender the work with conditions requiring the Secretary of State's approval before an authority can award the work in-house, to preventing the authority from tendering for the work in the future.[145]

143 Department of the Environment, *CCT and Local Government in England : Annual Report for 1995*, page 3.

144 Ibid., pages 3-4, and DoE, Circular 5/96, subsequently replaced by DETR Circular 16/97, (WO Circular 62/97).

145 Department of the Environment, *CCT and Local Government in England : Annual Report for 1995*, pages 10-11.

The extent of the Secretary of State's powers under the 1988 Act were considered in *R v Secretary of State for the Environment ex parte Knowsley Borough Council,* [146] Mr Justice Popplewell found that notwithstanding that the authority had acted reasonably, the issue was whether the Secretary of State had acted reasonably when determining what constituted anti-competitive conduct and no fetters were placed on this discretion. This was a view the Court of Appeal concurred with. The court also decided that the Secretary of State had the power to require local authorities to seek express consent before re-awarding the contract to the in-house DSO.

Thus, once the Secretary of State forms the view that an authority has acted anti-competitively in relation to the tendering process, authorities will find it very difficult to challenge the exercise of the wide discretion under Section 14. Indeed, the High Court recently confirmed in *R v Secretary of State for the Environment, ex parte Oldham Metropolitan Borough Council,* [147] that

146 *The Times*, May 28th, 1991, QBD. The facts of this case were that Knowsley MBC awarded its refuse collection contract to its in-house DSO which was the lowest bid after adjustments taking into account other costs in tender evaluation. The Secretary of State formed the view that some of these costs should not have been taken into account and eventually issued a direction under Section 14 of the 1988 Act that it constituted anti-competitive behaviour. The Direction required the contract to be re-tendered and consent of the Secretary of State to be obtained prior to any decision to award the contract to the in-house DSO. Mr Justice Popplewell held that the question raised on judicial review was whether the view taken by the Secretary of State was reasonable and not whether the steps taken by the local authority were reasonable. Thus, the Secretary of State was the arbiter of what was anti-competitive conduct and upheld the Secretary of State's discretion. However, he ruled that the requirement to seek consent before re-awarding the contract in-house was *ultra vires*. The Court of Appeal (unreported, 31st July 1991) confirmed the High Court's decision save that it upheld the cross appeal by the Secretary of State on the basis that the requirement to seek consent prior to awarding the contract in-house properly served the purposes of the 1988 Act and that such a condition was not *ultra vires* and could be included in a Section 14 Direction.

147 *The Times*, 16th December 1996, QBD. The facts of this case were that Oldham MBC refused to provide workforce information relating to a transfer of an undertaking to enable tenderers to assess their liabilities in the event of TUPE applying unless the tenderer undertook to submit a TUPE bid. The tenderer gave such an undertaking and duly received the TUPE information, and then submitted a non-TUPE bid in connection with the £1.5million building maintenance contract. The Council rejected the bid on the basis that it breached the undertaking and awarded the contract to its in-house Direct Labour Organization. The tenderer complained to the Secretary of State who ultimately served a direction under Section 19(B)(2)(a) of the Local Government, Planning and Land Act 1980 prohibiting the Council performing the work itself on the basis that the Council's conduct had been anti-competitive. The Council commenced judicial review proceedings. Mr Justice Laws decided that the Secretary of State was entitled to form the view that the provision of TUPE information without strings would encourage private contractors to tender. As a matter of law, following the approach set out in *R v Secretary of State for the Environment Ex parte, Knowsley Metropolitan Borough Council* (unreported, CA July 31st 1991) the Council's refusal to provide TUPE information to private bidders save on terms that they submitted a TUPE bid and its extraction of the undertaking was in law capable of amounting to anti-competitive conduct and the Secretary of State was entitled to make a Direction.

the Secretary of State has the power to ban DSOs from submitting an in-house bid where he has ordered a re-tender due to conduct he regards as anti-competitive.

During 1995, the Department of the Environment concluded investigations into 66 cases of alleged anti-competitive conduct. Most complaints were made by private contractors. An analysis of these complaints indicate that the greatest concern (33 per cent) related to complaints about the award of work to in-house teams who were not the lowest tenderer; 13 per cent related to onerous contract conditions; 11 per cent were related to disputes about the viability of private contractors' bids; 11 per cent concerned TUPE (which had fallen from 48.5 per cent in 1994 largely due to the TUPE Issues Paper of 21st January 1994); 9 per cent related to exclusions from the tender list; and 4 per cent concerned contract packaging. This left 6 per cent as 'other' complaints.[148]

In 1995, the Secretary of State served a combined total of twelve notices under Section 19A of the 1980 Act and Section 13 of the 1988 Act compared with 20 such notices for 1994. In 1995, a combined total of seven directions under Section 14 of the 1988 Act and Section 19B of the 1980 Act were served (compared with nine in 1994). Generally, the directions required the work to be re-tendered with prior approval of the Secretary of State required before the work could be awarded in-house.[149]

Authorities performing a defined activity in-house must also meet financial objectives set down by the Secretary of State as previously mentioned. Increasingly, the Secretary of State has shown his willingness to rely on Section 14 (and Section 19B of the 1980 Act) to close loss-making DSO's/DLO's.[150] In 1995, a combined total of 125 notices were served under Section 13 (and Section 19A) on local authorities which had materially failed to meet their financial objectives. In a combined total of 49 cases, directions were given. Of these, four required the in-house DSO/DLO to cease trading. This represents a marked increase on the 1994 combined totals of 102 notices and 39 directions respectively.[151]

Fair Wages Resolution

An important factor restricting private sector interest in performing local authority work was the Fair Wages Resolution.[152] Between 1891 and 1983

148 Department of the Environment, *supra* n.143, page 12.

149 Ibid., page 12.

150 Sparke, A., *supra*, n.7, pages 52-53.

151 Department of the Environment, *supra*, n. 143, page 13.

152 Johnson, A., *supra*, n.32, page 25.

the House of Commons passed a succession of Fair Wages Resolutions which required central government to require private contractors to observe 'fair' terms and conditions of employment in respect of their employees. In 1946 a new Fair Wages Resolution defined fair wages by reference to either the relevant collective agreements or the general rate for the job in similar industries. It also required contractors to recognise their employees' freedom to join a trade union.[153] Although the Resolution did not apply to other parts of the public sector, encouraged by central government they often included a fair wage clause in their contracts.[154] Indeed, many local authorities adopted such clauses to promote the 'model employer' concept in the private sector together with equal opportunities, training and health and safety policies.[155]

The significance of the resolution where it was enforced was that it regulated the market in such a way as to reinforce in-house provision because where services were labour intensive, the proportion of a contractor's costs attributable to wages reduced the scope for profit making. The contracting-out which occurred on an ad hoc basis in the 1950's and 1960's was essentially an expedient response to labour shortages. Moreover, in the main, private contractors at that time tended to recognise trade unions and their employees' rates of pay were broadly the same as those negotiated nationally for local authority employees.[156]

In 1982, the Conservative government having criticised the International Labour Organisation Convention No. 94 (1949) on Labour Clauses in Public Contracts, because it conflicted with its 'free market' ideology, revoked the Fair Wages Resolution.[157] The message the government wished to set was clear. 'It is that those placing contracts should not attempt to interfere with pay and conditions agreed by contractors and their employees. We hope that other public sector employers will behave in the same way.'[158]

NON-COMMERCIAL MATTERS

The failure of local authorities to follow the government's example, led it to propose legislation in its green paper in 1985[159] to prevent the use of 'contract

153 Ibid., page 25.

154 Davies and Freedland, *supra*, n.33, page 31.

155 Fredman and Morris, *supra*, n.39, page 144.

156 Johnson, A., *supra*, n.32, page 26.

157 Davies and Freedland, *supra*, n.33, pages 539-541.

158 Michael Allison, Minister of State at the Department of Employment, H.C. Debs, Vol. 34, cols 564-565, December 16, 1982, c.f. Fredman and Morris, *supra* n.39, page 148.

159 Department of the Environment, *Competition in the Provision of Local Authority Services*, February 1985. c.f. Davies and Freedland, *supra*, n.33, page 541.

compliance' designed to promote the 'model employer' concept.[160] This was implemented by virtue of Section 17 of the Local Government Act 1988. This section defines a number of matters as 'non-commercial' which a local authority and certain other public bodies are prohibited from having regard to when awarding a contract for goods and services.

Broadly, the matters specified as 'non-commercial', amongst other things, include, the terms and conditions of employment of workers or the composition of the workforce, the arrangements for promotion, transfer or training of or the other opportunities afforded to the workforce;[161] and 'the conduct of contractors or workers in industrial disputes'.

A notable exception to the above prohibition, is where authorities may ask prospective tenderers six approved race-relations questions specified by the Secretary of State to enable them to discharge their duty under Section 71 of the Race Relations Act 1976.

Consequently, it may be unlawful under Section 17 of the 1988 Act (and anti-competitive) for authorities to require a private contractor to employ the authority's existing workforce or to replicate its existing terms and conditions of employment. Moreover, authorities are precluded from requiring compliance by private contractors with the Sex Discrimination Act 1975.[162]

160 Contract compliance is the use of public procurement to further social or political goals in the private sector, through the imposition of contract conditions which do not relate to the subject matter of the contract but rather relate to non-commercial or political matters. In the UK, contract compliance was frequently used prior to the Local Government Act 1988 to promote equal opportunities and health and safety. It was also used to stray into the arena on national politics by some Labour controlled Councils to ban tenderers with commercial links with the former apartheid regime in South Africa. For further background details see Sparke, A., *supra*, n.7, Chapter 5; and P.E. Morris, *Local Government and Contract Compliance in Local Government Review*, September 15, 1990, pp. 728-734.

161 The Secretary of State points out in the Department of the Environment, Circular 5/96 (which has statutory force), paragraph 28, pages 6-7 that Part II of the Local Government Act 1988 prohibits local authorities making certain demands regards workforce matters or requiring, through contractual conditions, that contractors comply with codes of practice or conduct on these matters. However, the Secretary of State makes an exception where it is essential for service delivery, to have regard to workforce matters, such as training insofar as it relates to technical capacity, race policy for housing services or TUPE or require that the successful contractor follows the relevant professional code of practice or European equivalent.

162 S.18(2) of the Local Government Act 1988, and Department of the Environment Circular 8/88, Circular 12/88 (Welsh Office), Annex B. Also see *R v London Borough of Islington, ex parte the Building Employers Confederation* [1989] IRLR 382, where the High Court held that a clause requiring compliance at all times with provisions of the Sex Discrimination Act 1975 was unlawful. It is possible that requiring compliance with the Disability Discrimination Act 1995 except for service delivery will similarly be unlawful, i.e. the contract should not place a duty on the private contractor relating to terms and conditions or composition of its workforce notwithstanding that it only seeks compliance with existing general law.

Government interference with authorities' powers to contract have no parallel in the private sector, which is free to insert into its contracts fair wage conditions and to promote good employment practices.[163] This issue has long been a source of contention between local government, trade unions and the government. As a result of their lobbying the government has reviewed the position to ensure that the tendering process is not used as a barrier to higher quality services, fair competition and employment protection.[164]

The Private Finance Initiative

Contracting-out in the public sector was taken a stage further in 1992 with the government's introduction of the Private Finance Initiative (PFI). The main purpose behind this method of public procurement was to promote efficient public services by the introduction of private sector capital and skills into the ownership and maintenance of capital assets by the transfer of risk to the private sector and the need to achieve value for money. This in turn would reduce public expenditure by removing capital projects from the public sector balance sheet. The novel feature of PFI is the transfer of the management and operation of services to the private sector under long-term contracts lasting up to 30 years. The government expected to award £ 14 billion worth of contracts by 1999. It is intended to facilitate a more innovative approach to public procurement which reinforces the role of the public sector as enablers and purchasers of public services rather than being direct providers. Trade Unions are hostile to the PFI and have sought to extract concessions from the government to protect the employment rights of staff transferring from the public to the private sector.

The PFI is compulsory in central government and the NHS where it has been used, for example, in the provision and running of new prisons and

163 Fredman and Morris, *supra*, n.39, page 152.

164 Oona King MP promoted a Private Member's Bill - the Local Authority Tenders Bill. This proposed amendment to section 17 of the Local Government Act 1988 to permit local authorities to take into account when inviting and awarding tenders for contracts, certain factors which are presently prohibited as being 'non-commercial' considerations under that section. This would have allowed local authorities to have regard to such matters as terms and conditions of employment of a contractor's workforce and arrangements for recruitment and training. The purpose was to enable local authorities to use contracts as a means of tackling unemployment, promoting equal opportunities, and providing for skills training. Although the Bill has received government backing it failed to reach the statute book due to lack of parliamentary time in July 1998. However, the government has taken the matter on board in the Local Government Bill 1998. Clause 17 will enable the Secretary of State to provide by statutory instruments, in respect of Best Value authorities, for a specified matter to cease to be a non-commercial matter for the purposes of section 17 of the Local Government Acts 1988. An order may apply in relation to specified authorities, functions or contracts.

hospitals. The first NHS PFI deal occurred in 1995 and involved South Buckinghamshire NHS Trust, where a consortium will build a new hospital and then run it and charge the Trust for services.[165] PFI in local government is currently voluntary and there was little interest in it until 1996/97 when the government made changes to the capital finance regime regulating local authorities. This removed the adverse capital finance implications whereby payments to private contractors would not count as capital expenditure which previously had required credit cover and reduced the amount councils could borrow. In addition, an important incentive has been the possibility of revenue support grant from the government for the capital part of the payments to a contractor in the form of notional credit approvals. The largest PFI externalisation in local government occurred in April 1997 when Lambeth Council contracted-out all its blue collar services. This involved the sale of the assets of the Council's DSO, the award of seventeen contracts for up to ten years worth £350 million and the transfer of about 1,800 Council employees to Lambeth Serviceteam Limited - a joint venture company in which the Council has less than a 20 per cent stake.[166]

The Labour government is committed to the PFI and partnerships between the public and private sector. This may become an increasingly important form of public procurement especially for capital intensive services. It remains to be seen whether PFI will reduce the distinction between the public and private sector, and deliver low-cost, high quality services.

Conclusion

Contracting-out and competitive tendering for services were not new phenomena in the public sector when the Conservative government took office in 1979. Public authorities had traditionally resorted to such options on an ad hoc and flexible basis as local circumstances dictated. For example, contracting-out had often been a response to a mixture of poor industrial relations, inefficient services, and/or recruitment and retention difficulties in connection with skilled personnel. Broadly speaking, it was not thought of as a mechanism to achieve cost savings. On the contrary, it tended particularly in the 1950's and 1960's to be a more expensive option because of the use of 'management contracts' and premiums paid for qualified staff.

After the 'winter of discontent' in 1978/79 there were considerable concerns about the cost, reliability and quality of public services. The government believed competition would reduce public expenditure, expose waste and improve public services. With the exception of the Civil Service, the government's initial approach was largely voluntarist, encouraging the public

[165] *The Times*, 11th January 1996, page 22.

[166] *The Lawyer*, 13th May 1997, page 6.

sector to embrace competitive tendering and contracting-out.

The NHS and local authorities opposed central government interference in local affairs and failed to adopt competitive tendering to any significant extent. This led the government to impose mandatory tendering. Unfortunately, this politicised the process in a way which had been unknown before and proved to be a constant source of friction between central government and the NHS and local government.

The link between the Conservative government's political or ideological objectives and its commitment to contracting-out and competitive tendering in the public sector is disputed. Domberger and Jenson believe that, 'Contracting is neither an ideologically driven crusade, nor an emphemeral management fad. It is a manifestation of the natural, long-term evolution of the economy. It reflects the advanced stage of development of the services sector'.[167] However, Professor Sue Richards notes, 'it was driven by a powerful combination of the intellectual critique provided by public choice economics, and the politics of discontent with professional bureaucracies through which public services had been administered since the creation of the modern welfare state'.[168] Nonetheless, it is worth remembering that had the government been motivated entirely by ideology it could have imposed mandatory contracting out as opposed to CCT.[169]

It is important to consider contracting-out and competitive tendering in context. After 1979 it was to become a central plank of the government's privatisation programme, and must be viewed against a background of other developments such as the Education Reform Act 1988, the National Health and Community Care Act 1990, purchaser-provider splits in the Civil Service which concerned efficiency within public sector bureaucracies, and the government's economic policies which have imposed 'cash limits' on the public sector.

Davies and Freedland believe that although CCT has been justified in terms of value for money, the primary goal of the policy was to facilitate an erosion of public sector collective bargaining. [170] Indeed, the alleged economic benefits of CCT need closer examination and more research is required into the cost benefits of CCT for both 'manual' and 'professional' services. Domberger and Jenson believe that overall the benefits of contracting are real and substantial. Indeed, as Professor Richards concedes, 'looking at the

[167] Domberger, S. and Jenson, P., 'Gaining from outsourcing' in *New Economy*, Autumn 1997, pp. 159-163 at p163.

[168] Richards, Sue, 'Lessons from the Tory experiment' in *New Economy*, Autumn 1997, pp. 138-141 at p.138.

[169] Ascher, K., *supra*, n.27, page 253.

[170] Davies and Freedland, *supra*, n.33, pages 547-548, 622.

process of contracting in local government, the NHS and central government ...some efficiency gain has almost certainly been achieved. However, insufficient attention to institutional factors has severely limited the reform programme's effectiveness'. Richards believes contractorisation in the NHS and central government has failed to deliver innovation and that costs often outweighed efficiency gains. She notes that on the other hand, local government has had to comply with government policy but that the restrictive framework which forced compliance has undermined an innovative approach to service delivery. [171]

What is undisputed is that CCT has led to greater commercialisation, customer focus and the creation of 'markets' where none had previously existed. Indeed, its real significance lies not so much in the savings but the cultural change which has evolved in terms of the need for improved public sector management, consumer responsiveness, quality initiatives linked to the Citizen's Charter, and the need to eliminate waste and inefficiency due to the need to keep internal trading accounts.

CCT has forced authorities to consult recipients of public sector services. It has also led authorities to examine a broad range of service delivery mechanisms in the interests of their ratepayers. CCT has been seen as a useful mechanism to depress labour and overhead costs and ensure 'good housekeeping'. Moreover, the regular re-tendering of services has tended to ensure that ossification and complacency in service provision is less likely.

Thus, between 1979 and 1988, the government reversed the previous bipartisan policy which had exhorted the public sector to promote 'good' employment practices in the private sector. The reason for this was that it conflicted with its free market and de-regulatory approach of which the privatisation of public services formed an integral part. It is against this background that the Conservative government's antithesis to the TUPE can be understood. The TUPE Regulations were viewed in the same light as the Fair Wages Resolution as likely to inhibit the government's contracting out and competitive tendering process. However, the proportion of contracts won by DSO's without any external competition is not generally increasing, which suggests that problems over TUPE have not had an overwhelming deterrent effect on the private sector bidding for contracts.[172]

Behind the TUPE Regulations there was a fundamental clash of philosophy between on the one hand, the Conservative government's commitment to de-regulating and de-rigidifying the labour market especially in the public

[171] Richards, Sue, *supra*, n.167 at pp 139-141.

[172] *Municipal Year Book 1996*, Newman Books, pp 128-129. Also see DoE Research Summary: *CCT and Local Authority Blue-Collar Services*. Research conducted by Austin Mayhead and Co Limited, March 1997, para 1.7.2 of the Executive Summary.

sector and, on the other hand, the EEC's commitment to ensure that development of social policy particularly in the field of employment law within the European Union keeps pace with economic integration.

The Labour Government accepted that 'CCT made the costs of services more transparent. But its detailed prescription of the form and timing of competition led to unimaginative tendering, and often frustrated rather than enhanced real competition'.[173]

Accordingly, on 30th November 1998 the Government introduced the Local Government Bill which will repeal what it regarded as the discredited system of CCT and replaced it with a new statutory duty to achieve best value for the public. This states,

> 'A best value authority must make arrangements to secure continuous improvement in the way its functions are exercised, having regard to a combination of economy, efficiency and effectiveness.'[174]

This represents an important step in the Government's wider modernisation programme for local government designed to allow for creative and innovative solutions to improve public services and strengthen accountability to local taxpayers. Best value is based on a system of performance plans, reviews and audit with input from various stakeholders including service users, public, private and voluntary sectors. The purpose of the reviews is to set improvement targets and determine the best method for delivering best value based on the White Paper's '4 C's.' This requires authorities to 'challenge, compare, consult and compete' in order to ensure continuous improvement.

The best value regime has been embraced enthusiastically by local government, trade unions, and the private sector. However, it is generally expected to be more onerous because, unlike CCT, the duty of best value will apply to all local authority services. Competition is described as, 'a key management tool for delivering best value and driving up standards, but unlike CCT, it will be fair competition and it will be a means to an end, rather than the end in itself.'[175] It is this element of best value which may potentially alienate staff and trade unions. However, the Government recognises that compensation must be undertaken in a climate where employees' basic rights are respected. This underpins the Government's review of the TUPE regulations with a view to securing greater certainty in protecting terms and conditions of employment where work is transferred.[176]

[173] The Department of Environment, Transport and the Regions, White Paper, Modern Local Government: In Touch with the People, July, 1998, para 7.22.

[174] Clause 3 (1) of the Local Government Bill 1998.

[175] Hilary Armstrong, MP, Minister for Local Government in opening speech during second reading debate of the Local Government Bill 1999, 12 January 1999.

[176] *Supra*, n. 173, para 7.23 to 7.25.

5. Disclosure of Workforce Information

Karl Larrad

INTRODUCTION

Disclosure of workforce information in the context of public sector contracting-out is an area fraught with pitfalls for the unwary. It involves the need for an awareness of the implications of the overlap between the Transfer of Undertakings (Protection of Employment) Regulations 1981 (TUPE)[1], legislation relating to compulsory competitive tendering (CCT)[2], the Data Protection Act 1984, and the common law duty of confidentiality owed by employers to their employees.

[1] SI 1981/1794 which implemented the Acquired Rights Directive 77/187 into UK legislation. Revised UK TUPE Regulations are likely to be implemented in 1999 following consultation in the Spring of 1999.

[2] Local Government, Planning and Land Act 1980; Local Government Act 1988; Local Government Act 1992 and numerous regulations thereunder. In addition, non-statutory guidance is contained in the DoE Issues Paper on CCT and TUPE, 21 January 1994, and guidance on Pensions, 15 March 1995 and 28 June 1995. On the 2 June 1997, the Minister for Local Government and Housing confirmed the government's intention to replace CCT with a duty to obtain best value. Accordingly, the Secretary of State withdrew Statutory guidance contained in Circular 5/96 (WO Circular 11/96) and replaced it with new guidance to cover the interim period until CCT is replaced. However, the replacement Circular 16/97 (WO Circular 62/97) does not alter guidance on TUPE contained in the previous Circular 5/96 and the TUPE Issues Paper. The Local Government Bill 1998 provides for the repeal of CCT on 2 January 2000 and its substitution by a statutory duty of Best Value which will apply from 1 April 2000.

This chapter is intended to give practical guidance in dealing with this complicated process with particular reference to local government CCT, in order to ensure legal claims from prospective tenderers for negligence, misrepresentation and/or statutory action by the Secretary of State due to a breach of the 'anti-competitive' behaviour rules are minimised. It should also prove helpful in market testing and outsourcing.

The information which must be disclosed will depend to some extent upon the facts and circumstances in each case. For example, public sector trade unions may have reached an understanding or have a collective agreement with the transferor in relation to the information disclosed. TUPE is a rapidly changing area of law and up to date legal advice should always be sought where appropriate.

Should workforce information be supplied to the transferee?

Most services subject to CCT are labour intensive and therefore disclosure of workforce information is crucial to enable a tenderer to know what its liabilities are likely to be and to price its bid. It includes information concerning the numbers of employees employed in the undertaking and their terms and conditions of service. TUPE does not expressly require the disclosure of workforce information by the transferor to the transferee although this is likely to change when the new TUPE Regulations are introduced in 1999. In a private sector business transfer from one employer to another there would be no objection to the disclosure of workforce information. However, in the context of CCT in the public sector, the issue is complicated by the fact that there may be four or more private sector bidders competing against an in-house bid.[3] Clearly, information relating to the labour costs of the in-house operation is commercially sensitive and disclosure to rival bidders may prejudice its competitiveness, if tenderers having received the information then submit a non-TUPE bid which undercuts the labour costs of the existing service provider. If TUPE applies to a bid, the provision of workforce information is unlikely to be detrimental, because labour costs are in effect fixed costs which the successful contractor will have to budget for in its tender.[4] Needless to say, this can create tensions and lead to conflicts between contract managers and client-side officers in relation to the nature of the information which is disclosed.

[3] Section 7(4) of the Local Government Act 1988 prescribes that at least three non-local authority persons must be invited to tender. If less than four non-local authority persons notify the authority of their interest then each must be invited. This provision will be repeated by the Local Government Bill 1998 on 2 January 2000. However, under the Best Value regime which will replace CCT authorities are likely to have to market test services against an in-house bid or simply contract-out as appropriate in order to satisfy District Audit that best value is being achieved.

[4] This view was canvassed by Patrick Elias QC in *R v The Secretary of State for the Environment*, ex parte Oldham MBC, CO/994/96, 26 November 1996, Times Law Reports, December 16, 1996.

The government's view contained in Department of the Environment, Transport and the Regions Circular 16/97 (which has statutory force) is that:-

> 'Prospective contractors may wish to submit proposals for carrying out a service which might, in their view, involve the transfer of an undertaking. In these circumstances, contractors will need information on the numbers of staff who would transfer, and their terms and conditions of service. The Secretary of State expects authorities to provide such detail as is necessary for contractors to prepare such tenders at the tender invitation stage, even though they may have formed a preliminary view that the Regulations are unlikely to apply, in which case an authority should state clearly that the availability of the information is to allow tenderers to make their own judgement on the application of TUPE. Where additional information is subsequently requested, and supplied, authorities should consider any additional time reasonably required to prepare bids.'[5]

The government suggests that workforce information must be supplied to any tenderer to enable it to consider the submission of a TUPE bid, if they wish to do so.[6] Further, where an authority refuses to provide tenderers with TUPE information as indicated in paragraph 44 of Circular 10/93 (superseded by paragraph 32 of Circular 16/97) or provides insufficient information to enable contractors to cost a TUPE bid, this is potentially anti-competitive, since this makes it difficult for contractors who may wish to submit a TUPE based bid.[7]

5 Department of the Environment: Circular 16/97, (WO Circular 62/97): Guidance on the Conduct of Compulsory Competitive Tendering, 3 December 1997, paragraph 32. This guidance replaces DoE Circular 5/96 and DoE: Guidance on the Avoidance of Anti-Competitive Behaviour: Legal, Construction and property and Housing Management Services: 12 December 1994; and DoE Circular 10/93 (WO Circular 40/93). Further guidance is provided in Annex A to the DoE's Issues Paper: Handling of TUPE matters in relation to CCT, 21 January 1994 which summarizes the main items of information which will most often be relevant and DoE guidance on 'Handling pension matters in relation to CCT' dated 15 March 1995 (and the WO on 17 March 1995) and DoE letter from J R Footitt, Local Government Division 3 to Local Authority Chief Executives, 'Handling of pension matters in relation to CCT' dated 28 June 1995.

6 DoE : Issues Paper : Handling of TUPE Matters in Relation to CCT, 21 January 1994, Issue 6, paragraph 13. The Issues Paper does not have statutory force in the terms of section 9 of the Local Government Act 1992, but it indicates the considerations which the Secretary of State will have in mind when coming to a view regarding issues of anti-competitive behaviour.

7 Ibid., Issue 3, paragraph 8.

Controversially, tenderers are permitted to submit non-TUPE bids, irrespective of whether or not they have received workforce information.[8] Indeed, they may choose to submit no bid at all. This could potentially prejudice the in-house bid in that a tenderer could obtain sufficient information to cost the in-house bid, and then submit a non-TUPE bid; or simply use it as a benchmark against which to bid rather than submitting a more competitive tender.[9] However, this is mitigated to the extent that a local authority may refuse to consider a non-TUPE bid if it thinks TUPE applies.[10] The government also believes that tenderers should be able to submit a non-TUPE bid together with a TUPE bid and that it may be potentially anti-competitive to insist on one bid only.[11] Thus, even if an authority believes TUPE will not apply, workforce information must be made available and there are in effect no circumstances in which such information can be withheld from tenderers.

The government's stance on workforce information was confirmed in *R v the Secretary of State for the Environment, ex parte Oldham Metropolitan Borough Council.* [12] In 1994 Oldham MBC invited tenders for a building maintenance contract which was worth £1.5 million p.a. A prospective tenderer requested information concerning the Council's staff levels in order to assess their liabilities in the event of their making a TUPE bid. The Council replied that it would release the information on an undertaking that the firm undertook to submit a TUPE bid. A bid was made on the basis they had no TUPE liability but was not evaluated by the Council, which claimed the tenderer had breached its undertaking. In February 1995 the contract was awarded to its own in-house DSO. The tenderer complained to the Secretary of State who eventually served a direction under Section 19(B)(2)(a) of the Local Government, Planning and Land Act 1980, that the Council had acted anti-competitively and prohibited it from carrying out the contract work itself. The Council sought judicial review. The High Court held that where a local authority declined to provide workforce information unless the tenderer submitted a TUPE bid was capable of amounting to anti-competitive behaviour. Mr Justice Laws accepted that,

> '... in some circumstances a tenderer will gain an edge of advantage by possession of TUPE related information from the authority. But as it seems to me the Secretary of State was entitled

8 Ibid., Issue 6, paragraph 13.

9 Cirell, S.D. and Bennett, J. *Competitive Tendering for Professional Services*, Vol II, FT Law and Tax, 1996, para K2.23, page K2/19.

10 DoE Issues Paper, *supra* n. 6, Issue 8, paragraph 18.

11 Ibid., Issue 10, paragraph 22.

12 CO/994/96, 26 November 1996, QBD; Times Law Reports, 16 December 1996.

to take the view that the provision of such information without strings would, in short, encourage outside bidders to enter the ring to tender as they saw fit.'[13]

When should workforce information be provided?

For those authorities subject to CCT, the Secretary of State makes it clear that he 'expects authorities to provide such detail as is necessary for contractors to prepare such tenders at the tender invitation stage'.[14] This requirement could be met by providing it to all tenderers with the invitation to tender documentation, subject to an appropriate confidentiality agreement having been entered into beforehand. This clearly places the onus on authorities to have TUPE information prepared well in advance of inviting tenders since any delay in providing it may constitute anti-competitive conduct. Moreover, in circumstances where a delay has occurred, authorities will have to consider an extension of time for the return of bids. Failure to do so could itself constitute anti-competitive conduct.

The onus is clearly placed on authorities to 'provide' TUPE information and it would be insufficient simply to invite contractors into an authority to examine it, or even wait for them to formally request it. This latter point is not free from doubt in so far as the DoE in its covering letter to the TUPE 'Issues Paper' has stated that, 'the government therefore takes the view that workforce information should be provided automatically or on request to any contractor and without restriction as to the bids which he may subsequently submit'.[15] This conflicts with the advice in DoE Circular 16/97 which makes no mention of providing information 'on request', and since the circular was

13 Page 21, G and page 22, A of the transcript. Leave to appeal was refused. This case is to be contrasted with the government's approach to the provision of workforce information in relation to competitive tendering in the NHS, set out in NHS Executive Guidance to NHS trusts, HSG [96]58 dated 15 November 1996 which endorses the approach taken by Oldham MBC. Indeed, in relation to the Civil Service, the government states in its document, Better Quality Services: A Handbook on Creating Public/Private Partnerships Through Market Testing and Contracting-Out, HMSO, 1998, at para 3.15, page 38 that, 'Departments should not provide the information that would be required under TUPE to a potential bidder who has said that it is not going to submit a TUPE - based bid'.

14 DoE Circular 16/97, paragraph 32. In relation to the Civil Service, the government states that, 'Departments should give potential bidders full and accurate information to allow them to calculate potential liabilities under TUPE'. C.F. Better Quality Services: A Handbook on Creating Public/Private Partnerships Through Market Testing and Contracting-Out, HMSO, 1998, at para 3.47, page 46.

15 Paragraph 10 of the covering letter from L.G. Packer, Head of Local Government Division 3, Department of the Environment to Local Authority Chief Executives dated 21 January 1994 entitled, ' Department of the Environment Issues Paper: Handling of TUPE Matters in relation to CCT' which accompanied the Issues Paper.

published subsequently and has statutory force it is considered to be the preferred approach.

In private sector business transfers it is usual for the transferor to continue to disclose changes in TUPE information up to the point of completion of the transfer. In the context of CCT, minor changes in TUPE information are not usually disclosed since they are unlikely to affect the tender price. However, significant changes in the information which would affect the pricing of tenders or the liabilities of the transferree should be provided to prospective tenderers before the tender return date. Material changes in TUPE information after the tender return date but prior to the award of the contract, such that they are likely to result in a substantial increase or decrease in liabilities on the transferee, should be disclosed to all tenderers and an extension of time granted for them to revise their bids if necessary. Failure to do so would not be in the best interests of the authority, which will wish to ensure that tenders are properly priced and resolved.[16] Furthermore, it will also wish to avoid claims for misrepresentation and allegations of anti-competitive conduct.

Confidentiality Agreements

As a matter of best practice TUPE information should only be disclosed to prospective tenderers subject to them entering into a confidentiality agreement executed under seal. [17] This should be entered into with prospective tenderers prior to tenders being invited to avoid any delay in the despatch of TUPE Information. This approach is endorsed by the government which notes that, 'authorities may wish to require an undertaking from tenderers that the information supplied will be used only for the purposes provided'.[18] It is important to ensure that such agreements adequately deal with security issues raised in the Eighth Data Protection Principle. Moreover, in relation to CCT it should not stipulate that TUPE Information will only be provided to

16 If at the evaluation stage it transpires that the leading tender is one to which the authority believes TUPE applies and the tenderer thinks it does not or vice versa, then the authority should contact the tenderer setting out its reasons and invite a revised bid. Also, all other tenderers should be given an extension of time to revise their bids. See Issue 7, paragraphs 14-17 of the TUPE Issues Paper, *supra*, n. 6.

17 This should avoid arguments over consideration, given that the tendering stage may not be regarded as contractual, in so far as the submission of a tender may only constitute an offer.

18 TUPE Issues Paper, *supra*, n.6 Issue 3, paragraph 9. In addition, authorities may wish to consider whether the confidentiality agreement should cover other commercially sensitive information which may need to be disclosed, such as overheads and running costs, details of leases etc. It is submitted that a confidentiality agreement which is legally enforceable is preferable to an undertaking from a tenderer.

tenderers on condition that they must submit a TUPE bid as opposed to a non-TUPE based bid since this is regarded as anti-competitive.[19]

What information should be provided to tenderers?

It is necessary to provide sufficient information to prospective tenderers to enable them to submit and cost a TUPE bid, should they wish to do so. It should allow a transferee's prospective liability in relation to transferred employees to be assessed. The government has listed 'the main items of information which will most often be relevant'[20] which is set out below:-

ANNEX A

WORKFORCE INFORMATION IN RELATION TO TRANSFEREES' PROSPECTIVE LIABILITY IN RELATION TO THE TUPE REGULATIONS

This note summarises the main items of information which will most often be relevant to transferees' prospective liability in relation to transferred staff. But each case must be considered individually, and any other relevant items of information must be made available.

(A) PRINCIPAL TERMS AND CONDITIONS OF EMPLOYMENT

- probationary period - if any
- retirement age
- pension arrangements
- periods of notice
- current pay agreements
- any agreed pay settlements yet to come into effect
- working hours
- annual leave entitlements
- sick leave entitlements
- maternity/paternity leave arrangements
- special leave arrangements
- terms and conditions of transfers
- season ticket loan scheme - if provided
- car leasing scheme - if provided

[19] *R v Secretary of State for the Environment, ex parte Oldham Metropolitan Borough Council*, QBD, Times Law Reports, 16 December 1996.

[20] TUPE Issues Paper, Issue 3, paragraph 8 and Annex A as subsequently amended to include reference to pension arrangements, *supra*, n.6.

(B) BASE DATA OF STAFF WHO WOULD TRANSFER

- numbers of staff who would transfer and, in respect of each person who would transfer, their:-
- age
- sex
- salary rates and number of staff on each rate
- reckonable service
- input hours
- regular overtime and wage rates
- other factors affecting redundancy entitlement
- any outstanding industrial injury, or other claims

(C) OTHER, GENERAL INFORMATION

- any relevant collective agreement
- sporting, social, welfare or other facilities provided which may be asserted to be employment benefits of staff
- facility time and facilities provided for trade union officials and health and safety representatives

It is important to note that the above list is not exhaustive and there may be other information which should be disclosed. It is not possible to be prescriptive about the information which should and should not be given. Each case must be judged on its merits. Indeed, prospective tenderers may find TUPE information prepared strictly in accordance with Annex A of the DoE Issues Paper unsatisfactory. It is common practice for contractors to send authorities detailed questionnaires which are far broader in scope than the information referred to in Annex A. As a matter of best practice, it is sensible to give full and relevant disclosure at the outset, in the transferor authority's standard format rather than responding to each prospective tenderers' individually designed questionnaire. This approach should save administrative time, minimize the risk of allegations of anti-competitive behaviour, and ensure the integrity of the tendering exercise in that each tenderer receives the same information.

Nonetheless, requests for additional information should be properly considered and provided to all tenderers if it is necessary for contractors to assess their liabilities and responsibilities. Paragraph 32 of DoE Circular 16/97 reminds authorities that 'where additional information is subsequently requested, and supplied, authorities should consider any additional time reasonably required to prepare bids'.

Format of Information

The government's TUPE Issues Paper offers no guidance on the format the information should take. Each authority will therefore have its own style of presentation. However, it is important that it is provided in a comprehensive and readily useable form. This may mean providing 'base data' for each individual anonymous employee such as hours of work, salary and so on. Formats which entail aggregated information, depending on the circumstances, may potentially be anti-competitive. Authorities will need to be able to justify their chosen format in the event of a complaint to the Secretary of State.

Data Collection and Verification

The collection and checking of TUPE information can be a lengthy process, and therefore needs to be commenced at least a couple of months prior to tenders being invited. This is a task for the personnel officer in liaison with the contract manager and client-side officer.

The reasons for this are as follows:-

- the information must be ready to send out with the invitation to tender;
- to ascertain which employees have TUPE rights, and what duties and liabilities will transfer to the transferee;
- the invitation to tender itself will need to contain information in respect of TUPE;
- to enable the transferor to respond to the transferee's requests for information in an efficient manner;
- to identify employees and others who may not have TUPE rights and to take account of this in any tendering exercise;
- to enable the transferor and transferee to inform and consult as required by TUPE.

It is not uncommon for personnel records to be deficient. Therefore, authorities should ensure, for example, that details such as continuous service include service with other local authorities and certain other bodies which is deemed to be continuous under the Redundancy Payments (Local Government) (Modification) Order 1983. Where practicable, it is advisable to check the accuracy of information with the employees affected. Internal Audit may wish to carry out their own checks and ensure, amongst other things, that persons on the TUPE list do not also appear on any list of prospective redundant employees prepared for the purposes of tender evaluation. In addition, audit will also require details of trainees and disabled staff who appear on the TUPE list since the extra costs of employing such staff may be deducted from the DSO's tender price in the tender evaluation process. Care and attention at this stage is vital if claims for negligence, misrepresentation, and/or anti-competitive behaviour are to be avoided.

Relevant Information

Details which are commonly sought by prospective tenderers in order to put together a fully costed tender and which should be disclosed include:-

Terms and Conditions of Service

Up-to-date copies of the relevant local and national terms and conditions of service should be provided. From July 1997, a new collective agreement known as the Single Status Agreement on terms and conditions of employment (the Green Book) was introduced for all local government employees, except craft workers. This harmonizes the former collective agreements covering administrative, professional, technical and clerical (APT&C) employees and manual workers. It is sensible to cross-reference this to an index page so there is no dispute about what a tenderer has actually received. It is also important that other collective agreements are included, together with any terms and conditions which are unique to the particular service being contracted-out, such as career grade schemes. Some authorities will have varied the national conditions of service for certain staff and the extent of this must be disclosed, together with any known changes which are likely to take effect in the future such as pending pay awards. Details of the Local Government Pension Scheme according to paragraph 32 of DoE Circular 16/97 should be disclosed to enable tenderers to cover pensions matters in their bids. Standard letters of appointment/contracts of employment applicable to each type of employee should be supplied to enable tenderers to be aware of job flexibility, and place of work. Various employment policies should be disclosed which may be either contractual or non-contractual such as disciplinary and grievance procedures, voluntary severance policy, redundancy policy, harassment and equal opportunities policy.

Base Data

The workforce information should appear on separate sheets for APT&C, Craft and Manual employees, to correspond with their respective conditions of service and the national and local agreements applicable to each group of employees. The lists should be further sub-divided into employees directly engaged on the service and those indirectly connected such as support services staff located in other departments. The information could be set out in a tabular format and include, amongst other things, the following details:-

- **Employee reference number**

  \- Employees' names and addresses should not be revealed, in order to protect their identity, and ensure compliance with data protection legislation.

- **Age** - Dates of birth need not be disclosed but should be checked with individual employees. Age is a relevant matter for disclosure because it enables a transferee to calculate redundancy liabilities. It could be projected forward to the potential transfer date. Employees in local government must retire at 65 years of age and persons who reach this age prior to the transfer date should not appear on the TUPE list.

- **Sex** - The gender breakdown of the workforce is relevant in order to ascertain the possibility of any discrimination or equal pay claims.

- **Salary rates and the number of staff on each rate**

  \- Some transferor authorities may choose to aggregate salary rates. However, this can be complicated and lead to a lack of transparency. It may be preferable in order to avoid allegations of anti-competitive conduct, to give salaries including grade and spinal column points and the extent of any grade for each individual employee. This could be projected forward to the proposed date of the transfer.

- **Reckonable service**

  \- Commencement dates are relevant for assessing the extent of employment rights and calculating redundancy pay. It is important that reckonable service details are checked with individual employees to ensure that continuous service includes service with other local authorities and certain other bodies which is deemed to be continuous under the Redundancy Payments (Local Government) (Modification) Order 1983. This information could be projected forward to the proposed transfer date.

- **Input Hours**

  - This is clearly different from 'contractual' hours. Strictly speaking, since it is only contractual hours which would transfer under TUPE it should not be necessary to disclose actual hours for each member of staff. However, failure to do so could lead to under-resourced bids and complaints of anti-competitive behaviour.

- **Regular overtime and wage rates**

  - Overtime is usually non-contractual. However, where it is regular or habitual it will need to be disclosed. Failure to disclose details could result in complaints of anti-competitive behaviour and/or claims for misrepresentation. One option is to disclose contractual hours, rates of pay for contractual hours, together with overtime rates, and average take home pay to enable contractors to compare it with what the employees would have taken home if no overtime had been paid.

- **Other factors affecting redundancy entitlement**

  - In addition to age, length of reckonable service, other relevant factors which need to be disclosed appear to be actual weekly pay (projected forward to the transfer date) excluding overtime unless it is contractual. Also, the number of weeks applicable for calculating redundancy pay should be given. The total number of weeks applicable can then be multiplied by the number of week's pay to give the redundancy pay entitlement which some authorities also choose to disclose. Other additional contractual payments which may affect redundancy payments should also be revealed. It is important to note that the local authorities' redundancy figures are likely to be in excess of the statutory redundancy figure since this is based on actual pay and continuous local government service.

- **Any outstanding industrial injury or other claims**

  - Liabilities for personal injury including disease cases and breach of statutory duty will transfer to the transferee. In *Taylor v Service Team Ltd and London Borough of Waltham Forest,*[21] a County Court held that liability for damages in tort for accidents at work transferred across to the transferee since it was connected with the contract of employment. It was also noted in *Secretary of State for Employment v Spence,*[22] that the obligations transferred under TUPE were not limited to contractual liabilities but could include tortious liabilities. Indeed, in *DJM International Limited v Nicholas,* [23] the EAT made it clear that non-contractual liabilities must be regarded as transferring, such as sex discrimination claims. Thus, it follows that any claims or prospective claims against the transferor such as industrial tribunal claims should be disclosed to the transferee. There may also be other claims such as unlawful deduction of wages.

Annex A to the Issues Paper makes it clear that 'other relevant items of information must be made available'. These might for instance include:-

- notice periods;
- details of full-time, job sharers/part-time employees;
- details of staff employed on non-standard, fixed term and other temporary contracts of employment. Under the Employment Rights Act 1996, the expiry of a fixed term contract without its renewal constitutes a dismissal. If a new contract is offered and accepted prior to the date of the transfer then the contract would continue after the transfer without a dismissal and the employee may have TUPE rights. However, if the transferor authority has no intention of renewing a contract which expires before the transfer then the details should not appear on the TUPE list;[24]

21 Romford County Court, 24th October 1997. Also, see Scorer, R. and Carmichael, D., Transfer of Undertakings: liability for personal injuries, in *Solicitors Journal*, 30th January 1998.

22 [1986] IRLR 248.

23 [1996] IRLR, 76.

24 The Local Government Management Board: *CCT, TUPE and the ARD: Legal and Practical Implications. An information Guide for Local Authorities*, 1st edn., 1996, page 32.

- details of trade union membership, although the transferor is only likely to have details so far as it is responsible for making deductions of trade union subscriptions; and details of shop stewards; details of recognised trade unions, details of facilities provided, and any agreements or arrangements reached with them, and details of forthcoming pay negotiations;

- details of disabled staff and nature of the disability. This could affect productivity levels and the liabilities and responsibilities of the transferee under the Disability Discrimination Act 1995 which may, for example, require 'reasonable adjustments' to be made;

- details of health and safety policy, representatives, prohibition/ improvement notices, committees, and any claims;

- details of staff on maternity leave at the date of the transfer since they may have the right to return to work either full-time or perhaps as job sharers with the transferee;

- details of any 'bars' between linked grades for each individual employee;

- details of staff acting up and receiving extra payment;

- details of staff on protected salaries;

- details of staff paid hourly, weekly or monthly;

- details of staff to whom personal commitments have been made, such as the payment of professional body fees, professional subscriptions, payment of course fees, books, time off work whether paid or not to attend courses, study time;

- details of staff who are parking permit holders and their nominal values;

- details of staff in receipt of various allowances such as car user allowances, clothing allowances, telephone allowances, first aid allowances, disturbance allowances, stand-by allowances, early duties allowances and so on;

- details of staff in the Local Government Pension Scheme together with details of the scheme. Paragraph 32 of DoE Circular 16/97 provides that tenderers should be given sufficient information about existing pension arrangements of transferring staff, to enable tenderers to cover pensions matters to their bids. The DoE issued a document to all Local Authority Chief Executives entitled, 'Handling of Pensions Matters in Relation to CCT', dated 15 March 1995 in which they permit authorities to require 'broadly comparable' pensions and that this would not in itself be regarded by the Secretary of State as anti-competitive conduct. Pension rights are not protected under TUPE,[25] but parts of the Local Government Pension Scheme which are not old-age, Invalidity or survivors' benefits will pass under TUPE. Therefore, contractors need to be aware of these benefits and their potential liabilities. These are: discretion for immediate payment of pension and payment of added years for redundant staff aged 50 and over; injury and incapacity benefits; enhanced redundancy calculations based on actual pay and full length of local government service;[26]

- details of bonus schemes. An explanation of who is covered and how the scheme works in practice will be required as part of the summary of terms and conditions relating to local agreements. Some commentators suggest that details of individuals' performances under a bonus scheme should not be revealed.[27] However, it is arguable that if the scheme is basically one which is contractual and guarantees extra pay and not really based on productivity then it should be disclosed. Of course, this will in effect reveal the total wages bill;

25 *Adams and Others v Lancashire County Council and Another*, Times Law Reports, May 19th, 1997, (CA).

26 For further guidance see Local Government Management Board, *CCT, Pensions and Transfers: An Information Guide for Local Authorities*, 1995, page 19. However, a recent EAT case, *Frankling v BPS Public Sector Limited* (unreported, EAT/442/98) held that rights to enhanced benefits payable on redundency do not pass under TUPE because they fell within Article 3/Regulation 7 exception (the exclusion of occupational pensions) as they were payable under an occupational scheme and related to old age. The *Frankling* case only relates to the NHS but will create uncertainty for central government and local government where similar arguments could be raised. It should be noted that these are certain differences for local government where employees aged 50 and over do not have an automatic right to enhanced redundancy pay on redundancy.

27 LGMB, *supra*, n.24, p 39.

- details of vacant posts. The transferor should reserve the right to fill these posts;

- details of job titles and job descriptions. This is not expressly referred to in Annex A. Some commentators argue that details of working practices should not be disclosed. Indeed to do so in a small service undertaking could identify individuals, in breach of the Data Protection legislation. On the other hand, given that such information is contractual, and indicates flexibility in terms of place of work, job or hours of work, failure to supply it could restrict tenderers from forming an opinion on future costs and the organizational structure which they will inherit. Therefore, those transferors which wish to avoid allegations of acting anti-competitively may err on the side of caution and disclose these details, albeit in an aggregated form;

- details of trainees. This information will also be required for the purposes of tender evaluation. An authority needs to be satisfied whether such persons have TUPE rights or not;

- details of secondees into and out of the service. Employees temporarily seconded into a service may not have TUPE rights, whereas those seconded elsewhere at the time of the transfer may well have TUPE rights and their details may therefore need to be disclosed;

- details of employees on long-term sick leave since such staff may have the right to return to work with the transferee. For example, staff on sick leave for a period in excess of one month could be supplied;

- tenderers may request details of staff allocated to specific work locations. Care needs to be exercised about disclosing information of this nature since it may give private contractors a competitive advantage;

- details of employees in other departments which provide support services to the service being transferred who may have TUPE rights;

- details of outstanding loans. For example, under national and possibly local conditions of service, employees in certain circumstances may be entitled to a car loan. The agreement usually provides that where employment with the authority granting the loan ceases prior to the repayment of the loan, the remaining balance plus accrued interest becomes repayable immediately. This raises the question as to whether the employee is required to repay the remaining balance in a TUPE transfer situation? Since employees should be in a no less favourable position following a TUPE transfer, it may not be appropriate to require an employee to repay the outstanding balance otherwise this would be detrimental to the employee. It is therefore a matter for agreement between the transferor authority and the transferee about how the outstanding sums owing to the transferor will be repaid.[28] One option would be to require the contractor to pay the transferor authority any outstanding sums. The contractor could then establish a 'broadly comparable' scheme for those employees concerned. Alternatively, the transferor authority could at its discretion permit the affected employees to continue to make payments on the same basis as before the transfer;

- percentage split of time spent working in the service. It is not strictly necessary to give this information, and it should be sufficient to indicate to prospective tenderers that it is believed that those staff on the TUPE list spend in excess of two thirds of their time on the service or whatever proportion they believe implies 'assignment' to the contract in accordance with the *Botzen* case.[29] However, where there is real uncertainty about whether certain staff have TUPE rights it may be prudent to indicate percentages of time they are believed to spend working in the service, and let the transferee decide the position. It should be remembered that this is a crude test and not necessarily indicative of TUPE rights;

- Atypical staff. Transferor authorities are advised to indicate the use of any consultancy, agency, locums, casual, temporary or relief staff who may be employees for the purposes of TUPE and who would transfer if their services are actually being used on the date of the transfer. Alternatively, there may be staff whom it is believed do not have TUPE rights but about whom the authority as a matter of law cannot be certain in this regard. In these circumstances it is advisable

[28] Ibid., p.36.

[29] Case 186/83, ECJ, [1986] 2CMLR 50.

to indicate in broad terms their numbers and hours involved. This should ensure that tenders are properly resourced. In the event of a transfer, details of such staff with their consent could be given to the successful contractor who may wish to make continued use of their services.

Information which does not need to be disclosed

The critical question to determine whether information should be disclosed is whether it would allow contractors to assess their responsibilities and full liabilities. This is usually straightforward. However, there are grey areas and each request for information should be judged on its merits and the onus placed on contractors to justify why they need it. The transferor authority will need to balance any decision to refuse to supply information with the potential risks of a successful challenge that refusal constituted anti-competitive conduct. Thus, while it is not free from doubt, it appears that the following types of information need not be disclosed in the first instance, because it will not necessarily assist prospective tenderers to assess their liabilities, and/or relates to how the service has been provided before the transfer:-

- Individuals' names, addresses and dates of birth. The TUPE information should anonymise employees by way of a reference number.

- Individuals' CVs, experience and qualifications. It should be sufficient to assure the transferee that the staff are skilled to perform the service being tendered, but transferors should beware of giving warranties in this regard.

- Disciplinary and grievance records.

- Details of individuals' sickness records. Arguably brief details of staff on long-term sick leave should be disclosed.

- Proposed new terms and conditions of employment which are conditional on the in-house team's bid being accepted by the authority.

- Details of irregular, non-contractual overtime.

- Details of the in-house team's current working practices and organizational structure (e.g. job descriptions and job titles). However, failure to disclose these details following a specific request may constitute anti-competitive conduct.

- Details of individuals' performances under a discretionary bonus scheme, provided it is not akin to a scheme which guarantees pay. However, disclosure will be required particularly if the bonus is contractual.

- Information which indicates where individual employees are located. Disclosure of this type of information, for example in relation to catering services, could impinge upon the competitive advantage of the existing service provider. However, there may be cogent reasons necessitating disclosure particularly if a contractor only wishes to tender for certain services at specific sites and where bids for part of the Service have not been ruled out by the authority.

TUPE Transfers : confidentiality of employee records

In each case public sector organisations will need to ensure they do not breach the common law principle of confidentiality or their obligations under the Data Protection Act where it is proposed to disclose TUPE information.

Confidentiality

There is a common law duty on employers not to disclose to third parties information given in confidence about employees unless their consent has been obtained or expressly authorised by statute.[30] Therefore, it is important to recognise the understandings and circumstances at the time when the information was gathered, which is normally at the recruitment stage. For example, express commitments not to disclose may have been given to an employee. Information is not necessarily confidential merely because it is personal. Information may be confidential because it is sensitive (for example, health records) or because it is disclosed under a specific obligation to keep it confidential or because a duty to maintain confidentiality is imposed on the person to whom it is disclosed.[31]

[30] *Dalgleish and others v Lothian and Borders Police Board* [1991] IRLR 422, where an interim injunction was granted restraining the employing board from disclosing the contents of staff records including the names and addresses to the Lothian Regional Council for the purposes of identifying alleged community charge defaulters. The judge took the view that such information was confidential in that it had been given to the employers in the context of the employment relationship.

[31] For a discussion of the equitable principle of breach of confidence, see Rabinder Singh: 'Standing up to Big Brother' in the *Solicitors Journal*, 21 October 1994, pp. 1074-1075.

Data Protection Act 1984

The 1984 Act concerns the protection of 'personal data' held on computer data bases, which includes details such as names and addresses held on computer about living, identifiable individuals, including public sector employees. It establishes rights of individuals who are subjects of the data - 'data subjects' and it introduces obligations on the part of the 'data users' who are those who control[32] the contents and use the personal data concerned. The 1984 Act also sets up a registration scheme whereby persons or organisations holding personal data must register with the Data Protection Registrar details of the information they hold, which includes intended uses and disclosures to third parties unless an exemption applies. Data users are also required to comply with the eight legally enforceable 'Data Protection Principles'. 'Data' which is subject to the 1984 Act includes, '... information recorded in a form in which it can be processed by equipment operating automatically in response to instructions given for that purpose' .[33]

Section 34(5)(a) of the 1984 Act permits disclosure of personal data which is 'required by or under any enactment, by any rule of law...' and allows such disclosures to be made without breaching the 1984 Act even where disclosure is not registered and/or would normally be in breach of the data protection principles. Paragraph 32 of DoE Circular 16/97 (which has statutory force) states that contractors 'will need information on the numbers of staff who would transfer and their terms and conditions of service' and provides for authorities 'to provide such detail as is necessary' for contractors to prepare tenders. However, this would not appear to be sufficient to permit the disclosure of personal data, except in an anonymous format, without breaching the 1984 Act. The TUPE regulations do not currently require disclosure about staff to prospective tenderers. Thus, where there is no legal obligation

[32] 'Control' means having the power to decide what information about an individual is to be recorded, whether it should be added to, amended or deleted and to what use the recorded information may be put either by the data user or by the others. It is not the same as physically controlling either the processing operations or the discs on which the data are acquired. Control may also be shared jointly or in common with other data users. 'Jointly' means that control is exercised by acting together. Control 'in common' is where data users share a pool of information, each changing, adding to or using information for its own purposes independently of the other. The extent of control between data users may vary, with one having more control over content, and another data user having more control over its use. Processing may be carried out by third parties on behalf of the data user. Such a third party may fall within the definition of a 'computer bureau' in the 1984 Act.

[33] Section 1(2) of the Data Protection Act 1984. The EC Data Protection Directive 95/46/EC was formally adopted by the EU in October 1995 and was to be implemented by October 1998 and would include not only electronic data which is covered by the 1984 Act but also manual records. (i.e. non-computerised). The Data Protection Act 1998 implements the Directive into UK law but is not yet in force.

to provide information, the 1984 Act will apply in the usual way to any disclosures of personal data through registration and compliance with the eight data protection principles.

Under the 1984 Act, information must be held for proper purposes and only disclosed in accordance with prior formal registration. Public sector organisations, as data users, will have to check that they have registered for the purposes of collecting personal data on employees, since the 1984 Act forbids the holding of personal data by any person who does not register as a data user.[34] Moreover, on registration the data user must give a description of and the purposes for which personal data or information contained in that data is held and the third parties to whom disclosure is intended.[35] Therefore, potential transferors should ensure that their registration permits disclosure to potential tenderers, otherwise workforce information held on computer cannot lawfully be disclosed.[36] Appropriate registrations under the 1984 Act should permit disclosure to past, current or prospective employers. The government argues that, 'the [1984] Act does not prevent the disclosure of information which is not of a "personal nature". The relevant information to enable tenderers to assess their responsibilities and prospective liabilities, should TUPE apply, should not normally involve personal information in the terms of the Data Protection Act, and authorities should normally be able to provide it within the requirements of the Act, and without breach of their duty of confidentiality to employees'.[37] In other words, if information is given in a de-personalised format the 1984 Act would not be contravened.

However, Cirell and Bennett argue that this could conflict with the Secretary of State's view expressed in paragraph 32 of Circular 16/97 that authorities should disclose information concerning the numbers of staff who would transfer, and their terms and conditions of service. This is because it may be possible to identify from general information, certain living individuals, particularly where small contracts are being tendered.[38] The government's view is that 'authorities may require an undertaking from tenderers that the information supplied will be used only for the purpose provided'.[39] However, this would not prevent a breach of the 1984 Act occurring.

34 Section 5(1) of the Data Protection Act 1984.

35 S. Cirell and J. Bennett : 'Entangled Laws: conspiracy or confusion?', *Local Government Chronicle*, 19 November 1993, pp. 20-21.

36 The penalties for using personal data for unregistered purposes include enforcement notices or de-registration by the Data Protection Registrar. Also the 'data subject' can claim compensation in the courts for unauthorised disclosure. Failure to register is a criminal offence, as is contravention of the Eight Data Protection Principles.

37 Department of the Environment, Issues Paper, *supra,* n.6, Issue 3, paragraph 9.

38 S. Cirell and J. Bennett, *supra,* n. 35, p.21.

39 Issues Paper, *supra,* n.6, Issue 3, paragraph 9.

Pre-Tender Stage

Disclosures of personal data must be registered as a disclosure to 'potential suppliers of goods and services'. Authorities must also comply with the Eight Data Protection Principles. The Data Protection Registrar considers that compliance by an authority with the First Data Protection Principle requires the data user, when considering the disclosure of personal data, to inform all such persons affected, that a tendering exercise is proceeding, and that workforce information may potentially be transferred to a number of prospective tenderers.

There will be no breach of the 1984 Act or the duty of confidentiality if the employee agrees to disclosure of information held about him. The Data Protection Registrar considers that most workforce information can be aggregated and anonymised to some extent, but cautions that some staff may still be readily identifiable, for example because they are close to retirement, or happen to be supervisors/managers on a certain grade.

The Issues Paper does not deal with the problem where information cannot be anonymised and where the 'data subject'objects to his personal data being disclosed. As Professor Napier argues, disclosure in such circumstances could constitute a breach of the First Data Protection Principle, which requires personal data to be obtained and processed fairly and lawfully.[40] This basically means that the employee should not have been misled as to the uses his information would be put to, at the time it was collected. The Data Protection Tribunal has ruled that the question of fairness is to be decided primarily by reference to the interests of the data subject, not the data user. In another Data Protection Tribunal decision, it was said that the words 'fairly obtained' which occurred in the First Data Protection Principle had to be construed by looking at the position at the date the information was obtained, not by reference to what happened at any later date.[41] Moreover, tenderers may claim that aggregated and anonymised information is not sufficient for their purpose and request information in a format which may identify living individuals, giving rise to a disclosure of personal data. Depending on how the Courts would construe section 34(5) of the 1984 Act, this is likely to constitute a disclosure of personal data which would be regulated by the 1984 Act.

[40] Data Protection Act 1984, Guidline No. 4; DPA 1984, Section 2(1), Schedule 1, Part II, paragraph 1(1). Also, see Association of Metropolitan Authorities, 'Tupe - the debate continues: A report from the AMA conference TUPE : what's going on?' Part Two held on 2 February 1994, page 23 (Prepared by Stephen Bubb and Deirdre Mason) 1st Edition, March 1994.

[41] *Innovations (Mail Order) Limited v Data Protection Registrar,* Case No DA/9231/49/1 c.f. 'TUPE - the debate continues', Association of Metropolitan Authorities, 1st Ed. March 1994, pages 22-23.

Equally, the Secretary of State may regard aggregated information in certain circumstances as anti-competitive. Where personal data identifying living individuals is disclosed to tenderers, authorities must ensure such disclosures are properly registered under the appropriate purpose(s) within the data protection registrations. Since the disclosing body is responsible for the security of workforce information and compliance with the Eighth Data Protection Principle (Security), the Data Protection Registrar suggests that it is essential that authorities only disclose information subject to tenderers entering into a confidentiality agreement which reflects these security obligations. In the event that a tenderer is unsuccessful, then they should be required to return all personal data to the authority without any further use. Prospective tenderers may need to register as data users for the personal data they receive from the authority during the pre-tender stage. This is because they will be processing the data in their own right to prepare a bid.

Award of contract to a private contractor

Once a private contractor has been appointed, then the local authority and the private contractor will need to determine how the registration elements of the 1984 Act are complied with. How a data user registers depends on who controls that personal data. For example, if a statutory function has been contracted-out, such as the collection of council tax, then the local authority will remain the data user for the personal data involved. This is because they are required under statute to carry out certain functions. The Deregulation and Contracting Out Act 1994 allows the Secretary of State to authorise the contracting-out of specified local authority functions such as Council Tax collection to a third party contractor. However, the effect of such contracting-out by virtue of section 72 is that anything done or omitted by the contractor is regarded as if it had been done or omitted by the local authority itself. In addition, if the contractor also has some control over the personal data, such as assisting in the collection of council tax, then they too must register as a data user. On the other hand, where an authority still retains complete control over the personal data involved for that service, but where the functions are performed on a day to day basis by a private contractor acting on the instructions of the authority, then the authority must register as a data user, and the contractor must register as a 'computer bureau'. In the context of CCT, the control of personal data is usually a joint agreement between the authority and the successful contractor registering as data users. The Data Protection Registrar suggests that the contract conditions should reflect the amount of control existing between the parties, and highlights the need to comply with the eight legally enforceable Data Protection Principles. In particular, the Eighth Data Protection Principle concerning security measures should be reflected in any CCT contract, stating that all personal data used by the contractor, enabling them to perform the service, should either be destroyed or returned after the expiry of the contract. Moreover, it should be stipulated that during the contract period, personal data must be used only for the purpose of the authority's contract.[42]

Which employees are employed in the undertaking or part transferred?

This question appears relatively uncontroversial. However, it is an area which can cause practical problems when preparing workforce information in the context of CCT or marker testing where only part of an undertaking may be contracted-out. This is because the employees who work in the undertaking which is being contracted-out may carry out work for other parts of the authority which does not form part of the contract. Prospective tenderers will need to know which employees will transfer under TUPE in order to assess their responsibilities and liabilities.

Legal Principles

The starting point is the Acquired Rights Directive (77/187/EEC) as amended (the Directive). The European Court of Justice has consistently held that the Directive must be interpreted according to the terms of its purpose. As stated in the second recital of its preamble, the aim of the Directive is, 'the safeguarding of the rights of employees'. This approach has been endorsed in numerous European Court of Justice cases.[43]

The TUPE regulations, were made to implement the Directive and should be interpreted purposively so as to accord with the interpretation of the Directive as laid down in the European Court of Justice, if that can be done without distorting [their] meaning.[44]

To that end Article 1(1) provides:

> 'This Directive shall apply to the transfer of an undertaking, business or part of a business to another employer as a result of a legal transfer or merger.'

42 Information in letter to author from Caroline Bishop, compliance officer, on behalf of the Data Protection Registrar, August 20,1996.

43 *Landsorganisationen i Danmark v Ny Molle Kro* 287/86 [1989] IRLR 37, ECJ, at para 12; *Foreningen af Arbejdsledere i Danmark v Daddy's Dance Hall A/S*, 324/86 [1988] IRLR 315, ECJ, at para 9; *Dr Sophie Redmond Stichting v Bartol*, C-29/91 [1992] IRLR 366, ECJ at para 11; and *Schmidt v Spar -und Leihkasse der Früheren Amter Bordesholm, Keil und Cronshagen* C-392/92, [1994] IRLR 302, ECJ, para 15.

44 *Webb v Emo Air Cargo Limited* [1993] IRLR 27, HL at para 21; *Buchanan-Smith v Schleicher and Co International Limited* [1996] IRLR 547, at para 13; *M.A. Dines v Initial Health Care Services Limited and Pall Mall Services Limited*, [1994], IRLR 336, CA, at para 37.

Article 3(1) provides:

> 'The transferor's rights and obligations arising from a contract of employment or from an employment relationship existing on the date of a transfer shall, by reason of such a transfer, be transferred to the transferee.'

Regulation 2(1) provides:

> '"employee" means any individual who works for another person whether under a contract of service or apprenticeship or otherwise but does not include anyone who provides services under a contract for services and references to a person's employer shall be construed accordingly.'
>
> '"Contract of employment" means any agreement between an employee and his employer determining the terms and conditions of his employment.'

Regulation 2(2) provides:

> 'References in these Regulations to the transfer of part of an undertaking are references to a transfer of a part which is being transferred as a business...'

Regulation 3(2) provides:

> 'Subject as aforesaid, these Regulations so apply whether the transfer is effected by sale or by some other disposition or by operation of law.'

Regulation 5(1) provides:

> 'A relevant transfer shall not operate so as to terminate the contract of employment of any person employed by the transferor in the undertaking or part transferred but any such contract which would otherwise have been terminated by the transfer shall have effect after the transfer as if originally made between the person so employed and the transferee.'

Regulation 5(3) provides:

> 'Any reference in [Regulation 5(1)] above to a person employed in an undertaking or part of one transferred by a relevant transfer is a reference to a person so employed immediately before the transfer, including, where the transfer is effected by a series of two or more transactions, a person so employed immediately before any of those transactions.'

WHO TRANSFERS?

The first point to note is that regulation 2(1) makes it clear that only 'employees' working under 'a contract of service or apprenticeship or otherwise', as opposed to a contract for services, are protected under regulation 5. This is broader in scope than the definition of employee contained in Section 230 of the Employment Rights Act 1996, which provides that an ' 'employee' means an individual who has entered into or works under (or where the employment has ceased, worked under) a contract of employment and 'contract of employment' means a contract of service or apprenticeship, whether express or implied and (if it is expressed) whether it is oral or in writing'. Therefore, workers who appear to be covered are casuals, temporary staff or trainees, and possibly agency staff depending on the construction of their contracts but not self employed persons such as consultants.[45]

However, this is not free from doubt given that Article 3(1) of the Directive covers not only those covered by a 'contract of employment' but also applies to rights and obligations arising from an 'employment relationship'. The scope of this latter term has not been defined by the UK courts.[46] It is a

[45] Traditionally, agency staff were thought to be neither employees of the agency, nor of the business for which they were employed. This view as a proposition of law is incorrect, and their status will depend on the nature of the agreement they have with the agency. In *McMeechan v Secretary of State for Employment* [1997] IRLR 353, the Court of Appeal ruled that an agency worker could be regarded as an employee of the agency. The Court of Appeal noted that there were two separate agreements, the general terms of employment with the agency, and the specific assignment. It decided there was no employee status under the general agreement but, for the duration of the particular assignment with a client, the worker was to be regarded as an employee of the agency.

[46] In *Cowell v Quilter Goodison Co Limited and QG Management Services Limited* [1989] IRLR 392, the Court of Appeal acknowledged that 'an employment relationship' could have a potentially broad application. Nevertheless, the Court rejected the argument that it was sufficiently broad to include an equity partner in a stockbroking partnership who provided services under a contract for services and was therefore excluded from the definition of employee in regulation 2(1) of TUPE.

matter for the courts to apply ordinary principles of national law to determine whether a person is an employee working under a contract of service or as self-employed under a contract for services.[47] In the UK, employment status depends on the common law position. The courts have developed a number of tests to distinguish employees working under a contract of service from the self-employed person who works under a contract for services.[48] Thus, it appears that self-employed staff are not covered by the TUPE regulations, unless the UK courts determine that such workers are employees under the usual legal tests. Professor McMullen takes the view that agency workers appear to be excluded under the TUPE regulations because they are not employees of the transferor. However, he holds out the possibility, yet to be tested in the courts, that regulation 2(1) of TUPE that covers an employed person who 'works for another person' is manipulable enough to cover agency staff working in the transferor's undertaking. He also notes that proposed revisions to the Acquired Rights Directive would prevent member states from, amongst other things, excluding temporary employment relationships within the meaning of Article 1(2) of Council Directive 91/383/EEC which might bring agency workers within the ambit of the TUPE Regulations.[49]

Casual or 'marginal' workers are an increasing feature of the flexible public sector labour market. Casual staff, although temporary, may or may not be employees, depending on all the facts surrounding their contractual relationship with their employer. Whether casuals doing occasional work do so under a succession of separate employment contracts or under one 'global' or 'umbrella' contract, or as self-employed under a contract for services depends on the facts of each case. Casuals who do not work for extended periods may do so under a contract of service when working, but not under a long-term 'umbrella' contract. Their continuity of service may be broken by a break in service which exceeds the statutory week (Sunday to Saturday)

47 *Mikkelsen v Danmols Inventar* [1986] CMLR 316.

48 For example, see *O'Kelly v Trusthouse Forte plc* [1983] IRLR, 369, CA; *Lane v Shire Roofing Co (Oxford) Limited* [1995], IRLR, 493, CA; and *Lee Ting Sang v Chung Chi-Keung* [1990] 2AC, 374, [1990] ICR 409, PC.

49 McMullen, J., 'Atypical Transfers, Atypical Workers and Atypical Employment Structures - A case for Greater Transparency in Transfer of Employment Issues' in ILJ, 25, 4, December 1996 at p.297. The case of *Governing Body of Clifton Middle School v Askew* [1997] ICR 808; EAT tends to support the view that agency workers supplied to a transferor are not covered by TUPE, because they may work for the transferor, but are not under a contract with it. The EAT decided that the words, 'or otherwise' in regulation 2(1) meant an equivalent contract.

during which they have no contract of employment with their employer, unless they can establish sufficient continuity under the Employment Rights Act 1996.[50]

Casual workers who work for extended periods probably do so as employees and may be able to establish two years' continuous service under an 'umbrella' contract, and thus be able to claim statutory employment rights upon termination. The reason for this is that gaps in employment may be bridged and contribute to continuity of service, if the gaps are short in relation to the weeks in which the employee was working for the employer. Other casuals who work on an irregular basis may do so as an employee during the actual periods of work, but with no continuity of service to bridge the gaps between periods of work. Usually there is no obligation on the employer to offer work, and no obligation on the worker to accept it. Notwithstanding the lack of 'mutuality of obligations' often associated with casuals, it is likely that such persons would be regarded by the courts as employees when they are actually working.[51] Furthermore, provided the work is sufficiently regular, continuity of service may accrue irrespective of the fact that these atypical workers will often be engaged on 'zero hours' contracts.[52]

[50] Continuity of service is governed by Schedule 13 to the EPCA 1978, (now Part XIV of the Employment Rights Act 1996). Marginal workers can potentially gain continuity under paragraph 9(1)(b) or (c) of Schedule 13 (now Section 212(3)(b) and (c) of the Employment Rights Act 1996). Broadly speaking, continuity is not broken by periods where there is no contract of employment provided the cessation is temporary, a strike or lockout, absence due to illness or injury not exceeding 26 weeks, absence due to custom or arrangement and pregnancy.

[51] D. Cockburn, M. Edwards, S. Levinson, V. Middleton, N. Rose, *Know-How For Employment Lawyers*, FT Law and Tax, 1st ed., 1995, pp. 103-108. Also see *Clark v Oxfordshire Health Authority*, [1998] IRLR. 125; CA. This case concerned a 'bank nurse' who was not regarded as employed under a 'global contract' of employment during the periods of her engagements, because of the absence of mutuality of obligations subsisting over the entire duration of the relevant period. This case only dealt with employment status when the nurse was not working, and did not deal with her status during a specific engagement. In *Carmichael v National Power plc* [1998] IRLR 301, the Court of Appeal determined that casual tour guides who worked on 'as required' basis which involved an implied term that the firm would offer a reasonable amount of guide work and that the guides would undertake a reasonable amount of such work when offered amounted to a contract of employment. Thus, a casual 'as required' contract, depending on how it is drafted, can have the requisite mutuality of obligation between the parties to be construed as an 'umbrella' contract of employment.

[52] In *Brown v Chief Adjudication Officer* [1997] IRLR 110, the Court of Appeal decided a casual worker employed on a day to day basis for over 3 months was deemed to be employed under a contract for an indefinite period. (See Section 86 of the Employment Rights Act 1996) and thus was entitled to statutory minimum notice of termination and statutory sick pay. For further discussion concerning casual workers see Frank Walton, *The Employment Contracts Handbook: Practical Guidance and Procedures,* Gee publishing Limited, Chapter 5 'Temporary Employment'.

Thus, it seems prudent to include in the TUPE information, any staff which are regarded as 'self-employed' and other atypical workers, including casual and relief staff. Casuals who are actually working on the day of the transfer are likely to be protected under TUPE because in many cases they will have employee status. It should be remembered that no minimum length of continuous service is needed to acquire TUPE rights. There may be some staff who work very infrequently with large gaps between engagements. In such cases it may be prudent simply to disclose the fact that use is made of such staff together with details of the nature of engagement and the number of hours they have worked.

Who is employed in that part of the undertaking transferred?

It is not always straightforward to determine who is employed in the undertaking transferred. Under TUPE, an employee of the transferor will only transfer if employed in an undertaking immediately before the transfer. This causes particular difficulties in relation to staff who do not work wholly in the undertaking or support staff who spend time supporting the undertaking but are usually based outside it. The first reported UK case which applied a percentage of time test was *Anderson v Kluwer Publishing Limited*.[53] The industrial tribunal held that an employee was employed in part of a business sold when he spent 80 per cent of his time there. The tribunal did not indicate what, if any, was the required minimum percentage to infer TUPE rights. Indeed, percentages quoted by commentators vary from 50 percent to 90 per cent or more. However, this case pre-dated the leading European Court of Justice case of *Botzen v Rotterdamsche Droogdok Maatschappij B.V* [54] which decided that the transfer principle relates to those employees 'assigned' to the transferred undertaking and did not refer to any percentage test.[55]

In *Botzen*, certain identifiable departments of a bankrupt company were sold, and the issue was whether employees employed in a staff department (for example, personnel, porter's services, general maintenance) that were not transferred but which had performed duties for the transferred departments had TUPE rights.

The Advocate General, Sir Gordon Slynn argued in his opinion that employees must be 'wholly' employed in the part of the business transferred. The only exception to this requirement would be where an employee was

[53] COIT 15068/85, Industrial Tribunal, 4 September 1985.

[54] Case 186/83. [1986] 2 CMLR; 50 [1985] ECR 519; ECJ.

[55] McMullen, J., *supra*, n.49, page 303.

required to perform other duties which could be regarded as 'de minimis'. He went on to say that if a worker in fact is engaged in the activities of the whole business or in several parts then he cannot be regarded for the purpose of the directive as an employee 'of' the part of the business transferred.[56] The ECJ upheld the European Commission's view:-

> 'that the only decisive criteria regarding the transfer of employees' rights and obligations is whether or not a transfer takes place of the department to which they were assigned and which formed the organizational framework within which their employment relationship took effect.'[57]

However, it formulated its own test of 'assignment':-

> 'An employment relationship is essentially characterized by the link existing between the employee and the part of the undertaking or business to which he is assigned to carry out his duties. In order to decide whether the rights and obligations under an employment relationship are transferred under Directive 77/187 by reason of a transfer within the meaning of Article 1(1) thereof, it is therefore sufficient to establish to which part of the undertaking or business the employee was assigned.'[58]

The ECJ therefore decided that Article 3(1) of the Directive did not cover employees who, although not employed in the transferred part of the undertaking, performed duties which involved the use of assets assigned to the part transferred or who, whilst being employed in an administrative department of the undertaking which was not itself transferred, carried out duties for the benefit of the part transferred.[59]

Given the above, how should an authority determine to which part of the undertaking a person has been 'assigned'? The test for 'assignment'appears to be fairly stringent. The UK courts may adopt the Advocate General's opinion in *Botzen*, namely that an employee had to be ' wholly' engaged in the part transferred except to the extent that his other duties which he was required to perform were 'de minimis'. This view would not preclude the

[56] *Botzen v Rotterdamsche Droogdok Maatschappij B.V.*, case 186/83 [1986] 2 CMLR 50, ECJ, pages 52-53.

[57] Ibid., p.57, para 14.

[58] Ibid., p.57, para 15.

[59] Ibid., p.57 at para 16. The ECJ has subsequently endorsed this approach in *Schmidt v Spar* [1994] IRLR 302, ECJ at para 13.

transfer of, for example, a wages clerk who works in a staff department, which is not transferred as a separate unit, provided he works exclusively on the wages of the staff of the part transferred.[60] The European Court of Justice view is arguably more stringent than this and requires full-time employment in the undertaking being transferred.[61]

The law has developed significantly in the last ten years. However, the *Botzen* test remains good law, but should be applied in the light of recent decisions of the European Court of Justice which has interpreted the Directive widely to protect employees' rights. Ultimately, whether a person is 'assigned' to a transferred activity is a question of fact for national courts to determine and it is difficult to detect any consistency of approach by the UK courts. *Botzen* has been followed in several UK cases such as *Gale v Northern General Hospital NHS Trust*.[62] This was a continuation of employment case. Mr Gale was employed by Sheffield Health Authority as a student nurse for most of his time at the Northern General Hospital. The hospital became an NHS Trust which offered Mr Gale employment on completion of his training. Mr Gale's employment was subsequently terminated and his claim for unfair dismissal was contested on the grounds that he lacked the requisite two years continuous service. The court rejected the contention that Mr Gale's employment with the Trust was continuous with the Health Authority since he had not been 'assigned' to the part of the health authority's undertaking which was transferred, namely the Northern General Hospital despite the fact he had worked there for nine months before the transfer and for one year thereafter. The reason for this was that under his contract he could be transferred to any other hospital by the District Health Authority. Thus, at the time of the transfer he was not part of the permanent staff of the hospital. He was not part of the 'human stock' belonging to the hospital but was somebody who, at the behest of the health authority, was completing his training there.[63]

This case makes it clear that merely working in the part of the undertaking at the time of the transfer does not necessarily infer 'assignment' as defined by *Botzen*. Thus, certain trainees, secondees or staff providing temporary cover who are attached to part of an undertaking at the time of a transfer may not be protected by TUPE. However, whether they are assigned to the part transferred will depend on the particular facts of each case including the whole employment relationship and not just what they were actually doing at the time of the transfer.

60 *Botzen, supra*, n. 56, p53.

61 Ibid., p.57, para 16.

62 [1994] IRLR 292, CA.

63 Ibid., para 12.

In *Sunley Turriff Holdings Limited v Thomson*[64], Mr Thomson was the company secretary and chief accountant of two associated companies, LC Limited ('LC') and LC (Scotland) Limited ('LC(S)'). His contract of employment was with LC, but he also worked for the LC(S). He continued to work for both companies when they went into receivership. When LC(S) was sold, the sale included a large part of the LC undertaking consisting of its work in Scotland. Notwithstanding the fact that his contract of employment was with LC, when he was made redundant he claimed he was employed in the part of the undertaking transferred. The Scots EAT applied the *Botzen* test and held that given the employee had done substantial work for LC(S), even though he had no contract of employment with the transferor he was employed in the transferred undertaking. This was because he was 'assigned' to the part of LC which had transferred when LC(S) was sold because he worked almost exclusively for that part, notwithstanding the fact that the employee continued to work for the transferor for two months after the transfer until his dismissal. The Scots EAT ruled that mistaken belief as to whether the contract transferred did not prevent the application of TUPE, without evidence of agreement between the transferor and the employee to the contrary.

The *Botzen* test was accepted by the EAT in *Michael Peters Limited v Farnfield.*[65] This was another case which considered the problem of what happens when part of a group of companies is transferred. Mr Farnfield was chief executive of Michael Peters Group plc, a holding company for 25 subsidiaries. He was responsible for overseeing financial management of all the subsidiary companies. When the parent company and its subsidiaries went into receivership the employee was made redundant. Four of the subsidiary companies, but not the parent company, were sold off. The employee claimed unfair dismissal contrary to regulation 8 of TUPE. The Industrial Tribunal found that TUPE applied on the basis that the sale of the four subsidiaries had involved the transfer of assets of the group and so the 'transferor' was the group which had been the employee's employer notwithstanding that the parent company was not a party to the sale agreement. The EAT upheld an appeal that the Industrial Tribunal was wrong to regard the four subsidiaries together with that part of the parent company's assets belonging to those companies as a 'single economic entity' in the context of EU competition law. Also it was impermissible to go behind the 'corporate veil' so as to find that the business of the subsidiaries was the business of the parent company thus making the parent company the transferor. Therefore, the transferor was not the parent company and Mr Farnfield was not an employee of the transferor and clearly not assigned to the part of the undertaking transferred.

[64] [1995] IRLR 184, EAT.

[65] [1995] IRLR 190, EAT.

Recent guidance has been provided by the EAT in *Duncan Web Offset (Maidstone) Limited v Cooper.* [66] This case concerned whether three employees had been assigned to Passmore Web Offset (Maidstone) ('Maidstone'). This was a subsidiary company owned by Passmore International Limited ('The Parent Company'). Other subsidiaries in the group included a company based in Basildon which was acquired in February 1993 and a company in St Albans until August 1993. In March 1994, Maidstone was sold by receivers to Duncan Web Offset who did not take on the employees concerned. Mr Cooper was the purchasing manager for the group who was based at Maidstone's offices and involved in the daily business of that company. After the Basildon firm was acquired, he spent a considerable amount of time there but from the appointment of the receivers of Maidstone in early 1993 until the transfer he was based in Maidstone doing Maidstone work. Mr Batemen worked for the St Albans company. When that company closed down in August 1993 he was told his employment would continue with Maidstone as head of human resources for both Maidstone and Basildon. He spent about 80 per cent of his time at Maidstone and after the receivers were appointed, he spent all of his time at Maidstone. Both Cooper and Bateman were paid by International. Mrs Russell spent one day a week at the Basildon company following the closure of the St Albans firm and the rest of her time at Maidstone as 'acting computer manager'. The industrial tribunal found that the employees were employed by Maidstone and assigned to Maidstone. Any duties carried out for other companies in the group were as employees of Maidstone.

The EAT agreed and stated that, 'It would take some persuasive evidence to suggest that an employee was not assigned to the business of his employer, where the whole of his employer's only business was transferred ... such evidence would have to have shown, at the very least, that the bulk of the employees' time and responsibilities were devoted to other entities within the group'. The EAT went on to say that, 'the employees were assigned to the only business which their employers did, even though some of their time was spent looking after other parts of the group'. [67] The EAT had been invited to give guidance to industrial tribunals about how to consider who was 'assigned' and who was not, but declined to do so 'because the facts will vary so markedly from case to case'. [68] However, Mr Justice Morison referred to three instances of how regulation 5 may operate in practice:-

66 [1995] IRLR 633

67 *Duncan Web Offset (Maidstone) Limited v Cooper* [1995] IRLR 633 at points 21-22.

68 Ibid., point 15.

- X transfers part of his business to Y. In order to determine which employees were employed by X in the part transferred it is necessary to ask:

  which of X's employees were assigned to the part transferred - *Botzen* CMLR 50. In determining this, an industrial tribunal may consider factors such as the amount of time spent on one part of the business or the other; the amount of value given to each part by the employee; the terms of the contract of employment showing what the employee could be required to do; how the cost to the employer of the employee's services had been allocated between the different parts of the business.

- A person is employed by X to work on Y's business and Y transfers that business to Z. On its face, TUPE would not apply so as to transfer the employee because for regulation 5 to apply, the employee must be employed by the transferor. However, TUPE will not be evaded by devices such as service companies or by complicated group structures which conceal the true position. Thus, it may be possible to say that if the person always and only worked on Y's business, then X was employing him on behalf of and as agent for Y. Or, it may be that the employee remained employed by X, who had other work for him to do.

- X employs a number of persons on X's sole business, the whole of which is transferred to Y. X is part of a group of companies. Some of X's employees worked partly for X and partly for other parts of the group. X's employees will almost certainly be transferred; but there may be cases where it could be said that despite being employed by X they were in reality assigned to the business of another part of the group. The contract of employment test is not the only matter for consideration. Put another way, an employee might be employed by one company but assigned to the business of another.[69]

As McMullen argues this approach appears to allow for a longer term and factual inquiry of the assignment of an employee to a particular undertaking.[70]

The issue of 'assignment' was considered in *Buchanan-Smith v Schleicher & Co International Limited*,[71] and *Securicor Guarding Limited v Fraser Security Services Limited*.[72] In *Buchanan-Smith*, Tarantor Limited carried on business servicing

69 Ibid., points 15 - 18.

70 McMullen, J., *supra*, n.49, page 306.

71 [1996] IRLR 547, EAT.

72 [1996] IRLR 552, EAT.

and selling machinery. In February 1993 the servicing part of T Ltd's operations was sold to Schleicher, and the sales part ceased trading. The employee, who before the transfer had been employed on both servicing and sales, started work with Schleicher. When she was made redundant in September 1993, she claimed a redundancy payment which depended on a two year qualifying period. The question was whether she had been transferred under TUPE with the servicing business. The Industrial Tribunal found that there had been a TUPE transfer but that she had not been protected by TUPE since she was not employed in the servicing part of the business and therefore lacked the requisite qualifying period.

However, the EAT applied the *Botzen* test as to whether the employee was 'assigned' or 'allocated' to the part transferred. This was a question of fact. It was not necessary for a person to work exclusively in an undertaking, or part transferred in order to be regarded as employed in all or part of that undertaking. Since the sales part in which she had been involved had ceased to trade at the time of the transfer, she was to be regarded as assigned to, and employed in the service part of the business which was transferred at the date of the transfer. The reason for this was because she organised and ran it. There appears to have been no analysis of the percentage of time spent working by the employee in the service part or the other criteria stated in the *Duncan Web Offset* case although the criteria were confirmed as relevant. The EAT took a purposive approach in that because the only other part of the business on which she had been active, the sales part, ceased trading at the same time as the transfer of the service part, it therefore followed she could not be assigned to the sales undertaking. It is difficult to reconcile this decision with *Botzen* and it was arguably wrongly decided.

Securicor Guarding Limited concerned two employees who were employed as security guards by Securicor and who both worked at Datamatic Limited's premises in Caerphilly with whom their employer had a guarding contract. Their contracts of employment specified that they were contractually based at different locations from Datamatic Limited's premises where one employee had worked for the past two years and the other for over five years. Both employees had a mobility clause in their contract of employment permitting Securicor to require the employees to work at the Company's head office in London, or at any one of the Company's other branches. In May 1994 the guarding contract was put out to competitive tendering by Datamatic Limited who awarded the contract in August 1994 to Fraser Security Services Limited.

The new contractor refused to employ the employees on the basis that TUPE did not apply. Securicor had not exercised their rights under the mobility clause prior to the award of the contract to Fraser because there were no other jobs on the same terms and conditions available. They were subsequently employed by Securicor as 'casuals' on worse terms and conditions of service.

The EAT held that TUPE applied and confirmed that a mobility clause in employees' contracts of employment whereby Securicor could require staff to work at other sites did not prevent security guards assigned to a particular site from transferring when a contract for the provision of security services was terminated and re-granted to a different supplier. Judge Clark held the guards were Securicor's 'human stock' assigned solely to Datamatic Limited's site unless and until transferred to another site.[73] The Judge argued, 'It would be standing TUPE on its head to hold that because the transferee will not honour a relevant employee's existing terms and conditions of employment, and because the contract between the employee and the transferor contains a mobility clause, that has the effect of compelling the *transferor* to retain the employee on his existing terms'.[74]

The approach in the *Botzen* case was recently applied in *Hassard v McGrath and Northern Ireland Housing Executive (NIHE)*.[75] The direct labour organisation (DLO) of the NIHE, a public body responsible for local authority housing in Northern Ireland, undertook the maintenance work. The DLO ceased to operate at the beginning of 1993, except for a small element of the work for which tenders for the maintenance work were invited from external contractors.

The NIHE's housing stock was split into modules, consisting of one or more housing estates. The Fermanagh District Council area was split into four modules. Hassard was employed as a joiner on general building work and worked virtually exclusively at Enniskillen on all four modules. Before June 1993, his time was divided between the four modules as follows: 8 per cent, 62 per cent, 17 per cent, and 12 per cent.

In 1993, private contractors were invited to bid for the work. The general building work for two of the modules was awarded to one contractor, and the other two modules were awarded to another firm. Thus, one firm became responsible for general building work on which Hassard had spent 73 per cent of his time in the preceding year, and the other contractor became responsible for work on which he had spent a quarter of his time. The tribunal held that each group of modules was part of an undertaking, and that Hassard was assigned to both parts of the undertaking. Therefore, he had a right to transfer to both contractors.

The Northern Ireland Court of Appeal overruled this decision and, following *Botzen,* held that an individual has to be assigned solely to all or part of an undertaking in order to be transferred. On the facts this was not the case, and therefore Hassard had no right to transfer to either contractor.

73 Ibid., para 26.

74 Ibid., para 30.

75 Northern Ireland Court of Appeal, 6 December 1996, unreported.

Re-tendering and TUPE Information

Prior to 1993, it was widely assumed that TUPE did not apply to the contracting-out of services for a fixed duration.[76] Accordingly, contractors may not be contractually bound to disclose relevant TUPE Information for the purposes of re-tendering unless authorities had the forethought to incorporate such a condition in their contract documentation. Clearly, unless TUPE information is available this may prevent prospective tenderers bidding for a contract because they would not be able to calculate the potential liabilities involved. It could also result in less competitive bids.

The government's TUPE Issues Paper argues at paragraph 10 that, 'the authority should do whatever it can to obtain the relevant information from the existing contractor. Should this not prove possible, the Department will expect the authority to assemble and supply prospective contractors with such information about the existing workforce, terms and conditions as is available to it from other sources, for example, from monitoring or other information provided by the existing contractor, subject to contractual or other legal constraints on disclosure'.

In the absence of an express contractual provision requiring disclosure of TUPE Information, there is no statutory requirement under the TUPE Regulations requiring the disclosure of workforce information and the 'anti-competitive behaviour' sanctions contained in the Local Government Act 1988 do not apply to private contractors. There is a risk that contractors may choose not to disclose information or disclose information which is misleading. In such circumstances, authorities must rely on persuasion. For example, they could threaten to exclude the contractor from re-tendering for the

[76] The reasons for this were twofold. Firstly the government improperly implemented the TUPE regulations and restrictively defined 'undertaking' as a 'commercial venture' which was thought to exclude public sector transfers. Secondly, Industrial Tribunals tended to conclude there was no transfer as a going concern. This was because a private contractor was simply required to undertake a service for a fixed duration for a fee, with the local authority retaining ultimate control. This position became untenable after development in ECJ Case Law such as *Dr Sophie Redmond v Bartol* [1992] IRLR, 366 and *Rask v ISS Kantineservice* [1993] IRLR 133 which indicated that the Acquired Rights Directive could apply to a non-commercial undertaking, and the contracting out of a canteen management function previously performed in-house respectively. However, uncertainty about the application of TUPE to 'second generation' contracting out has been created by the decisions of *Süzen v Zehnacker* [1997] IRLR, 255 and *Betts v Brintel Helicopters Limited* [1997] IRLR 361 which are discussed in chapter 2. This was resolved by the ECJ decision in *Sanchez Hidalgo v Association de Servicios Aser* [1999] IRLR 136, which held the Acquired Rights Directive could apply to second generation contracting-out where there was a transfer of an economic entity which meant an organised group of persons and other assets enabling an economic activity with a well-designed purpose to be performed.

contract unless they disclose the TUPE Information. However, this is unlikely to have the desired effect if the contract is terminated prematurely for poor performance and the authority does not wish the contractor to re-tender or the contractor itself does not to wish to re-tender.[77]

Therefore, the only sensible approach is to heed the advice at paragraph 11 of the Issues Paper which recommends that authorities ensure they include a contract condition requiring disclosure of TUPE Information. Failure by a contractor to comply with this would enable the authority to sue for breach of contract.[78] Many authorities also include a clause requiring the contractor to indemnify the authority against any liability it may incur due to the contractor's failure to disclose information within a reasonable time, or any inaccuracies in it.

Authorities should also be alive to the possibility of a contractor, towards the expiry of a contract, increasing the remuneration of staff, removing its best employees from the contract and/or substituting poor quality employees or employees with long reckonable service. Such measures may serve to increase redundancy costs for incoming contractors and thereby inhibit prospective tenderers from bidding and/or increase the price of bids. It is difficult to prevent this in practice and it underlines the importance of regular monitoring throughout the contract period. A contract condition could be used which stipulates that employees or service delivery structures must not be changed except in good faith for bona fide or operational or economic reasons and that the contractor shall not unreasonably increase the remuneration of staff or alter the assignment of employees to a particular contract without legitimate organisational or economic reasons.[79] However,

[77] Competition Advisory Service, CIPFA, Finance Bulletin, June 1996, '20 TUPE Questions' page 25, para 11.

[78] Examples of contract conditions requiring TUPE Information for re-tendering purposes can be found in Andrew Sparke, *The CCT Guide,* 2nd ed, Butterworths, 1996, at Appendix III, pages 216-217; The Local Government Management Board: *CCT, TUPE and the ARD : Legal and Practical Implications* 1996, at Appendix D, page 62. Also see precedent contract conditions for blue collar CCT contained in *Local Government Precedents and Procedures,* General eds Alan Aisbett, Clive Grace, Alan Harrison, *FT Law and Tax, 3 Vols,* 1996.

[79] An appropriate clause can be found in precedent D14/4 at D/346 of chapter D.14, 'TUPE and Tendering Procedures' In Alan Aisbett, Clive Grace, Alan Harrison (General editors) *Local Government Precedents and Procedures*: FT Law and Tax, 3 Vols, 1996 Prof. McMullen points out that an unresolved question is how far the employment tribunal can consider the genuineness of an assignment of an employee to an undertaking being transferred. He believes there are good policy reasons why an employment tribunal should be able to look at this issue, rather than relying on a snapshot profile of the workforce immediately preceding the transfer. Some support for this view is contained in the decision in *Cariswav Cleaning Consultants Ltd. v Richards and Cooper Cleaning Services* (EAT/629/97), c.f. J. McMullen (ed.), *Business Transfers and Employee Rights*, February 1999, Bulletin No.2, pp.7-8.

local authorities must ensure they do not contravene Section 17 of the Local Government Act 1988 which prevents them taking into account 'non-commercial' considerations such as matters relating to a contractor's workforce.

Contracting-in and Equal Pay

There is no reason in principle why TUPE may not apply when a service is won-back in-house.[80] Thus, in-house tenders for contracts currently in the private sector need to be based on a careful analysis of the potential liabilities they stand to inherit. One particular problem for local authority in-house bids, where contracts are in the private sector, is whether to bid on the basis of local authority terms and conditions of employment or those revealed in the TUPE Information. Private sector terms and conditions of service are likely to be worse than local authority terms and conditions of employment. The reason for this is because TUPE may not have applied on the first round of tendering and therefore staff may have been recruited on inferior terms and conditions, and/or by the recruitment of new staff on the contractor's existing terms and conditions. Even if TUPE did apply, it is likely that terms and conditions will have been varied downwards. If in-house teams bid on the basis of national terms and conditions of employment they are unlikely to be successful. However, if they bid on the basis of the contractor's terms and conditions revealed in the TUPE information they may at some future date fall foul of the Equal Pay Act 1970, which provided for equal pay between men and women doing the same or similar work. This is particularly a risk in blue-collar CCT areas such as catering where the workforce is predominately female on low pay. Thus, an authority could find itself faced with equal pay claims backed by trade unions or brought by staff individually using male comparators on better national conditions of service elsewhere within the local authority. This could result in an authority having to pay out large sums in back pay. These risks need to be fully understood since they could undermine the viability of any successful in-house bid and possibly lead to statutory action by the Secretary of State.[81]

80 This was confirmed in *Ayse Süzen v Zehnacker Gebäudereinigung GmbH Krankenhausservice Lefarth* GmbH, case C-13/95, ECJ, 11 March 1997, [1997] IRLR, 255, and *Gomez Montana v Claro Sol SA and Red Nacional de Ferrocarriles Espanoles* [1999] IRLR 132, ECJ. Also see *Council of the Isles of Scilly v Brintel Helicopters Limited and Ellis* [1995] IRLR 6, where the EAT held that TUPE applied where a fire fighting and baggage handling contract was terminated and the service was contracted back in-house.

81 While it may be possible to minimise the risks of claims for breaches of equal pay legislation by reaching an agreement with recognised trade unions prior to bidding, it should be noted that it is not possible to contract out of individual employees' legal rights under the Equal Pay Act 1970. This view is supported by *Land v Knowsley Borough Council, Industrial Tribunal,* unreported, September, 1996.

Employee objection to the transfer

At common law, an employee could not be forced to transfer from one employer to another without his agreement. Thus, '... the right to choose for himself whom he would serve... constituted the main difference between a servant and a serf'.[82] Therefore, the transfer or sale of a business resulted in the termination of a contract of employment. TUPE as originally drafted removed this common law right to object to the transfer since it provided for the statutory novation of a contract of employment so that the transferee assumed the rights and obligations in respect of the contract of employment between the employee and the transferor. However, the ECJ held in *Katsikas v Konstantinidis* [83] that the Acquired Rights Directive was not intended to remove the right of an employee to object to the identity of his new employer following a transfer where his terms and conditions of employment otherwise remain the same, and in such circumstances an employee would not transfer. It was for Member States to determine what happened to the contract of employment in the event of an employee refusing to transfer.

The government therefore introduced an amendment to TUPE[84] and regulation 5(4B) now provides that the effect of an objection under regulation 5(4A) is for the transfer to terminate the contract of employment without a dismissal by the transferor. Therefore, it is treated as a voluntary resignation, and there can be no claim for unfair or wrongful dismissal against either the transferor or the transferee. Moreover, any statutory redundancy payment in these circumstances would be unlawful so far as local authorities are concerned.

This was qualified by *Merckx v Ford Motor Co Belgium SA*, [85] where the ECJ held that when an employee refuses to consent to the transfer, it is for the Member State to determine the fate of his contract of employment with the transferor. However, where an employee refuses to transfer because his level of remuneration cannot be guaranteed after the transfer this is to be regarded as a 'substantial change in working conditions to the detriment of the employee' within the meaning of Article 4(2) of the Acquired Rights Directive. In these circumstances the employer is responsible for the termination.

Regulation 5(5) of TUPE, which transposes Article 4(2), preserves an employee's right to allege constructive unfair dismissal and terminate his contract of employment without notice, if he can establish a substantial change

[82] *Nokes v Doncaster Amalgamated Collieries* [1940] AC 1014.

[83] [1993] IRLR 179.

[84] Section 33 of the Trade Union Reform and Employment Rights Act 1993 which introduced new regulation 5(4A) and 5(4B).

[85] [1996] IRLR 467.

in his terms and conditions or a change in the identity of the employer to his detriment. This has been thought to only apply where an employee actually transfers, in which case any claim would be against the transferee. However, *Merckx* appears to suggest that a similar right exists where an employee objects to being transferred because of a change in remuneration: this must be regarded as substantially detrimental to the employee and the transferor remains potentially liable for the termination of the contract of employment which will be deemed to be a dismissal due to post-transfer changes in employees' working conditions. This may also include, for example, the withdrawal of a bonus scheme or occupational pension scheme.

It is not clear what constitutes an objection for the purposes of TUPE. In *Hay v George Hanson (Building Contractors) Limited* [86] the EAT held that no particular form of objection was required in accordance with regulation 5(4A) provided there was an actual refusal to consent to the transfer communicated to the transferor or the transferee, before the transfer occurs. Expressions of concern or unwillingness are insufficient. It could be by 'word or deed or both'. Lord Johnstone noted that it was 'singularly unfortunate', given the draconian nature of the objection, under regulation 5(4B), that there is no legal obligation that the employee should be informed of the consequences by the transferring employer. In these circumstances, an employee should be requested to put their objection in writing to avoid doubt at a later date. Details of objectors should be disclosed to potential tenderers. The objection may be a legitimate concern that they are not in their view 'assigned' to the work being transferred and therefore they should not appear on the TUPE list. Conflicts of this nature must be resolved by negotiation and the prospective transferee made aware of the problem.[87]

Transferors sometimes prefer to give affected employees the choice of receiving an ex gratia severance payment instead of transferring under TUPE. But there are potential problems for transferees who subsequently recruit *Katsikas* objectors who believe all liabilities have been discharged prior to the transfer by the transferor. In *Senior Heat Treatment Ltd v Bell*, [88] most of the affected employees chose to opt-out of the transfer in favour of receiving a voluntary 'redundancy' payment. They immediately secured jobs under new contracts of employment with the transferee. When they were dismissed a year later they claimed for redundancy and unfair dismissal relying on previous service with the transferor under TUPE. The question was whether

86 [1996] IRLR, 427.

87 For a consideration of how the right to object may be exercised in practice see Paul Goulding; 'TUPE : the employee's right to object' in *Solicitors Journal*, 9 May 1997, pp. 424-425.

88 [1997] IRLR, 614, EAT.

their continuity of service had been broken by the 'redundancy' payment and their objection pursuant to regulation 5(4A). The EAT noted that whether the employees had objected to the transfer was a matter for the Tribunal to decide. Given that the employees had accepted new jobs almost immediately with the transferee they could not be said to have objected to the transfer. This suggests that Tribunals will not take objections at face value but will look to the substance, rather than the form. Further, the employees were entitled to claim a second redundancy payment based on continuous service with their previous employer, because continuity was not broken by the non-statutory 'redundancy' payment they had received since they had not been dismissed for redundancy.

RETENTION OF STAFF

While staff have no right to insist on redeployment, the transferor could, where practicable, voluntarily offer redeployment away from the part of the undertaking transferred. Indeed, there may be appropriate flexibility and mobility clauses which could be invoked by the transferor prior to the transfer which would enable the employee to be moved to another part of the transferor's undertaking. Provided the employer does not breach the employees contract of employment there is nothing to prevent the transferor retaining certain staff, and in such circumstances they would not transfer since they are not persons under regulation 5(1) whose contracts of employment would otherwise have been terminated by the transfer.[89] This would enable an employer to retain key staff for the purposes, for example, of winding down work-in-progress. However, such staff could find themselves with a diminishing workload and face redundancy together with a potential loss of the right to transfer under TUPE.

On the other hand, the courts are increasingly adopting a purposive approach to protecting employee rights under TUPE and it could be argued that they are persons whose contracts of employment have been terminated by the transfer, even though the termination occurred after the transfer, since their dismissals are a result of the transfer. Consequently, such persons may transfer across to the transferee at that time.[90]

89 *Direct Radiators Limited v Howse and Shepherd*, [1986] EAT unreported, 130/86, which suggested that if an employee continued to work under the same contract of employment after the transfer, TUPE would not apply.

90 P. Elias Q C and J. Bowers, *Transfer of Undertakings: The Legal Pitfalls*. 5th ed., Longman, pages 38-39. The *Direct Radiators* case was considered in the *Sunley Turriff* case and in a decision which was not intended to contradict *Direct Radiators* the EAT held that where the company secretary of a group which went into receivership continued to work for the parent company for nearly two months after transfer, the EAT held that the employee nonetheless was protected by TUPE.

In the light of the *Sunley Turriff* case it may be prudent before the transfer, for the transferor to obtain their employees' express agreement that they should not be treated as employed in the undertaking which is transferred or at least secure a variation of their contract if necessary, otherwise they may be entitled to transfer under TUPE.[91] Moreover, the transferor would need to ensure that any agreement did not contravene regulation 12 which prohibits contracting out of TUPE and which renders any agreement to do so unenforceable.

It follows that staff who are to be retained should not be included on the TUPE list. Depending on the circumstances, it may be advisable to disclose details of employees who are retained to complete works-in-progress since they may assert protection under TUPE and transfer across to the transferee some time after completion of the transfer. A common sense approach will need to be adopted in connection with those staff who do not wish to remain with the transferor and in such circumstances it is probably preferable to allow them to transfer.

Implications of disclosing inaccurate information

Any material inaccuracies could result in claims for misrepresentation or negligent misstatement by a transferee. Such potential litigation is not theoretical as the former Humberside County Council found when BET sued it on the grounds that it had been supplied with TUPE information which grossly understated labour costs. The case was settled out of court and interim damages of £3m were paid. Complaints of anti-competitive behaviour could also be made to the Secretary of State. Authorities are unlikely to warrant the accuracy of information, but should ensure that the contract provides for the contractor to warrant the accuracy of TUPE information which is required for re-tendering purposes, and to provide an appropriate indemnity.

Warranties and Indemnities

Before submitting a bid, prospective tenderers, mindful of the *caveat emptor* rule, will be keen to calculate the potential liabilities which they will inherit under regulation 5. Contractors may wish to apportion risks and liabilities through the disclosure of TUPE Information process, and the use of warranties and indemnities.

A warranty is basically a representation that information supplied by one party to the other is true and accurate at the time it is given. Contractors will often seek to extract warranties because they reverse the *caveat emptor* rule. Therefore, any information which is given should be carefully checked for accuracy. If a warranty proves to be inaccurate the contractor will have a

91 *Sunley Turriff Holdings Limited v Thompson* [1995] IRLR 184 at para 14.

claim for damages against the authority for any loss caused by the breach of warranty.

Warranties often cover the number of employees 'assigned' to the undertaking to be transferred; the accuracy of employees' details such as age, continuity of service and notice periods; terms and conditions of employment; current or anticipated litigation such as Industrial Tribunal claims and other County and High Court claims; the extent and nature of union recognition and collective bargaining agreements; details of past and current industrial disputes; and compliance by the transferor with its duties under TUPE including consultation with recognised trade unions, and/or elected representatives under regulation 10.

Indemnities are often used to indemnify a party from potential liabilities which it may inherit and which cannot be properly assessed in advance of the transfer, and therefore cannot be included in the bid price. Essentially, they are an agreement that one party who incurs a liability will be indemnified by the other party, and be able to recover the costs involved. Indemnities could cover, amongst other things, claims for unfair dismissal under regulation 8 from staff, whether they be agency, relief workers or employees, who believe they should have transferred under TUPE; the cost of protective awards under TUPE; costs arising from existing equal pay or discrimination claims or indeed other outstanding litigation relating to the contract of employment; and claims arising out of the provision of inaccurate TUPE information, or failure to provide, for re-tendering purposes, accurate information within a reasonable period.

However, the availability of warranties and indemnities is largely dependent on the strength of the bargaining position of the parties. Public sector authorities who tend to be in a stronger position are unlikely to be inclined to provide contractors with warranties or indemnities. Moreover, authorities may not have the necessary statutory powers to give indemnities,[92] and many authorities advise that contractors should consider this as a commercial risk they must bear. It is worth noting that it is the government's policy not to give indemnities against the possibility that TUPE applies except where these

[92] It appears that local authorities are not empowered to grant indemnities unless there is express statutory power to do so. See *Credit Suisse v Allerdale BC* [1996] 4AllER 129 and *Credit Suisse v Waltham Forest LBC* [1996] 4llER 176 which held that an authority could not rely on section 111 (1) of the Local Government Act 1972 to give an indemnity. Moreover, in *Sutton LBC v Morgan Grenfell & Co Limited*, C.A. *The Times*, 7th Nov, 1996, the Court of Appeal noted that it was inconceivable that Parliament ever intended by section111 of the Local Government Act 1972, which did no more than put into statutory form what was implied at common law, to give local authorities power to incur unlimited financial liability when it had so clearly regulated its powers of spending, borrowing and granting of financial assistance.

are expressly provided for in statute. Furthermore, since indemnities are 'blank cheques', unless qualified in some way, their use could bring them into conflict with their district auditors. Consequently, indemnities in public sector contracting-out tend to be given by the private contractor rather than vice versa. Typical indemnities which an authority may insist upon from a contractor include claims against the authority in respect of the contractor's non-compliance with the Employment Rights Act 1996, or any application of TUPE, and/or the Acquired Rights Directive; and failure to provide occupational pension benefits not less favourable in aggregate than those currently provided by the authority where those employees have transferred under TUPE; and failure to disclose for re-tendering purposes accurate TUPE information within a reasonable time from the request.[93]

Consequently, the scope for a contractor to obtain warranties, which is usually done via a disclosure letter, are restricted because authorities rather than responding to detailed questionnaires tend to supply information in their own standard format. This will usually make it clear that it cannot give a warranty as to the accuracy of the TUPE information. This is sensible from the authority's point of view because the information represents a 'snapshot' in time, and may be supplied perhaps as many as eight months prior to the contract commencement date. For example, employees leave and vacancies may or may not be filled. In addition, employees may object to the transfer, and there can be no guarantee that those employees on the TUPE list actually have TUPE rights. Furthermore, there may be employees not included on the list who may assert that they should transfer under TUPE. These uncertainties are exacerbated when staff are not spending all their time working within the undertaking, and there are genuine doubts about whether certain staff have TUPE rights. If a contract is awarded to a private contractor it is advisable to list the transferring staff in a schedule to the contract to ensure certainty as to which staff actually transfer.[94] Nevertheless, authorities may provide in their contract documentation for the successful contractor to warrant the accuracy of TUPE information which it may require for re-tendering purposes.

[93] *Better Quality Services: A Handbook on Creating Public/Private Partnerships Through Market Testing and Contracting-Out*, London, HMSO, 1998, para 3.42, page 44.

[94] LGMB: *CCT, TUPE and the ARD : Legal and Practical Implications*, 1996, page 40, para 5.14. For a more detailed discussion of indemnities and warranties see John McMullen, *Business Transfers and Employee Rights*, 2nd ed., 1992, Butterworths, pages 287-292. Other useful sources for precedents are *Butterworths Forms and Precedents* (4th ed.) Vol 9 and J. Green (ed.) *Practical Commercial Precedents*, Vol 1, Longman, e.g. Precedent D5, D5020, D5-125-127.

Failure to provide warranties and indemnities may inhibit competition, and/or increase tender prices, and local authorities need to be mindful that they are not acting anti-competitively in relation to their conduct in this regard.[95]

PROVISION OF TUPE INFORMATION: CCT AND ANTI-COMPETITIVE CONDUCT.

The Department of the Environment has completed 101 cases of alleged anti-competitive behaviour where TUPE was seen as the major issue. The DoE do not keep details of what proportion of these cases related to the provision of TUPE information. It is understood that a considerable majority of these cases arose, amongst other things, because authorities insisted upon undertakings from contractors that they would submit a TUPE -related bid before they were provided with workforce information.[96] The non-provision of information to contractors has occasionally been a problem, but to a lesser extent.[97]

It appears that the Department's guidance on the handling of TUPE matters in relation to CCT, 21 January 1994, has considerably helped to resolve these problems. Out of the 101 completed TUPE-related cases, the majority stemmed from work tendered in 1993/94. Only six of these cases were completed in 1995 and only one in 1996. Overall, TUPE-related cases have resulted in nine notices, leading to six Directions, although only two of these were concerned with the non-provision of TUPE information. All six directions required the relevant authorities to re-tender the work and obtain the Secretary of State's consent before awarding it in-house. Five of these directions were given in 1994, with the other being given in 1995.[98]

Although TUPE appears to be less contentious than it was in the recent past, it is understood that the DoE do receive occasional complaints that an authority has not provided workforce information, or concerning the

[95] For example, the DoE has stated in its Issues Paper at Issue 1 that if there is genuine uncertainty about the applicability of TUPE to a contractor's proposals in its tender submission, and both the authority and the contractor wish to proceed on the basis that TUPE does not apply, it may be reasonable for the authority at that stage in the process, to require an indemnity against the possibility that TUPE may apply, but only to the extent that it may face claims for failing to consult staff as required by Regulation 10 of TUPE. The DoE points out that if authorities require other forms of indemnity, or as a matter of course, they may be acting anti-competitively.

[96] For example, see *R v Secretary of State for the Environment. ex parte Oldham Metropolitan Borough Council*, *The Times*, 16 December 1996, QBD.

[97] Letter to author from Philip Brown, Local Government Competition and Quality Division, Department of the Environment, 23 January 1997.

[98] Ibid.

timeliness of the TUPE information provided insofar as it has not been provided until a late stage in the tendering process, giving the contractor insufficient time to incorporate it within its bid. Complaints may arise due to the contractor's ignorance of the type of information they are entitled to receive. Contractors often request price sensitive information or information which is unnecessary for them to calculate their liabilities under TUPE.[99] In these circumstances, the Department's policy is to advise contractors to resolve their differences informally, but they will make preliminary enquiries if appropriate. Provided authorities have acted in accordance with the Department of the Environment's Issues Paper on the handling of TUPE matters in relation to CCT and paragraphs 30 to 32 of DoE Circular 16/97, then most complaints are likely to be resolved satisfactorily. However, if an authority has provided poor quality or misleading information, particularly where this is inaccurate or insufficient, or provided it late in the tendering stage, then complaints may be upheld. Authorities may have to grant extensions of time for the return of tenders if this is reasonable to enable contractors to make bids as necessary.[100]

Transfer of Employees' Personnel Records

Employees' personnel records should not be disclosed during the tendering process. However, once a contract has been awarded to a private contractor, one of the first things they are likely to wish to do is to examine the personnel records of transferring staff. This raises the question as to what extent personnel files should be disclosed to the transferee employer. It is not possible to give prescriptive advice as to what should and should not be given. The approach adopted may depend on whether the authority is acting as transferor or transferee and this should be dealt with in the contract conditions.

In considering what should be disclosed the following factors should be noted:

- wait for the transferee to formally request the personnel files;
- consider the managerial requirements of the new employer;
- consider the interests of the transferring employees and the views of the trade unions;

99 Competition Advisory Service, CIPFA, Finance Bulletin, June 1996, para 18, page 27.

100 Letter to author from Philip Brown, Local Government Competition and Quality Division, Department of the Environment, 23 January 1997. Also see Competition Advisory Service, CIPFA, Finance Bulletin, June 1996, para 18, page 27.

- administrative practicability for the authority's personnel officers, including the need to retain records of former authority staff;

- the common law principle of confidentiality. For instance, references provided by former employers arguably should not be disclosed without their consent and usually this will be impracticable to obtain; or information given by an employee in confidence.[101]

Types of Information

- **Factual Information**

  There can be no objection to the transfer of factual information such as dates of birth, length of continuous and pensionable service, annual leave, salary, methods of payment, next of kin details. These details should transfer to the new employer in whatever is the most appropriate manner. Personnel officers should be alert to avoid transferring any information which may have been provided in confidence. It may be prudent to get the employees' consent to the transfer of such records.

- **'Personal' Information**

  This could include grievance and disciplinary matters. A case could be made for not disclosing this type of information to the new employer. Difficulty may arise as to whether details of recent disciplinary cases should be supplied to the new employer. It is advisable for 'live' disciplinaries and grievances to be settled prior to the transfer date. Details of 'spent' matters such as disciplinary warnings should not normally be given to the new employer. Ultimately, it is a matter for negotiation between transferor and transferee, bearing in mind that contracts of employment are novated under TUPE.

  Whether annual appraisals should be disclosed potentially gives rise to a conflict between confidentiality, and the needs of management. It may be advisable to disclose the most recent annual reports provided the employee does not object. Generally speaking, the originals of documents should be retained by the transferor because at some future date it may potentially face legal action by transferred staff, or indeed

[101] Cabinet Office (MPO) Guidance on the Handling of Staff Records where work is being transferred out of Government Departments, dated February 1986. Also see *Better Quality Services: A Handbook on Creating Public/Private Partnerships Through Market Testing and Contracting-Out*, HMSO, 1998, paras 3.47-3.50, pp.46-47.

the staff may transfer back in a re-tendering situation. In cases of doubt, the objective should be to reconcile the interests of the transferee employer with those of the transferred employees.

The TUPE regulations do not expressly provide for what is to happen to personnel records. However, regulation 5(1) provides that a contract of employment is statutorily novated so that the contract of employment will continue with the new employer substituted for the former employer. Regulation 5(2)(a) provides that on completion of a TUPE transfer, all the old employer's rights, powers, duties and liabilities under or in connection with a contract of employment transfer to the new employer. Regulation 5(2)(b) provides that on completion of a relevant transfer 'anything done' in respect of a transferred employee or his/her contract of employment before the transfer which would otherwise have been terminated by the transfer should be regarded as having been done by the transferee employer. It is therefore implicit that the transferee employer is entitled to know what the transferor has done in respect of the employee or his/her contract. It is not clear whether this could be stretched to include everything in an employee's personnel file.

The critical question appears to be whether the 'anything done' on the file was done by the old employer in relation to the employee's contract of employment or that employee? If the answer is 'yes', the information should probably be disclosed. This would encompass grievance, disciplinary and attendance records. If the answer is 'no', the information may not have to be disclosed.[102] Of course, there may be matters on the personnel file which were not done by the old employer. For example, information provided by the employee, and which is not in connection with the contract of employment. This could include next of kin details or correspondence by an employee which is unrelated with their contract of employment. Arguably, such information should not be transferred without the consent of the employee. If the information is of a confidential nature, such as health records which were not intended to be disclosed to third parties, the new transferee employer for the purposes of the TUPE Regulations is not a third party but somebody who stands in the shoes of the old employer, and the new employer would be bound by the implicit confidentiality of any such information.

[102] Frank Walton, *Employment Law and Practice*, published by GEE, para 3.7, page T161.

Conclusion

The Department of Trade and Industry in its TUPE consultation paper [103] accepts that there appears to be a strong case for amending the Acquired Rights Directive and/or the TUPE Regulations to require employers in contracting-out situations to give tenderers comprehensive and accurate TUPE information to facilitate a level playing field in the tendering process. This is reflected in amendments to the Directive which provide that 'Member States may adopt appropriate measures to ensure that the transferor notifies the transferee of all the rights and obligations which will be transferred to the transferee under this Article, so far as these rights and obligations are or ought to have been known to the transferor at the time of the transfer'.[104]

Any amendment to the TUPE Regulations by the government will need to balance the reasonable needs of the transferee, and those of the transferor bearing in mind commercial sensitivity, data protection, and confidentiality issues. This area is already highly regulated in the public sector by way of circular advice, and legislative change is arguably unnecessary. Experience suggests that difficulties are mainly confined to situations involving contracting-out to an external service provider, and potential problems which can then arise when TUPE information is required from them in order to re-tender the contract. It is suggested that this can best be dealt with through the use of contract conditions and the inclusion of an appropriately worded indemnity clause in the contract. These should be included irrespective of whether TUPE applies on the first round of tendering.

[103] Department of Trade and Industry : *European Acquired Rights Directive and Transfer of Undertakings (Protection of Employment) Regulations 1981 (The TUPE Regulations) : Public Consultation, (Ref URN 98/513), December 1997, paras 49-51.*

[104] Article 3(2) of the text of the Council Directive 77/187/EEC as amended by Directive 98/50/EC.

6. Dismissal and the Acquired Rights Directive

Colin Bourn and Paul Thorpe

It would serve little purpose for the Acquired Rights Directive to protect the terms and conditions of transferred employees, if those employees could be freely dismissed by the transferor or the transferee. Consequently Article 4 of the Directive provides as follows:

(1) 'The transfer of an undertaking, business or part of a business shall not in itself constitute grounds for dismissal by the transferor or the transferee. This provision shall not stand in the way of dismissals that may take place for economic, technical or organisational reasons entailing a change in the workforce.

Member states may provide that the first sub-paragraph shall not apply to certain specific categories of employees who are not covered by the laws or practices of the Member States in respect of protection against dismissal.

(2) If the contract of employment or employment relationship is terminated because the transfer within the meaning of article 1(1) involves a substantial change in working conditions to the detriment of the employee, the employer shall be regarded as having been responsible for the termination of the contract of employment or the employment relationship.'

This provision is implemented principally by TUPE regulations 8(1) & (2) which provide, that a dismissal before or after a relevant transfer shall be unfair if the principal reason for it is the transfer or a reason connected with it. This broad protection is qualified by regulation 8(2) which provides that where such a dismissal takes place for an economic, technical or organisational ('eto') reason entailing changes in the workforce, regulation 8(1) shall not apply and that dismissal shall be regarded for the purposes of the unfair dismissal legislation as having taken place for some other substantial reason and judged to be fair or unfair according to ERA 1996 s.98(4). The above provisions operate not only in the context of straightforward dismissals by the employer but also in the context of constructive dismissals, provided for in regulation 5(5) and discussed below.

There are therefore three possible categories of dismissal arising from a relevant transfer, namely, (1) those automatically unfair dismissals which occur for a reason connected with the transfer, (2) those taking place for an 'eto' and (3) those brought about by a substantial (repudiatory?) change in working conditions. In each case, however, the normal two years' service qualification for unfair dismissal applies according to the Court of Appeal in *MRS Environmental Services Ltd v Marsh.*[1] The Collective Redundancies and Transfer of Undertakings (Protection of Employment) (Amendment) Regulations 1995 modify TUPE so as to state that the normal qualifying period for unfair dismissal applies in the transfer situation.[2]

In examining the effect of the ARD and TUPE upon the right of an employee not to be dismissed in connection with a transfer a number of questions arise. *Who* is intended to enjoy protection of the Directive and the Regulations? *When* does the protection operate? *What* is the extent of the protection? *Why* might an employee be fairly dismissed?

WHO ENJOYS THE PROTECTION OF THE DIRECTIVE?

Whilst it usually obvious whether a person is 'employed by the transferor in the undertaking or part transferred'[3] this is not necessarily the case as regards either persons working in 'atypical' forms of employment or in administrative functions connected with, but not included in, that part of the undertaking which is to be transferred. The transferor may wish to inflate the number of persons covered by the transfer, or to get rid of troublesome or difficult employees by a sudden late reassignment as in *Carieswav Cleaning Consultants Ltd. & Richards* (EAT/629/97) where such a reassignment was held to be fraudulent and therefore void.

The Directive uses the word 'employees' but does not define it. Consequently, this being a measure of minimum harmonisation, the definition of employee is

1 *The Times* July 22nd, 1996, overturning *Milligan and Bailey v Securicor Cleaning Ltd.* [1995] IRLR 288

2 SI 1995 2587 modifies TUPE Regulation 8(5) accordingly.

3 TUPE Reg.5(1).

left as a matter for the Member States to define according to their national law.[4] Whilst it would have been possible to adopt the definition of employee in ERA, which confines itself to those working under a contract of employment, TUPE would appear to cast the net more widely to include 'atypical' forms of employment where there might otherwise be a doubt as to whether they met the definition in the ERA. TUPE 2(1) defines employee as a person who works for another 'under a contract of service ... *or otherwise*', but excludes persons working under a contract for services.[5] Part-timers, home-workers and temporary workers would all appear to be covered, though the status of agency workers paid by the employment agency but working in the transferred part of the undertaking immediately before the transfer would appear to be open to question:[6] if they are employees, they are employees of the agency. Thus a transferor might at the present time seek to fill vacancies from an agency in anticipation of a transfer, if circumstances allow, in order to minimise potential liabilities on a transfer. Casual workers, who may be employees during the periods of time when they are working, but who lack a 'global' contract,[7] may be included within the transfer if they are employed 'immediately before' the transfer, so satisfying the test in TUPE Regulation 5(3).

The Amended Directive

The 1998 text for an amended Directive, like the 1994[8] and 1997 proposals, leaves the definition of employee to the Member States, but provides that employees shall not be excluded on the basis of their hours of work, where they work on fixed–term contracts, or are temporary workers, in the terms of Directive 91/383 on encouraging improvements in health and safety. The first of these categories extends the notion of a fixed term contract to include not only contracts with a specified end date, but contracts to complete a specified task or which terminate on the occurrence of a specific event. However, what would the position be if such an employee had signed a waiver clause regarding redundancy and unfair dismissal rights on the non-renewal of such a contract, especially as such clauses are specifically endorsed by the

4 *Mikklesen v Danmols Inventar A/S* C-105/84, [1985] ECR 2639, [1986] 1 CMLR 316.

5 In *Cowell v Quilter Goodison & Co Ltd. and QG Management Services Ltd* [1969] IRLR 392 an equity partner in a firm was found to be outside the definition of employee in TUPE Reg. 2(1) as being a self-employed person.

6 *McMeechan v Secretary of State for Employment* [1997] IRLR 354, CA.

7 *Clark v Oxfordshire Health Authority* [1998] IRLR 125, CA, *McCleod v Hellyer Bros. Ltd.* [1987] IRLR 232, CA c.f. *Carmichael & National Power plc* [1998] IRLR 301, CA.

8 COM (97) 60 final.

1995 amending Regulations,[9] which provide for an amended regulation 8(5). As the amended Directive will not contain any such derogation, regulation 8(5) may in future be called into question. The changes proposed by the Commission would noticeably increase the potential of the Transfers Directive to embrace atypical and temporary forms of work, as does the inclusion of 'temporary' workers. Directive 91.383 defines these as including

> 'Temporary employment relationships between a temporary employment business which is the employer and the worker, where the latter is assigned to work for and under the control of an undertaking and/or establishment making use of his services.'

Under the amended Directive, if the transferor sought to minimise liabilities for itself or a potential transferee by employing agency workers, those employees would enjoy the right to follow the part of the undertaking in which they are working, though this would not presumably render them employees of the transferee. Should the transferee terminate the contract with the agency in respect of those staff, if this occurred in connection with the transfer they would have been automatically unfairly dismissed. Liability for those dismissals would arguably pass to the transferee in such circumstances, These amendments would bring the law more into line with present day flexible employment practices, even if they do not necessarily catch all forms of atypical work.[10]

ASSIGNMENT TO THE TRANSFERRED UNDERTAKING

Only those employees assigned to the transferred part of the business will be transferred, according to the Court of Justice in *Botzen v RDM*.[11] The Court excluded from the coverage of the Directive those employees who, not being assigned to the part transferred, nonetheless performed certain duties involving assets assigned to the part transferred, or undertook administrative duties in connection with the transferred parts of the business. Thus a trainee nurse who happened to be working in a hospital at the moment when it was transferred to an NHS Trust, was held not to have been transferred to the

[9] See n. 2.

[10] Professor Hepple in his evidence to the House of Lords Select Committee (1995) (HL Paper 38, p.11of the Minutes of Evidence) would go further and argues for a Community wide definition of 'any agreement in return for gain to do or perform personally any work or services for another.' i.e. which does not contain an express exclusion of persons working under a contract for services.

[11] C-186/83, [1985] ECR 519, [1986] 2 CMLR 50.

employment of the trust because his contract of employment did not solely require him to work there.[12] In *Michael Peters Ltd v Farnfield and Michael Peters Group plc*,[13] a group holding company which had twenty-five subsidiaries became insolvent. The businesses of four subsidiaries in the group were to be sold. The group managing director was not assigned to any of the four subsidiaries, although he did work on their behalf. The industrial tribunal found that the four subsidiaries and the parent company could be treated as a single economic entity,[14] so that the managing director's contract transferred when the subsidiaries were sold. The EAT was reluctant to pierce the corporate veil and on appeal held that it was not possible to treat the parent company and its four subsidiaries as a single economic entity. By contrast, in *Sunley Turriff Holdings Ltd. v Thompson*[15] the EAT upheld an industrial tribunal decision which had taken cognisance of the fact that whilst on the face of a sale agreement only a separately incorporated Scottish subsidiary was transferred, in reality all the business of the parent company in Scotland was transferred, along with the employee's contract. The *Sunley* case notwithstanding, complex corporate structures can serve to limit the impact of the Directive, a situation so far little changed by any purposive interpretation.

Mr Justice Morrison sets out a series of three alternative scenarios in *Duncan Webb Offset (Maidstone) Ltd. v Cooper.*[16] The first was the transfer of part of a business, to which *Botzen* would apply, the difficulty being to determine the factual extent of assignment. The second scenario canvassed was where an employee engaged in the affairs of one company in a group, has his contract of employment with a separate service company. An example of this second scenario is provided by *BIFU v Barclays Bank Ltd*,[17] in which those working in the merchant banking arm of Barclays, BTZ, were not employed by BTZ but by Barclays Bank and subsequently by another subsidiary BTZ (Services) Ltd. On their transfer to BTZ (Services) Ltd. it was held that there was no need for their union to be consulted, nor was their an obligation to consult on the transfer of business from Barclays to BTZ. Thus the corporate veil served to defeat the operation of TUPE, as would equally have been the case in respect of any dismissals. In *Duncan Webb* Mr Justice Morrison posits that although

12 *Gale v Northern General Hospital NHS Trust* [1994] IRLR 292, CA.

13 [1995] IRLR 190.

14 Consistently with the position under EC competition law. See Weatherill and Beamont, *EC Law*, Penguin, 2nd ed., p. 674.

15 [1996] IRLR 184.

16 [1995] IRLR 633.

17 [1987] ICR 495.

such an employee would not normally be employed by the transferor, he may be deemed to be employed by the service company as agent for the transferor, as was found to be the case in *Zabaxe Ltd. v Nicklin.*[18]

The third scenario occurs where an employee in a subsidiary company, the business of which is transferred, also does work for other companies in the group, as was the case in *Duncan Webb Offset* itself. Here, it was decided according to whether the pattern of the employee's work was such that he could be considered not have been assigned to the part of the enterprise in which he was employed.

An employee who refuses to transfer

Whilst in *Daddy's Dance Hall*[19] the Court of Justice had held that the transfer of the contracts of employees was independent of the will of the parties, what if the employee objects to being so transferred? In *Katsikas v Konstandinis*[20] the Court held that where an employee objects to the transfer of his contract, Article 3(1) does not oblige him to transfer. The Court had already held in *Mikklesen v Danmols Inventar*[21] that where an employee relinquishes his employment voluntarily from the date on which the transfer occurs, he would not enjoy the protection of the Directive and in *Berg & Buschers*[22] that it is not the purpose of the Directive to ensure that the employment relationship with the transferor is continued where the employee does not wish to transfer to the transferee. It followed, reasoned the ECJ in *Katsikas* that the Member States are not obliged to provide that the employment contract continues with the transfer, but may determine the fate of such employees. The response of the UK government was to insert a new regulation 5(4A) in TUPE nullifying the requirements for the transfer of the employee's contract to the transferee but also providing in regulation 5(4B) that he shall not be treated for any purpose as having been dismissed by the transferee.

Any such objection must be conveyed to the transferor before the transfer, either by word or deed, according to the EAT in *Hay v George Hanson (Building Contractors) Ltd,*[23] which held that it should normally be possible to distinguish between the withholding of consent and the mere expression of unwillingness

18 EAT 123/89.

19 [1988] IRLR 315 ECJ.

20 C-132/91, [1993] IRLR 179 ECJ.

21 C-105/84, [1986] 1 CMLR 316 ECJ.

22 C-144/87, [1989] IRLR 447 ECJ.

23 [1996] IRLR 427 EAT.

or concern about the prospect of a transfer. Often an employee who objects to a transfer may be angling to receive a redundancy payment, as in the *Hay* case. Where an employee is successful in receiving a redundancy payment (albeit one to which he would have no statutory right, following regulation 5(4)(B)) the question arises as to whether such a payment could break the employee's continuity of service under ERA 1996 s.214(2). In *Senior Heat Treatment Ltd v Bell*[24] three employees objected to a transfer, took voluntary redundancy terms on offer and then immediately started work for the transferee, but were subsequently dismissed after less than a year. The employer argued that the receipt of redundancy payments had broken their continuity. However, the EAT upheld a finding by the Industrial Tribunal that as there was a transfer and consequently no dismissal, no entitlement to statutory redundancy payments could arise and therefore there was no break in continuity.[25] It follows that transferees should be aware that the receipt of voluntary redundancy payments from the transferor by employees who do in fact transfer, albeit perhaps indirectly, will not break their continuity of employment, if overall there is found to be the transfer of an undertaking.

Where an individual refuses to transfer on the grounds of the new proprietor's identity, he may only bring himself within the scope of Regulation 5(5) if that change is significant and to his detriment. An employee might object to the identity of the transferee, as opposed to its record as an employer, where its public reputation was such that a stigma might attach to any of its employees, as in *Malik v B.C.C.I. SA (in liquidation)*.[26] Otherwise, apart from the example cited in Parliament of the employer who had run off with the employee's wife, it is difficult to think of an example which has strictly to do with the transferee's identity as such, except, say, where the transferee has an involvement in the arms, drugs or tobacco trades. Where the employee has more substantial objections to the transfer, he may fall outside the scope of the decision in *Katsikas* and therefore of regulation 5(4A), as in *Merckx and Neuhys v Ford Motors Belgium SA*[27] (discussed below), where a non-contractual change in conditions was sufficient to ground a claim under Article 4(2) that the employer was responsible for the termination.

24 [1997] IRLR 614 EAT.

25 The EAT also argued that it was for this reason that s.94 of the ERA had been repealed, which formerly assimilated the position where an offer was made by a new owner of the business, to that of an offer to renew a contract of employment made by an existing employer.

26 [1995] IRLR 375 CA.

27 *Supra.*

Constructive Dismissal

TUPE Regulation 5(1) provides that a relevant transfer shall not operate so as to terminate the contract of employment of any person employed by the transferor in the undertaking or the part transferred, but that continuity of employment with the transferee shall be preserved. Regulation 5(5) provides that this right shall be without prejudice to any right of the employee arising apart from these regulations to terminate his contract without notice if a substantial change is made in his working conditions to his detriment.[28] In this way the possibility that changes associated with the transfer could give rise to 'constructive dismissal' arises. A statutory 'constructive' dismissal occurs, according to E.R.A s95(1)(c), where the employee terminates the contract of employment, in circumstances where he is entitled to so terminate it without notice, because of the employer's conduct, i.e. where there is a repudiatory breach of contract according to the Court of Appeal in *Western Excavating v Sharp*.[29] Though a constructive dismissal is always wrongful, it is not necessarily unfair.[30]

The question arises as to whether a statutory dismissal which occurs under Regulation 5(5) is identical with, or in some way different from, constructive dismissals under ERA s.95(1)(c).[31] Whilst Regulation 5(5) speaks of rights 'arising apart from these Regulations', thereby implying a reference to the common law standard laid down in *Western Excavating v Sharp,* which requires there to be a serious breach of contract, the case law of the ECJ calls that analysis into question. In *Merckx and Neuhuys v Ford Motors Belgium SA*[32] a Ford dealership was transferred from a subsidiary to a wholly independent agent. The plaintiff salesmen objected to transferring to the new employer on the basis that, whilst they would retain all their contractual rights under Convention Collective No. 32, which implemented the ARD in Belgium, the

28 This provision implements Article 4(2) of the Directive, which provides that ' If the contract of employment or the employment relationship is terminated because the transfer within the meaning of Article 1(1) involves a substantial change in working conditions to the detriment of the employee, the employer shall be regarded as having been responsible for termination of the contract of employment or employment relationship.'

29 [1978] ICR 221, [1978] IRLR 27, CA.

30 (Harvey: 401).

31 In *Crown Leisure v Waldron* (1993) EAT/307/91 Mr Justice Hicks was of the view that regulation 5(5) imposed no new requirements beyond the ordinary domestic provisions, but this view may be argued not to survive *Mercx*. The observation of Brown-Wilkinson L J (as he then was) in *Delabole Slate co. v Wilson* [1985] IRLR 305 that Regulation 5(5) encompassed 'any detrimental change in his working conditions' would seem to anticipate the decision in *Merckx*.

32 [1996] IRLR 467, ECJ.

transferee would not guarantee their existing levels of bonus and commission, which depended on turnover. Sales earnings might fall as there was no guarantee that the existing client base would be retained or the existing level of turnover achieved. The Court of Justice held that though an employee cannot be obliged to transfer to the new employer, it follows from the decision in *Katsikas v Konstandinis*[33] that such employees do not enjoy the protection of the Directive, unless they fall within the scope of Article 4(2). Article 4(2) provides that

> 'If the contract of employment or the employment relationship is terminated because the transfer within the meaning of Article 1(1) involves a substantial change in working conditions to the detriment of the employee, the employer shall be regarded as having been responsible for termination of the contract of employment or of the employment relationship.'

The Court held that a change in the level of remuneration is such a substantial change in working conditions, even though it did not entail a breach of contract. As Davies[34] observes, the implication for the British courts is that they will have to give a broad interpretation to TUPE Regulation 5(5). Elias and Bowyers argue[35] that an employee contemplating inferior non-contractual conditions, such as promotion opportunities or seniority arrangements, might formerly have been able to claim that such a change rendered the employment not a suitable alternative to his present employment, thereby preserving a claim for redundancy compensation. This is an additional reason for taking a broad interpretation of the Directive's provisions, as otherwise there would in this respect be a worsening of the legal position of employees. Davies also makes the point that even though the courts have confirmed that there is no obligation for transferees to provide pensions in respect of post-transfer service,[36] the wider interpretation of Article 4(2) may provide a legal basis for the Government's cautious view that contractors for CCT work should provide equivalent pensions.

33 C-132/91,C-138/91 & C-139/91, [1993] IRLR 179.

34 Opting out of Transfers, Paul Davies, (1996) *I.L.J.*, 25, No. 3, pp.247-254.

35 Elias and Bowyers, *Transfer of Undertakings, the Legal Pitfalls*, FT Law and Tax, 1995, p.76

36 *Adams v. Lancashire County Council and BET Catering Services Ltd* [1997] IRLR 436, CA, [1996] IRLR 154, HC, *Walden Engineering Ltd. v Warrener* [1993] IRLR 420, *Eidesund v Stavanger A/S* E-2/95 [1996] IRLR 654, EFTA.

In general, an employee will leave in response to an actual breach of contract by the employer, but a constructive dismissal can also arise from an anticipatory breach, where an employee leaves in response to an indication from the employer that he intends to break the contract at some point in the future. This concept is of particular relevance where an employer seeks to push through changes in terms and conditions, with the threat in the background of discharging dissenting employees with due notice, which would not involve an actual breach of contract, as occurred in *Greenaway Harrison Ltd. v Wiles*.[37] Where, however, such a threat occurs in connection with an impending transfer the doctrine may not hold good. In *Sita (G.B.) Ltd v Burton & Ors*[38] two employees resigned two weeks before a transfer in anticipation of detrimental changes to their terms and conditions. The EAT held that as TUPE provides for the protection of employees' existing terms and conditions against the new employer, these employees held no more than 'a fear of change' based on the transferee's behaviour and remarks in the weeks immediately prior to transfer about his intentions as to the terms and conditions of employees. In *Europiéces SA v Sanders* [38a] the ECJ held that it was for the national court to determine if a contract of employment proposed by the transferee entailed a substantial change in working conditions contrary to Article 4(2) of the Directive.

Automatically Unfair Dismissals

When the transfer is the reason for the dismissal, the dismissal is rendered automatically unfair by Regulation 8(1). However, the transfer must indeed by the reason for the dismissal, if Regulation 8(1) is to apply.[39] Where an employee is dismissed for a reason connected with the transfer, an employee is to be deemed to have been employed 'immediately before' the transfer in the terms of Regulation5(3), according to the House of Lords in *Litster v Forth Dry Dock and Engineering Co. Ltd.*[40] In *Litster* the words of Regulation 5(3) were construed purposefully, so as to give effect to the Article 4 of the Directive as interpreted by the Court of Justice in *P. Bork International A/S v Foreningen af Arbejdsledere i Danmark*. [41] In *Bork* the Court of Justice had held that although only workers who have a current contract of employment at the date of the transfer may invoke the Directive, this is subject to the mandatory rules of

[37] [1994] IRLR 80, EAT.

[38] [1996] IRLR 501, EAT.

[38a] C-399/96.

[39] *Secretary of Employment v Spence* [1986] ICR 651, CA, approved by the House of Lords on this point in *Litster v Forth Dry Dock and Engineering Co. Ltd*. [1989] IRLR 161 at 171.

[40] [1989] IRLR 161.

[41] Case C-101/87, [1989] IRLR 41.

the Directive concerning the protection of workers against dismissal by reason of the transfer. Therefore an employee whose contract had been terminated beforehand in circumstances where the transfer itself constitutes the ground for dismissal, must be considered as still employed. Consequently, the transferor's rights and obligations towards him are transferred under Article 3(1). In *Litster* the Lords therefore held that regulation 5(3) must be construed as if it read 'employed immediately before the transfer or would have been so employed if he had not been unfairly dismissed before the transfer for a reason connected with the transfer'. In *Litster* the employees had been collusively dismissed an hour before the transfer and in those circumstances the Lords held that liability for those dismissals transferred to the transferees. Thus a dismissal which is contrived, delayed or anticipated to avoid falling within the scope of the Directive will nonetheless be caught by it, as was the case in *Litster*, where a gap of one hour between the dismissals and the transfer was set up by collusion between the transferor and the transferee. Time is not of the essence of this matter, it is the reason for the dismissal which is important, although, other things being equal, the greater the distance in time the less likely is it to be assessed as a fact that the dismissals were occasioned by the transfer.

Where a business is insolvent it is not always easy to determine whether the dismissal occurs by reason of the transfer or for some other reason, which, though proximate in time, is not actually the transfer itself. This difficulty is especially pronounced in cases of sale by receivers, who may find it necessary to dismiss employees in order to stem losses, or make the business more efficient or saleable. Having made those dismissals the business is then sold to new owners, giving rise to the question as to whether the dismissals were due to the transfer or to other valid managerial reasons. Thus in *Longden & Paisley v Ferrari Ltd. and Kennedy International Ltd.*[42] the eventual transferee informed the receiver for Ferrari, two weeks before the final date of transfer, of the names of those employees whom it regarded as essential to be retained. Other employees were then dismissed by the receiver, because of the financial situation of the company and pressure from the bank. The majority of the EAT held that the Industrial Tribunal had not erred in concluding that those employees were not employed immediately before the transfer, nor that they were dismissed by reason of the impending transfer but by reason of financial exigencies. Similarly, the EAT held in *Ward v Beresford & Hicks Furniture and Salvi International Ltd (in liquidation)*[43] that one batch of employees dismissed two weeks before the transfer on financial grounds were not dismissed in

[42] [1994] IRLR 157.

[43] Unreported 16.12.96 EAT 860/95, Lexis transcript.

connection with the transfer, whereas another batch dismissed on the day of the transfer were unfairly dismissed under regulation 8(1). The decision of the Court of Justice in *Jules Dethier Equipment v Dassy and Sovram SPRL* has given support to a wider view of the options open to receivers and liquidators, in that it has held that the notion of an economic, technical or organisational reason for the dismissal applies as well to the transferor as to the transferee. Such a reason must obviously relate genuinely to the conduct of the business in the period before a transfer is accomplished. To constitute an 'eto' reason by the transferor, the dismissal must relate to the exigencies of running the business in the period prior to the transfer. If the transferee, anticipating its operational needs, requests the transferor to dismiss employees prior to the transfer, the transferee's reason for the dismissal must be connected with the transfer and would, in the UK context, fall foul of regulation 8(1).

A further problem can arise where there is a prospect of a transfer but no certainty about the identity of the eventual transferee. In such circumstances the EAT *in Harrison Bowden Ltd. v Harrison Bowden*[44] held that it was not important whether the identity of the transferee was clear at the point of dismissal, whereas another division of the EAT in *Ibex Trading v Walton*[45] held that Regulation 8(1) referred to *the* transfer and that a transfer which was a mere twinkle in the eye at that stage in the proceedings might never occur. The EAT in *Michael Peters Ltd. v Farnfield and Michael Peters Group plc* opined that *Harrison Bowden* and *Ibex* were not inconsistent, there being no necessity for an actual contract to be in place, if it is projected, but it must presumably amount to more than 'a twinkle in the eye'.

Liability for Dismissals

If an employee is dismissed by the transferor for a reason unconnected with the transfer, liability stays with the transferor, according to the EAT in *Tsangalos v Amalgamated Chemicals Ltd.*[46] Where the dismissal takes place for a reason connected with the transfer, liability for that dismissal transfers to the transferee, in accordance with regulation 5(1). For such a transfer of liability to occur, regulation 5(5) provides that the employee must have been employed by the transferor 'immediately before' the transfer. In *Litster v Forth Dry Dock and Engineering Co. Ltd.*, the House of Lords held that this provision is to be interpreted so as to give effect to Article 4(1) of the Directive, citing the decision of the European Court of Justice in *P. Bork International A/S v Foreningen af*

[44] [1994] ICR 187.

[45] [1994] IRLR 564.

[46] [1997] IRLR 4, EAT.

Arbejdsledere i Danmark.[47] This line of reasoning receives support from the decision in *Jules Dethier Equipment SA v Dassy and Sovram SPRL (in liquididation)*[48] in which the European Court of Justice held that where employees were unlawfully dismissed by the liquidator prior to the transfer and not taken on by the transferee, the employees could claim against the transferee that their dismissal was unlawful. The House of Lords, relying on part on the decision in *Jules Dethier*, also concluded that liability for dismissals by reason of the transfer passes to the transferee, in the joined cases of *British Fuels Ltd v Baxendale and Another* and *Wilson and Others v St Helens Borough Council*.[49]

That liability for a pre-transfer dismissal transfers to the transferee was confirmed by the Court of session in Scotland in *Allan v Stirling District Council*,[50] reversing an earlier EAT decision in which it was suggested that there might be joint liability between the transferor and the transferee. Whilst the Directive allows Member States to legislate to that effect this option was not exercised by the UK. Liability transfers irrespective of whether the employee was informed of the identity of the transferee or of the fact of the transfer.[51]

The 1994 proposals for an amended Directive would have made the transferor as well as the transferee liable for obligations which arose from contracts of employment. However, the transferor would only have been liable for obligations falling due after the date of transfer in so far as these arose from obligations relative to periods before the date of transfer. Member States would have had an option to limit the liabilities of the transferor to pre-transfer obligations which fell due within a year of the transfer. The 1997 amendments would have obliged Member States to legislate for joint and several liability of the transferor and transferee in respect of obligations which arose from a contract of employment and fell due before the transfer, but the text of Directive 98/50[52] is merely permissive, providing that Member States may provide for joint and several liability and for the notification of all rights and obligations to the transferee by the transferor. A failure to notify such rights will not invalidate their transfer. These provisions have given rise to controversy as to the equitable distribution of liability between transferor and transferee but the chosen solution prefers to respect the diversity of national practice, placing no obligation on the UK government to make any change in national law in this respect.

47 *Supra*.

48 C-319/94 [1998] IRLR 206.

49 *The Times*, October 30th, 1998, [1998] IRLR 706.

50 [1995] IRLR 301, CS, [1994] IRLR 208, EAT.

51 *Secretary of State for Trade and Industry v Cook* [1997] IRLR 150 EAT, expressly dissenting from the contrary decision in *Photostatic Copiers (Southern) Ltd. v Okuda* [1991] IRLR 11 EAT.

52 Article 3(1)&(2)

Are Dismissals Connected with a Transfer a Nullity?

The House of Lords in *Litster* did not clearly decide whether the implication of Article 4(1) of the Directive that the transfer 'shall not in itself constitute grounds for dismissal by the transferor or the transferee' implies that such dismissals are a nullity or merely unfair. Regulation 8(1) states in terms that such dismissals are unfair. However, the Court of Appeal in *Meade and Baxendale v. British Fuels Ltd.* held that such dismissals were a nullity, with the result that the previous conditions continued to apply. Any failure to pay the contractual sums due would sound in damages for breach or under the terms of ERA 1996 s.13. Conversely, if the dismissals were to have been held effective but unfair, the employees could have been re-engaged on fresh terms, albeit that they may have received some unfair dismissal compensation.[53] The concept of dismissals being a nullity if they are connected to a transfer was heavily criticised by Mr Justice Morrison in the EAT in *Cornwall County Care Ltd. v Brightman and others*[54] as having 'unsatisfactory practical consequences'. Morrison J argues that an employee dismissed in fact in such circumstances would not have been dismissed in law and his appropriate remedy would be a claim for unlawful deduction of wages under ERA 1996 s.23. The employer would then presumably argue for a dismissal, which the employee could not contend was unfair without accepting the dismissal, thereby making it effective and losing the remedy which was originally sought. Morrison J further contends that it is unsatisfactory if the legal consequences of a dismissal under regulation 8(1) (nullity) and under regulation 8(2) (effective and putatively fair) should be so different and cannot have really been intended by Parliament. If the employee knew that an 8(1) dismissal was effective but unfair he would know where he stood and could receive compensation for his losses, whether he ultimately takes work with the transferee on new terms or no. In the *Cornwall Care* case Morrison J held that the employees, whose dismissal was connected with the transfer of the County Council's care homes to a wholly owned private company outwith the formal local government structure, were unfairly dismissed and re-employed on new but inferior terms, so that the unfair dismissal compensation in effect 'buys-out' their loss once and for all. The ECJ in *Jules Dethier Equipment SA v. Dassy and Sovram SPRL (in liquididation)*[55] held that liability for the dismissal of employees dismissed

[53] The extent of that compensation would depend on service and salary but particularly on the extent of the discrepancy between the old and the new terms and the consequent level of economic loss experienced in the change of terms.

[54] [1998] IRLR 228.

[55] C-319/94 [1998] IRLR 206.

for a reason connected to the transfer transferred to the transferee. According to the ECJ it is the secondary, rather than the primary, obligations under the contract of employment which transfer to the transferee under these circumstances and it is clear from the final conclusions of the Court that the reference it makes to the contracts remaining 'extant', must be construed in this way.

The House of Lords in *British Fuels Ltd. v Baxendale and Another* and *Wilson v St Helens Borough Council*[56] drew support from the decision of the ECJ in *Jules Dethier* and held that there was much force in the criticisms of the Court of Appeal made by Morrison J in the EAT in *Cornwall County Care v Brightman.* Lord Slynn, giving the judgment of the House, held that where ' the transferee does not take on the employees who are dismissed on transfer the dismissal is not a nullity though the contractual rights formerly available against the transfereror remain intact against the transferee.' Lord Slynn rejected the argument put on behalf of the employees that the Court of Justice has concluded in a series of cases[57] that the combined effect of Articles 3(1) and 4(1) of the Directive is to render any dismissal by reason of the transfer a nullity. Lord Slynn did not accept that the transferee was obliged to take on all the transferor's workforce, even though the Court of Justice held in *Danmols Inventar* that the Directive aims

> 'to ensure as far as possible , that the employment relationship continues unchanged with the transferee, in particular by obliging the transferee to continue to observe the terms and conditions of any collective agreement and by protecting the worker against dismissal solely motivated by the transfer.'

Lord Slynn concluded that passages such as the one quoted above mean only that where an employee is taken on, 'the contract is automatically transferred, so that in the absence of permissible variation, the terms of the initial contract go with the employee'. The transferee must perform the obligations of the transferor and he cannot use the transfer as a justification for dismissal, but if he does it is question for national law as to what are the rights of the employee. That this may result in different remedies in the various Member States did not occasion anxiety, because the measure is said to be one of partial harmonisation or approximation and does not create a

56 *The Times*, October 30th, 1998.

57 *Wendleboe v L.J. Music APS* C-19/83 [1985] ECR 457, *Foreningen af Arbejdsledere I Danmark v A/S Dansmols Inventar (Mikklesen'scase)* 105/84 [1985] ECR 2639,*Ny Molle Kro* C-287/86 [1987] ECR 5465, *D'Urso v Ercole Marelli Electtromeccanica Generale* C-362/89[1991] ECR 1-4105, *P. Bork International* C-101/87[1988] ECR 3057.

uniform European law on transfers, nor a Community right to employment which does not exist under national law. As there is no remedy of specific performance in contracts of employment in Britain, under national law an employee dismissed by reason of a transfer is effectively, but unfairly, dismissed, provided he satisfies the necessary qualifying periods. The transferee must honour the statutory and contractual obligations of the transferor as regards employees who are not taken on because they have been dismissed for a transfer related reason by the transferor or the transferee, unless either the employee objects to employment with the transferee (*Katsikas*) or the dismissal is for an economic, technical or organisational reason entailing changes in the workforce. The situation of an employee dismissed before the transfer for a non-transfer related reason remains governed by national law.[58]

The Lords in *Baxendale* revisited the *Litster*[59] case and concluded that, taken as a whole, the import of that judgment is that the dismissal for a reason connected with the transfer of an employee deemed to be employed immediately before the transfer is effective, but unfair. The contract may have been kept alive in the run-up to the transfer, but only for the purpose of ensuring that any breach of the rights of the employee could be enforced against the transferee and not for the purpose of enforcing an obligation to continue the working relationship with the transferee, an obligation not found in domestic law.

No reference was made to the Court of Justice under Article 177 on this issue, because, according to Lord Slynn, that Court had already indicated the answer to this point of law with sufficient clarity. Indeed, both on law and policy grounds that would appear to be the correct conclusion, in that, as their Lordships recognise an obligation to take on all the workforce may not be in the best interests of either the employer or the totality of workers, present and future. The Directive recognises, the need for change in the labour market in its preamble and attempts to balance the protection of employee interests against the need for change and adjustment in times of economic transition, introducing the concept of an economic, technical or organisational reason. An obligation to take on all the workforce would make little difference as regards those employees whom it was the transferee's intention to dismiss, as the transferor is as responsible for the consequences of a pre-transfer dismissal as for a post-transfer dismissal if the reason is connected with the transfer. The question of adjustment of terms is considered in the next chapter, but this can be a contentious issue even where only a reduced workforce is taken on by the transferee.

58 *Secretary of State for Employment v Spence* [1986] ICR 651, [1986] IRLR 248.

59 *Litster v Forth Dry Dock and Engineering Co Ltd.* [1989] ICR 341, [1989] IRLR 161.

Compromise Agreements

The use of compromise agreements under ERA s.203(3) in connection with dismissals by reason of a transfer has given rise to controversy, in that regulation 12 of TUPE provides that any provision of any agreement to exclude or limit the application of regulations 5, 8, 10 or 11 are void. Whilst regulation 8(1) stipulates that a dismissal shall be deemed unfair 'for the purposes of Part V of the 1978 Act' (now Part X of the ERA 1996) and the rights under Part X of ERA are qualified by the provision on compromise agreements, the Court of Justice in *EC v UK*[60] held that in the absence any financial penalty in a directive, Article 5 of the Treaty requires the Member State to take all measures necessary to guarantee the application of Community law. The Court further held that infringements of Community law should be penalised under procedural and substantive conditions analogous to those applicable to infringements of national law. The use of compromise agreements would, however, appear to be integral to comparable national law. In *Thompson v Walon Car Delivery and BRS Automotive Ltd.*[61] the EAT decided that a compromise agreement signed and cleared the day *after* the transfer could not avail the transferee, to whom liability had already transferred the day before. It is implicit in that decision, though not explicitly argued, that such compromise agreements can comport with TUPE. Thus if the transferor signed a compromise agreement before the date of the transfer, this action, it is submitted, would be deemed to have been taken by the transferee under regulation 5. As compromise agreements are an integral part of national unfair dismissal law, the reasoning in *EC v UK* suggests that they are valid, in spite of the restriction in regulation 12 on contracting out of the rights conferred by TUPE or precluding the presentation of a complaint to an tribunal.

Dismissal for an ETO reason

Article 4(1) of the Directive allows that dismissals which take place for an economic, technical or organisational reason entailing changes in the workforce ('eto') may constitute grounds for dismissal by the transferor or the transferee. This provision is implemented by regulation 8(2), which provides that where an employee is dismissed for an 'eto' reason, that dismissal shall, subject to the test of reasonableness in ERA 1996 s.98(1)(4), be regarded as having taken place for some other substantial reason under ERA 1996 s.98(1)(b). Thus if the employer can successfully advance an 'eto' reason for the dismissal, it will be potentially fair. In *Gibson & Ciro Citterio (Menswear)*

60 Case C-382/92 [1994] IRLR 392.

61 [1997] IRLR 343, EAT.

plc[61a] the EAT held that even where an 'eto' reason is established tribunals must go on to scrutinise the employer's action in terms of ERA s.98(4) to establish whether the dismissal fell within the band of reasonable responses in the circumstances of the case.

'Eto' reasons are not defined in the Directive and are capable of covering a wide range of dismissals which might be perceived as economically rational by the employer. According to the Court of Appeal in *Warner v Adnet Ltd*[62] the categories of dismissal covered by regulations 8(1) and 8(2) are not mutually exclusive and a dismissal which is connected to a transfer may nonetheless be for an 'eto' reason. The European Court of Justice in *Jules Dethier Equipment SA v Dassy*[63] held that the transferor as well as the transferee may dismiss employees for 'eto' reasons, so that a dismissal by an administrative receiver to reduce costs or stabilise the financial position of a company could be for an 'eto' reason, provided that the transfer itself is not the reason for the dismissal. The courts have set two principal boundaries to the scope of 'eto' reasons by requiring that they shall pertain to the conduct of the enterprise and that they must entail a change in the numbers and functions of the workforce. Dismissals undertaken to effect or facilitate a sale,[64] or to attract a good price for the business,[65] have not been held to constitute an economic reason. In *Ibex Trading v Walton*[66] employees who refused a pay cut proposed by the receivers in order to prepare the business for sale, were held not to have been dismissal for an 'eto' reason. In *Wheeler v Patel*[67] the EAT held that an 'economic' dismissal must relate to the conduct of the business and that 'technical' and 'organisational' must be construed accordingly.

The suggestion in the opinion of Advocate General Slynn (as he then was) in *D'Urso v Ercole Marelli Electtromeccanica Generale*[68] that not all dismissals for an 'eto' reason fell within the Directive, but only those which would have been made in any case (and which could not therefore pertain directly to the transfer), was rejected by the EAT in *Trafford v Sharp and Fisher (Building Supplies) Ltd.*[69] In *Trafford v Sharp* the transferees reduced the workforce some three weeks after the transfer, having had a chance to inspect the books and to make their appraisal of the business. The EAT rejected the argument

61a EAT 1267/97 (Lexis).

62 *The Times*, March 12th, 1998.

63 C-319/94 [1998] IRLR 266.

64 *Anderson and McAlonie v Dalkeith Engineering* [1984] IRLR 429 EAT, *Wheeler v Patel and J. Golding Group plc* [1987] IRLR 211 EAT.

65 *Gateway Hotels v Stewart* [1988] IRLR 287 EAT.

66 [1994] IRLR 564 EAT.

67 *supra.*

68 C-362/89 [1992] IRLR 136 ECJ.

69 [1994] IRLR 325.

that the words of regulation 8(2) should be made subject to the proviso that the dismissal for an 'eto' reason would have been made in any case, and held that economic reasons entailing a change in the workforce may outweigh the purpose of safeguarding the rights of employees. However, whilst on the facts of this case the reasons for dismissal were held not to be directly related to the transfer, the distinction between a dismissal in connection with a transfer under regulation 8(1) and an 'eto' reason under regulation 8(2) may be blurred and not easy to discern in practice.

An 'eto' reason must entail 'changes in the workforce' of the transferor or transferee. The Court of Appeal has held that the transferee must make changes in the numbers and functions of the workforce as a whole to constitute an 'eto' and cannot merely substitute one employee for another. *In Berriman v Delabole Slate Slate Ltd.*[70] a quarryman was transferred and the employee proposed to harmonise his terms and conditions with those of the existing workforce, which would have entailed a significant reduction in pay. The employee resigned and claimed to have been constructively dismissed. Even though this was a constructive dismissal the Court of Appeal held that the burden of establishing an 'eto' fell upon the employer. Neither the temporary fall by one whilst a replacement was sought for the applicant, nor the proposal to harmonise the terms and conditions of transferred workers with those of the existing workforce, was held to constitute an 'eto'. The Court was of the opinion that such a construction was in accord with the purpose of the Directive to safeguard employees' existing terms of service and that such harmonisation did not fall within the bounds of an 'eto' reason. The employer in *Porter and Nannaayakkara v Queens Medical Centre*[71] successfully argued that the intention to provide a more community oriented pediatric service than was provided by the transferor entailed a change of function for employees which demanded a different mix of skills. In *Porter* the medical staff were dismissed and invited to apply for one of the new posts in the reorganised service. Thus a dismissal of existing staff and reselection amongst them would only appear to constitute an 'eto' if the nature of the jobs applied for is so different that the functions of the workforce as a whole can be said to have changed. Changes in the individuals who compose the workforce cannot constitute an 'eto' unless there is a change in their functions sufficient to say that there is genuinely a change in the workforce.[72] In *Gibson v Cito Citterio (Menswear) plc*[72a] the applicant was deprived of the status 'key holder' at the shop where she worked by the transferee and consequently lost her key holder's allowance of £20 p.w. The EAT upheld a finding that this amounted to a change in the workforce.

70 [1985] IRLR 305 CA.

71 [1993] IRLR 486 EAT.

72 *Crawford v Swinton Insurance Brokers Ltd.* [1990] IRLR 42 EAT.

72a EAT 1276/97 (Lexis).

Can the transferee rely on the transferor's reasons and vice versa?

Regulation 8(2) provides that where an 'eto' reason *entailing changes in the workforce of the transferor or the transferee, before or after the relevant transfer* is the reason for dismissal it shall fall within ERA s.98(1)(b). The question then arises as to whether the 'eto' reason of the transferor has to be its own reason or can it rely on the 'eto' reason of the transferee and vice versa. In *BSG Property Services v Tuck*[73] neither transferor nor transferee believed that TUPE applied to the transfer of a contract for maintenance work, which was to be carried out by self-employed sub-contractors to the transferees. Consequently, the transferors gave notice before the transfer which expired a day after the transfer took place. As the notice was effective after the transfer, liability for the dismissal unequivocally passed to the transferee, but it was the transferor's non-'eto' reasons on the date of dismissal which were held to be the reason for dismissal. Thus the transferor must rely on its own 'eto' reasons on this analysis and it follows that the transferee would in turn have to rely on its own 'eto' reasons for the dismissal. Yet the wording of the regulation does not at first seem to mandate this conclusion, as it refers indifferently to changes in the workforce of the transferor and the transferee before or after the dismissal. However, there are two difficulties in that argument. First, if the transferor relies upon the prospective operational reasons of the transferee, is not the transferor facilitating the sale and falling on the wrong side of *Wheeler v Patel,* however good the reasons in themselves. Second, the transferor is at risk that the dismissals will be found to be unfair and would be advised to seek indemnification from the transferee. If the transferee has genuine 'eto' reasons, it has in any event nothing to lose by dismissing post the transfer, except that the pool of employees from amongst which those dismissed are selected should include all the transferee's workforce.

Are redundancy rights protected

The concept of an 'eto' reason for dismissal is a wider provision than that merely of redundancy, but as Nolan J (as he then was) observed in *Gorictree Ltd. v Jenkinson*[74] it is one of the most common of the economic, technical or organisational reasons to which regulation 8(2) applies. Yet in *Canning v Niaz*[75] the EAT in Scotland had held that redundancy compensation was excluded by the terms of regulation 8(2), which provides that 'the dismissal shall for the purposes of s.98(1)(b) ... be regarded as having been' for some

73 [1996] IRLR 134 EAT.

74 [1984] IRLR 391.

75 [1983] IRLR 431 and in *Meikle v McPhail* [1983] IRLR 351.

other substantial reason. As was held by the EAT in *Gorictree v Jenkinson*, the fact that '*for the purposes of* s.98(1)(b)' the dismissal is to be regarded as having been for some other substantial reason does not preclude that, for the purposes of Part XI of the 1996 Act, the facts of the case might give rise to a valid claim for redundancy.[76] As McMullen[77] argues, it is wrong to suggest that if in the ordinary case an employee would be entitled to claim a redundancy payment he will be disentitled in circumstances of a transfer. This, he argues, cannot be right since it cannot be the purpose of the A.R.D. to derogate from existing standards of labour law. It is also worth observing that the concept of an 'eto' is narrower than 'some other substantial reason', positively from the point of view of protecting employee rights, in that it does not cover a range of economic dismissals which could under the ERA be potentially fair, yet would be automatically unfair under regulation 8(1); that is, those economic reasons which do not 'entail changes in the workforce'.

Redundancy is par excellence a reason for dismissal which entails a change in the workforce, but it is worth noting in this context that according to the decision of the EAT in *Church v West Lancashire NHS Trust*,[78] where the employer has selected amongst the whole or part of the workforce, rather than dismissing those employees whose own jobs are no longer needed to be done, the statutory test of redundancy is not satisfied, even though the selection for redundancy might be fair. This situation, which may leave such employees with no statutory right to compensation, is unfortunate and the *Church* case is on appeal at the time of writing.

The fairness of 'eto' dismissals

By making the remedy for an 'eto' dismissal subject to the test of fairness in s.98(4) the normal procedural and substantive standards which apply in the unfair dismissals at large apply equally to dismissals under regulation 8(2). An absence of appropriate selection methods for redundancy or of adherence to the usual standards of consultation may result in a finding of unfairness, as in *Trafford v Sharpe & Fisher*.[79]

76 In *Anderson v Dalkeith Engineering Ltd* [1985] ICR 66 Lord McDonald in the EAT in Scotland admitted the force of criticism of the decision in *Canning*. In *McGrath v Rank Leisure* [1985] ICR 524 Waite J. held that such a result must be consonant with the presumed intention of both UK and European legislators.

77 J. McMullen, *Business Transfers and Employee Rights*, Butterworths, 1992, p. 216.

78 [1998] IRLR 4.

79 [1994] IRLR 325.EAT.

Elias and Bowyers[80] argue, by analogy to the decision in *Marshall v Southampton and South West Hants Health Authority (No 2),*[81] that the cap on unfair dismissal compensation may be such as to deprive employees of an effective remedy under Community law for transgressions of the Directive. However, the Employment Relations Bill 1998 proposes to raise the limit for unfair dismissal compensation to £50,000.[82] The High Court in *Betts v Brintel Helicopters*[83] held that it did not have power to grant an injunction restraining a dismissal in breach of TUPE, jurisdiction being exclusively reserved under TUPE to the industrial tribunals and limited to the remedies available in that forum.

However, if the dismissals were deemed a nullity, it is arguable that to adequately protect the Community rights granted under the Directive, an injunction restraining such an unlawful dismissal may issue, the Court of Justice in *EC v UK*[84] having held that in the absence any specific penalty in a directive, Article 5 of the Treaty requires the Member State to take all measures necessary to guarantee the application of Community law. However, in *Griffen v South West Water Services Ltd* Blackburn J. in the High Court held that an injunction would not lie in respect of a breach of the Collective Dismissals Directive 75/129 as the directive cannot be interpreted as 'requiring one mode of sanction rather than another, at any rate where the sanction selected is capable of guaranteeing real and effective judicial protection and a real deterrent effect.'[85] In spite of the critical findings of the Court of Justice in *EC v UK* Blackburne J. did not feel it was open to him to ignore the sanctions laid down by Parliament for a breach of the Directive. A similar reluctance to grant an injunction in the context of a business transfer is evident in *Newns v British Airways plc*[86] where the Court of Appeal refused an injunction to restrain the transferor from transferring a contract of employment to the transferee. It was argued on behalf of the plaintiff that the transfer of his contract constituted an unlawful breach of contract which could be restrained by injunction but Scott L J held that the effect of TUPE was to effect a statutory novation of the contract which an employee has, in general, no right to restrain.

80 Elias and Bowyers, *Transfer of Undertakings, the Legal Pitfalls*, FT Law and Tax, 1995, p. 80.

81 [1991] ICR 136.

82 ERA 1999, Section 124(1)(b).

83 [1996] IRLR 45 HC.

84 Case C-382/92 [1994] IRLR 392.

85 [1995] IRLR 15 HC at paragraph 162.

86 [1992] IRLR 575 CA.

The mere change in identity of the employer cannot be restrained, although where that change is in some relevant way significant and detrimental to the employer, regulation 5(5) may come in to play. The door was left partially open, however, in that it was raised as a possibility that where the employer acted in breach of the duty of mutual trust and confidence, such a breach of contract might be restrained. A transfer which was not done in good faith, for example as in *Litster*, where there was collusion between the transferor and the transferee to defeat the claims of the employees, may be significant and detrimental to employees and might, on the above analysis, be capable of being restrained by injunction. Whether the normal tests for the grant of an injunction in relation to a contract of employment would be met, i.e. that personal mutual trust and confidence should have survived,[87] is, however, open to question.

Injunctions to prevent or delay a transfer

The Directive provides no specific remedies, though in *EC v UK* the Court of Justice held that in such circumstances Article 5 of the Treaty requires that the Member states take all measures necessary to guarantee the application and effectiveness of community law.

Conclusions

The protection of employees from dismissal within the context of a transfer is marked by the same attempt to reconcile the protection of employee rights with economic efficiency which characterises the Directive as a whole. These pressures are reflected in the preamble to the Directive, which speaks of economic trends bringing changes in the structure of enterprises, within which context employee rights are to be safeguarded. The Directive, as interpreted by the Court of Justice and by the domestic courts, has attempted a sophisticated reconciliation of these competing pressures as regards dismissal. Whilst transfer related dismissals *simpliciter* are proscribed, those responsible for the management of the undertaking have been left with carefully delineated powers to shape the size and functions of the workforce. The management of declining enterprises may shape human resources to the level of demand, even while putting a business up for sale, so long as this not done at the behest of the transferee or in collusion with it. Likewise, receivers of insolvent enterprises may slim down the workforce in the face of declining demand and financial exigencies, so long as these arise from the short-term management of the undertaking. The transferor may reduce the numbers

87 c.f. *Jones v Gwent County Council* [1992] IRLR 521.

and change the functions of the workforce in accordance with operational needs, although it may not dismiss in preparation for the transfer, nor simply replace the workforce with a cheaper or what is felt to be a better alternative. Where the transferor does dismiss for a transfer-related reason, liability for that dismissal transfers to the transferee. Transferees may not refuse to take on employees without incurring liability for automatically unfair dismissal, unless it is possible successfully to argue the existence of an 'eto' reason. Post-transfer dismissals are subject to the same test and there is no guarantee that the simple effluction of time will ensure that any dismissal is not seen as being connected to the transfer. Thus the transferor and transferee employers must be able to establish that any dismissals occur for reasons connected with the operation of the business and not the transfer itself. However, as genuine redundancies arising from the operational needs of the transferred business would qualify as an 'eto', a well-prepared employer need have little to fear from the protection given to employees against dismissal.

In out-sourcing situations this protection means that the original employer may not dismiss in preparation for the transfer of work but the transferee can dismiss if it can show that it genuinely can operate with fewer employees, or that its plans for the business imply a reorganisation of the functions of the workforce. A decision to dismiss staff in the expectation of replacing them at lower pay after the transfer would be effective but entail a risk that the dismissals would be attributed to the transfer and thus be found automatically unfair. The irony is that, following the *Suzen* case, if the transferee decides not to take on the greater part of the workforce, or any of the relevant fixed assets, the employees will not enjoy any protection against dismissal and can be replaced at will by others willing to work for less money. The amended Directive will, of course, incorporate the essential features of the decisions in *Suzen* and *Henke*, so that the number of employees enjoying protection from unfair dismissal in contracting out and in governmental reorganisations will continue to be at the present lower level. The proposal that employers and employees' representatives in insolvency situations could agree whether and to what extent dismissals could take place for 'eto' reasons, has, however, found no place in the amended Directive.

7. Preservation, Variation and Harmonisation of Terms and Conditions

Colin Bourn and Paul Thorpe

The Acquired Rights Directive attempts to protect the position of employees affected by the transfer of the undertaking in which they are employed by preserving their existing terms and conditions of employment and by precluding transfer-based dismissals. Article 3(1) provides that the transferor's rights and obligations arising from a contract of employment shall be transferred to the transferee, whilst Article 4(1) precludes dismissals connected with a transfer *per se*, whilst allowing employers to advance economic, technical or organisational reasons for such dismissals.

TUPE provides in regulation 5(1) that a relevant transfer shall not operate so as to terminate the contract of any person employed by the transferor in the undertaking or part transferred, but that any such contract shall have effect after the transfer as if originally made between the employee and the transferee. Regulation 5 (2)(a) further provides that the transferor's rights, duties, powers and obligations under or in connection with any such contract of employment shall be transferred to the transferee, and regulation 5(2)(b) that anything done before the transfer is completed by the transferor in respect of that contract or a person employed in the undertaking shall be deemed to have been done by the transferee. The transfer of rights, powers, duties and obligations achieved by TUPE is comprehensive, extending not only to contractual matters, such as non-payment of wages, but also to statutory obligations owed to transferred employees, such as those which arise in relation to unfair dismissal claims. Liability also transfers for non-contractual actions, in that regulation 5(2)(b) covers 'anything done by the transferor... in respect of a person employed in the undertaking', thereby including, for example, liability for discriminatory actions by the transferor, even where those actions were taken in respect of a contract no longer extant at the date of the contract which could not be terminated or otherwise affected by the transfer.[1]

Transfer of Contractual Provisions

Whilst straightforward rights to wages and salary are clearly transferred, indirect payments or other rights, such as bonuses or profit sharing payments, can give rise to problems. Where these are calculated on the profits or turnover of the transferor and the transferor's business is merged into that of the transferee, it is no longer possible literally to compute the bonuses due. In such cases the most appropriate response would be for the transferee to offer an alternative scheme, which though strictly in breach of contract would yield equivalent benefit,[2] which would limit any claim for damages and might be argued not to constitute a repudiatory breach. Likewise, share options schemes can only be exercised against the transferor under the rules of the applicable scheme, so that once a person is no longer an employee he normally ceases to be eligible.[3] Such rights arguably arise 'in connection with the contract' even if contained in a separate scheme document but it would be extremely unlikely that any court would allow them to be exercised against the transferee company, so that unless exercisable against the transferor, such rights would be incapable of being exercised after the transfer.

Although the terms of a bonus scheme may remain formally identical after a transfer, the change in business circumstances may mean that income of the employee is less, giving rise to a substantial change in working conditions to the detriment of the employee contrary to Article 4(2), according to the Court of Justice in in *Merckx and Neuhys v Ford Motors SA.*[4] In that case, even though the bonus arrangements did not change, the transfer of the business to another undertaking led the employees to believe that their income would fall, which, even though there was no breach of contract, the Court held was contrary to Article 4(2).

1 *DJM International Ltd. v Nicholas* [1996] IRLR 76 EAT.

2 Elias and Bowyers, *Transfer of Undertakings: the Legal Pitfalls*, FT Law and Tax, 1996, p.60.

3 *Micklefield v SAC Technology Ltd.* [1990] IRLR 218 HC, *Chapman v CPS Computer Group plc* [1987] IRLR 462 CA.

4 C-171/94 [1996] IRLR 457. And see chapter 6 for discussion of this case in the context of constructive dismissal.

Where an employee has a contractual right to enhanced redundancy terms, this obligation will be transferred, according to the EAT in *Whitewater Leisure Management Ltd. v Frankling.*[4a] In that case the employee was made redundant by the transferee three months after it had taken over responsibility for the provision of leisure services in Brent. The employee was entitled to an enhanced redundancy payment under local authority terms and conditions, because Brent had had a policy of disapplying the statutory maximum for a week's pay in calculating the sums due. The transferee resisted the claim for enhanced redundancy terms on the ground that *Allsop v North Tyneside Metropolitan Borough Council*[4b] was authority for the proposition that blanket enhanced redundancy terms of this type were *ultra vires* the local authority and could not therefore transfer. The question turned upon the construction of regulation 5 of the Local Government (Compensation for Redundancy and Premature Retirement) Regulations 1984, which the transferee argued only gave the authority a discretion to award such payments, so that a blanket application of enhanced terms was *ultra vires*. The EAT rejected this construction of the Regulations, distinguishing *Allsop* on the ground that in that case the local authority had exceeded the maximum permissible limits. The EAT held that it was not contrary to the Regulations to adopt a blanket policy in these circumstances and therefore the valid contractual obligations of the local authority were transferred to the new contractor. This is clearly a significant matter in terms of the liabilities of contractors for local authority work and must mean that greater care needs to be taken in computing possible liabilities where a contractor foresees imminent redundancies. However, *Frankling v BPS Public Sector Ltd.*[4c] is authority for the proposition that where enhanced redundancy terms form part of a premature retirement package, those terms are excluded as relating to old age benefits under Article 3(3).

Restrictive covenants and share options can likewise give rise to problems when the identity of the employer changes. If the employee is required not to compete with the transferor nor to solicit its customers, to what do such clauses refer in the context of a transfer of the business? If the identity of the business is preserved, there may be no difficulty in applying the terms of the covenant. The Court of Appeal confirmed in *Morris Angel and Son Ltd. v Hollande*[5] that such agreements relate to the business transferred and not to the transferee's pre-existing business, even though regulation 5(1) provides

[4a] EAT/964/98.

[4b] [1992] ICR 639.

[4c] [1999] IRLR 212, EAT.

[5] [1993] IRLR 169 CA.

that 'the contract shall have effect after the transfer as if originally made between the person so employed and the transferee'. If it is not possible to identify the relevant pool of customers or business after the transfer, the covenant will arguably fail. A transferee may be tempted to agree revised restrictive covenants with employees in view of the above difficulties, yet this course of action may also encounter difficulties because the revised covenants would constitute a change in contractual terms by reason of the transfer. Thus, when Credit Suisse took over BZW the transferee sought to agree a non-competition covenant, which would come into operation at the close of a three months' notice period. The EAT, in *Credit Suisse First Boston (Europe) Ltd. v Padiachy*,[6] took the view that this clause was void as having occurred by reason of the transfer even if the package of terms was advantageous overall, such changes being contrary to the decision of the Court of Justice in *Daddy's Dance Hall*.[7]

NON-CONTRACTUAL MATTERS

The subject matter of discrimination claims can constitute action taken in respect of a person employed in the undertaking under regulation 5(2)(b), even though the matter arose in connection with a contract which was not in force at the time of the transfer.[8] Similarly, matters which give rise to a personal injury claim constitute action done in relation to a transferred employee.[9] However, criminal liabilities are not transferred under TUPE regulation 5(4) and neither are the obligations in respect of pensions.[10] As it is the obligations owed to the employee which are transferred, neither vicarious liabilities owed to a third party by the transferor in respect of the employee transferred, nor obligations owed to trade unions,[11] outside of those covered under regulation 6 as regards collective agreements, transfer.

6 [1998] IRLR 504.

7 14.

8 See 1.

9 *Secretary of State v Spence* [1986] IRLR 248 per Balcombe J at 14.

10 See chapter 5.

11 *Jowett (Angus) & Co. Ltd. v NUTGW* [1985] IRLR 326 as regards protective awards made consequent upon a failure to consult the trade union.

Variation and Harmonisation of Terms

For many contractors, competitive tendering for public sector work will only be commercially attractive if it can be undertaken at a lower labour cost, [12] just as an employer who takes over an ailing competitor may need to cut costs if the business is to be viable. A tender may have been very keenly priced in order to obtain the work, which puts pressure on labour costs. There may also be pressure to bring the new workforce into line with existing employees as regards pay and, in particular, fringe benefits.

The approaches adopted by employers, employees and trade unions will be constrained by the application of the Acquired Rights Directive (ARD)[13] and the Transfer of Undertakings (Protection of Employment) Regulations (TUPE) which implement the ARD in the Britain. Regulation 5 provides for the automatic transfer of rights and obligations arising from the contract of employment, where regulation 12 renders void any agreement which purports to exclude or limit its application. Regulation 12 also renders void any agreement to exclude the effect of regulation 8, or to preclude a complaint being made to an industrial tribunal under regulation 11 or to avoid the consultation provisions under regulation 10.

In *Foreningen of Arbejdsledere Danmark v Daddy's Dance Hall*[14] the European Court of Justice (ECJ) held that the provisions of the Directive were mandatory and that an employee could not waive the rights conferred on him, even if the disadvantages of so acting are offset by the advantages, so that overall he is left in no worse position. This protection is expressed to be a matter of public policy and outside the control of the parties to the employment contract. Nonetheless, the Court of Justice held that, as Directive 77/187 only aims at partial harmonisation, it does not preclude an alteration in the employment relationship agreed with the new proprietor of the undertaking insofar as such an alteration is permitted by national law in cases other than transfers of undertakings. It is necessary therefore to enquire how far, and in what circumstances, the common law permits such alterations in the terms of the employment relationship apart from the effect of ARD and TUPE.

12 In a survey of employers and trade unions involved in contracting out situations, Hardy, Adnett and Painter report that 46% of the employers contacted had changed pay levels post-transfer and 20% had changed job descriptions. Whilst 64% of those employers contacted who had decreased pay expressed satisfaction with CCT as a process, only 5% of employers who had made no change in pay expressed that view, 50% rating it as merely satisfactory and 37% as unsuccessful. Hardy, Adnett and Painter, *TUPE and CCT Business Transfers: UK Labour Market Views*, Staffordshire University Institute of Industrial and Commercial Law, 1997.

13 77/187/EC.

14 C-324/86, [1988] ECR 739, [1988] IRLR 315 ECJ.

The position at common law

At common law a transferee employer in such a situation has several options. The transferee may seek to negotiate and agree the necessary changes, possibly via a trade union if one is recognised. Failing that, the employer may seek simply to impose new conditions on the transferred workers, or may explicitly give notice of termination of the previous contract and offer a fresh contract on new terms.

Where changed terms are negotiated directly with employees the contractual requirements of consent and consideration are met,[15] as the new terms are agreed in exchange for the promise of continued employment on fresh terms. The same is true when change is negotiated with a trade union, at least where the employees' contracts contain a term, whether express or implied, that relevant terms negotiated between the employer and the trade union are to be incorporated into the individual's contract of employment. If an employer were to agree revised terms with the 'appropriate representatives' provided for under the 1995 Consultation Regulations,[16] such an agreement would not effect an alteration of the terms of the contracts of employment of individual workers without their express consent, there not normally being any appropriate implied term vesting the statutory representatives with such authority.

Where an employer, perhaps despairing of reaching an agreement, seeks to impose fresh terms unilaterally there will be a breach of contract. Where the employee continues to work under protest and does not accept the changes to his terms, an action becomes possible under s.13 of the Employment Rights Act in respect of an unauthorised deduction from wages. Such a claim can be made even though the employee continues to work and may continue so long as the employer has not effected a lawful variation of the terms of the contract. In *Rigby v Ferodo Ltd.*,[17] an employee made a breach of contract claim when his pay had been unilaterally reduced. The House of Lords rejected the employer's argument that such an action was effective to terminate the contract automatically, limiting the employee to damages during the notice period, at the end of which the contract would have lawfully terminated.

15 *Stylck v Myrick* (1809) ' Camp. 317 and *Hartley v Ponsonby* (1857) 7 E. & B. 872 can be distinguished as concerning a situation where the employees were already committed to completing a voyage which could not therefore serve as consideration for a promise of increased pay by the captain of the vessels. An indefinite contract can be terminated by agreement and a new contract entered into incorporating such terms of the old contract as are relevant, the consideration being the mutual agreement to carry forward the employment on this basis.

16 SI 1995/2587 amending TUPE 1981 Reg. 10(2A).

17 [1987] IRLR 516 and also *Burdett-Coutts v Herts. C.C.* [1984] IRLR 91.

Lord Oliver, giving the judgment of the House, held that

> 'Whatever may be the position under a contract of service where the repudiation takes the form either of a walk-out by the employee or a refusal by the employer any longer to regard the employee as his servant, I know of no principle of law that any breach which the employee is entitled to treat as repudiatory of the other party's obligations brings the contract to an end automatically.'[18]

Lord Oliver could not accept the proposition that a 'combination of a breach going to an essential term, a desire in the party in breach to bring the contract to an end or to continue it in a different form and no practical option in the other party but to accept the breach', automatically brings the contract to an end. He concluded that he saw no reason in law or logic why the contract of employment, leaving aside cases of outright dismissal or walk-out, was not amenable to the famous proposition that 'an unaccepted repudiation is a thing writ in water and of no value to anybody'.[19] The contract therefore continued until it could be validly varied. Consequently, the employee was not limited simply to damages in the notice period, there being no termination of the contract at common law without an acceptance of the breach by the employee.

Yet in *Alcan Extrusions v Yates*[20] the employees suffered a change in their shift patterns, but continued working under protest and successfully claimed to have been dismissed under ERA s.95(1)(a). The EAT applied the principle enunciated in *Hogg v Dover College*,[21] that where an employer imposes radically different terms which have the effect of withdrawing and thus terminating the original contract, the employer's actions can amount to a dismissal under s.95(1)(a) and do not simply give rise to a repudiatory breach which the employee must accept, so as to bring about a termination under s.95(1)(c). A dismissal under s.95(1)(a) is a dismissal in terms which needs no acceptance by the employee. Whether a change in terms is sufficiently radical to amount to a withdrawal of the old contract was held to be a question of fact and degree. In *Hogg* the EAT relied on *Marriot v Oxford and District Co-operative*

18 At page 518.

19 *Howard v Pickford Tool Co Ltd*. [1951] 1 KB 417 CA at 421 *per* Lord Asquith.

20 [1996] IRLR 327, noted by White in *ILJ*, 25, 3, pp. 252-258.

21 [1990] ICR 39 EAT. The employee, a department head in a school, returned from a period of sick leave and was offered only a part-time post as an ordinary teacher. He did that work under protest whilst claiming to have been unfairly dismissed under ERA s.95(1)(a).

Society (No 2)[22] in which the Court of Appeal held that the imposition of inferior terms could amount to a termination of the contract, although the employee in *Marriot* did subsequently resign, giving due notice, on finding other employment. However, the decision in *Marriot* arose from the circumstance that, under the 1965 Redundancy Payments Act an employee had, at that time, to leave without giving notice, if he was to bring himself within the compass of a 'constructive dismissal' by reason of redundancy. After *Marriot's* case the statute was amended so that 'constructive dismissal' could occur when the employee was simply *entitled* to leave without notice. In *Western Excavating v Sharpe*[23] Lord Denning sought to resile from his analysis in *Marriot*, stating that in the circumstances 'we had to stretch it a bit. It was not the employer who terminated the employment. It was the employee: and he was entitled to do so by reason of the employer's conduct.' Thus, although *Hogg* and *Alcan* are restricted to contractual changes which constitute an effective withdrawal of the old contract, so that the employment relationship must be deemed to be continued by means of a fresh contract, the decisions are questionable. Why should the claim that a repudiatory breach brings the contract to an end be rejected in *Rigby v Ferodo*, whilst a similar argument by the employee is accepted in *Hogg* and *Alcan*? *Hogg* and *Alcan* were both statutory claims for unfair dismissal, whereas *Rigby* was a common law claim for damages, but this should in principle make no difference, as the statutory test for constructive dismissal relies on the contractual test of repudiatory breach, according to Lord Denning in *Western Excavating*.[24]

The import of the above cases is that where an employer fails to reach an agreement with the employees and imposes substantial changes in the contract of employment, if the employee accepts the repudiation and leaves, there will be a dismissal under either ERA s.95(1)(c) in relation to unfair dismissal and/or s.136(1)(c) in relation to redundancy. If the employee chooses to work on under protest, on the authority of *Rigby v Ferodo* there is no dismissal unless the employee accepts the repudiation by acting in ways incompatible with the continuance of the contract of employment. In the event that the employee works on under protest, he may make a claim for an unlawful deduction from wages under ERA s.13, the former Wages Act 1986

22 [1970] 1QB 186.

23 [1978] IRLR 28.

24 Even though the EAT in *Robert Cort v Chapman* [1981] IRLR 437 held that where an employee's contract is repudiated, the effective date of termination is the date at which the act of termination took place, even if the employee does not accept the repudiation at all or only at some later date. The decision in *Robert Cort* pertains only to the effective date of termination for the purpose of claiming unfair dismissal and has no bearing on whether or not the contract has itself been determined.

provisions.[25] If the actions of the employer amount to a withdrawal of the old contract, so that whilst the employment relationship may persist, the original contract is brought to an end, *Hogg* and *Alcan* are authority (though not unimpeachable authority) for the proposition that there is a dismissal under ERA s.95(1)(a), even though the employee continues working under protest. Such an employee may therefore argue in the alternative; either there is a withdrawal of the old contract and a dismissal or there is no dismissal and a claim may be made under the former Wages Act provisions until such time as the employer chooses explicitly to terminate the contract under s.95(1)(a) and perhaps to offer a fresh contract on new terms.

Consensual Change and the Application of TUPE

In *Foreningen of Arbejdsledere Danmark v Daddy's Dance Hall*[26] the European Court of Justice (ECJ) first pointed to the possibility that even consensual change may not be permitted in the circumstances of a transfer. In this case, even though there was an agreed 'trade-off' between the employees and the transferee, such as both parties might normally have been able to achieve, the ECJ held that it was not possible to derogate from the ARD even in a manner not on balance unfavourable to the employee. The Court argued that the safeguarding of the rights arising under the employment contract or relationship 'is a matter of public policy and, as such, outside the control of the parties to the employment contract.'[27] The provisions were held to be 'mandatory' and that it was not possible 'to derogate from them in a manner detrimental to the workers.'

Nonetheless, the Court recognised that the Directive aimed only at partial harmonisation and was not intended to set a uniform level of protection throughout the Community. Therefore, the Directive can only serve to protect the worker in relation to the transferee, in so far as he was protected in relation to the transferor under national law. In *Rask and Christensen v ISS Kantinsenservice*[28] the ECJ reiterated that, as the Acquired Rights Directive is

25 Employees made a successful claim under the Wages Act provisions, when they were dismissed by reason of redundancy by a local authority, in the belief that TUPE did not apply, when their jobs as swimming pool attendants were transferred out to a private contractor on inferior terms. The contractor subsequently went bankrupt and the management of the swimming pools was resumed by the local authority. The employees successfully brought an action against the Council for the shortfall in pay when they had worked for the private contractor. *Fuller v London Borough of Croydon* London south Industrial Tribunal, December 21st 1995.

26 C-324/86, [1988] ECR 739, [1988] IRLR 315 And see *Langeland v Norske Fabricum A/S*, EFTA Court Case E/3-95.

27 At point 14.

28 C-209/91 [1993] IRLR 133.

a measure of only partial harmonisation, only the protection afforded to employees under the legal system of the Member State is transferred upon a relevant transfer.

> '(I)n so far as national law allows the employment relationship to be altered in a manner unfavourable to employees in cases other than a transfer of an undertaking, in particular as regards their conditions of pay, such an alternative is not precluded merely because the undertaking has been transferred in the meantime and the agreement has therefore been made with the new employer...provided that the transfer itself may never constitute the reason for that amendment.' [29]

In view of the fact the Directive aims only at partial harmonisation, it can only be relied upon to protect an employee in his relations with the transferee to the extent that such an employee was protected in his relations with the transferor, under the legal rules of the Member State. Therefore, insofar as the national law permits the employment relationship to be altered in situations outside a transfer, such alterations are not precluded merely because the undertaking has been transferred, providing that the transfer itself may never constitute the reason for that amendment.

In *Wilson v St Helen's Borough Council*[30] the EAT applied the reasoning in *Daddy's Dance Hall* to a situation in which, due to financial pressure, responsibility for a residential community home was transferred from Lancashire County Council to St Helens Borough Council, the transferee being willing and able to finance only a much reduced establishment. Following discussions with the trade unions a new and reduced set of posts with generally lower gradings was implemented by the transferee. The Industrial Tribunal found that employees were dismissed by the transferor on grounds of redundancy and a proportion offered new contracts on fresh terms by the transferee.[31] The EAT proceeded on the basis that there had been a variation of terms and, following *Daddy's Dance Hall,* found the agreed contractual variations void on public policy grounds, having arisen from the transfer itself. The employer's argument that the employees had affirmed the changes by working to the new grades for eighteen months was rejected, as the new practices arose from the transfer. The EAT also held that there

29 At para 28

30 [1996] IRLR 320, EAT

31 McMullen, *Business Transfers and Employee Rights*, Butterworths, 3rd edn, 9/16 observes that only those retained employees whose functions had been changed to such an extent as to constitute new positions, would in law have been dismissed by reason of redundancy.

was no place for the operation of an 'eto' type reason in relation to a variation of terms, absent a dismissal. The case was remitted to an industrial tribunal to determine entitlements under the Wages Act 1986 as regards unlawful deductions from pay.

McMullen describes this as a 'woeful outcome', whilst Rubenstein,[32] offers trenchant criticism of the decision, whilst admitting that Mr Justice Mummery had Community law on his side, arguing that the refusal to allow a consensual variation of terms on a transfer is a form of 'betterment' which tends to defeat the purposes of consultation on the implications of the transfer, insofar as any resulting agreement would be legally ineffective. Rubenstein goes on to argue that the EAT. seems to have fallen into the same trap as it fell into in *Milligan v Securicor Cleaning*,[33] i.e. in exceeding the provisions available to employees under domestic law.

Wynne-Evans[34] goes further in his criticism of *Wilson*, for what he sees to be a misapplication of the purposive interpretation of the ARD. He argues that minimum harmonisation, allowing to the transferee whatever rights were possessed by the transferor, implies that consensual variations should be possible under the common law even when they occur in the context of a transfer.[35] However, he has to concede that the proviso stated by the ECJ in *Daddy's Dance Hall* and *Rask*, that this position only obtains 'provided that ...the transfer itself is not the reason for the alteration' requires clarification at ECJ level. Wynne-Evans argues that Community law is only supreme in its own terms and that purposive interpretation can lead to difficulties where there is confusion as to the policy and purposes of the Directive. He implies that the EAT had too raw an understanding of the policy of the Directive in *Wilson* and looks to the eventual resolution of this issue by the ECJ. Wynne-Evans also makes the point that in the circumstances of a dismissal, the transferee can plead 'eto' reasons, whereas such recognition of the economic logic facing an employer is absent where there is simply a change in terms.

In *Meade and Baxendale v British Fuels Ltd.*[36] the employees worked for NFD, which was subsequently merged with another company to form BFL. They were purportedly dismissed by the transferor by reason of redundancy and offered new employment with the transferee on inferior terms and

[32] Editorial, IRLR, (1996), 25, 6, p. 1.

[33] [1995] IRLR 288.

[34] (1996) ILJ, 25, 3, pp. 230-234.

[35] Wynne-Evans outlines the practical consequences of the EAT decision in *Wilson*, as including the difficulties posed to transferees in making changes needed to ensure the survival of the undertaking and the discouraging fear of retrospective claims for breach of contract or under the erstwhile Wages Act provisions.

[36] [1996] IRLR 541.

conditions, the employer claiming that the redundancy and severance payments had 'bought out' their prior service with the transferor. The EAT held the dismissals effective, if unfair, reasoning that there was nothing in the Directive or TUPE, as construed by the Lords in *Litster,* [37] which required such dismissals to be rendered a nullity. *Wilson* was distinguished on the basis that there was no submission or findings in that case concerning dismissal.[38]

The Court of Appeal heard both *Wilson* and *Meade and Baxendale*[39] together, but the judgment was rather disappointing, providing no answer to the question raised by *Wilson* as to the validity of variations of terms following a transfer. Beldam LJ, giving the judgment of the Court, approached both cases as a matter of the effectiveness and fairness of dismissals in a transfer situation. In *Wilson* the Court of Appeal held that the tribunal had found as a fact that the reason why the employees' contracts had been terminated, either by the transferor immediately prior to the transfer on grounds of redundancy, or by the transferee in offering employment on substantially different terms, was an 'eto' reason brought about by the shortfall of funds of both local authorities. As the reason for these putative dismissals was not the transfer but an 'eto' reason, namely, the shortage of funds, the dismissals were effective and the transferee was free to re-engage the employees on fresh terms. The dismissals in *Meade and Baxendale*, prior to the harmonisation of the terms of Meade and Baxendale with those of the existing employees of the transferee, were held to have been occasioned by the transfer and therefore ineffective. The employees therefore continued to be employed on their previous terms and conditions. Thus the Court of Appeal analyses the issues of variation as questions of the validity of the dismissals and whether or not they take place for a reason connected with the transfer or by way of an economic, technical or organisational reason.

The impact of *Wilson* and *Meade and Baxendale* can be seen in *Brightman and Adams v Cornwall Care Ltd* [40] in which the County Council formed a company as charitable trust to run its twenty care homes, in order to put itself in a position to lower labour costs towards those commonly paid in the private sector. The union withdrew from discussions about new terms and conditions on hearing of the *Wilson* decision, the transferee employer then dismissed the workforce and offered to re-engage them on less favourable

[37] *Litster and others v Forth Dry Dock and Engineering Co. Ltd.* [1989] IRLR 161, HL.

[38] Alternatively, the EAT held that if the effect of Community law were to render the dismissals a nullity, the offer of employment by the transferee would amount to an attempt to preclude the operation of Regulation 5, an action rendered void by Regulation 12.

[39] [1997] IRLR 505.

[40] Case no: 1700776/96, 11th April 1997.

terms and conditions. All the employees accepted under protest, but subsequently, with the support of their trade union, brought an action in the industrial tribunals complaining that their dismissals were automatically unfair under regulation 8(1) and seeking a declaration that they were still entitled to their old terms and conditions. The Industrial Tribunal concluded that the dismissals, found to be unfair under regulation 8(1), were a 'sham', the new employer always having intended to retain their services. The Tribunal found that the variation in the terms was ineffective, and the employees entitled to the continuation of their previous terms. The EAT upheld the unfair dismissals but held that it was illogical to conclude that there was an unfair dismissal, but that the employees were still entitled to be employed on the terms and conditions which they enjoyed before the transfer. Morison J in the EAT argued, that the Court of Appeal in *Wilson* and *Meade and Baxendale* having apparently accepted that a regulation 8(1) dismissal may become effective if accepted by the employees, it was unreal to suppose that having worked to the new terms, the employees could contend that they were still employed on the old ones. The reality was, the EAT held, that the employees were dismissed and the unfair dismissal award represented once and for all compensation for any losses.

When the *Wilson* case was heard by the House of Lords,[41] Lord Slynn held that the need for radical staffing changes to ensure the continued running of the home, either by Lancashire County Council or St Helens Borough Council, constituted an economic or organisational change which entailed a change in the workforce, whether or not, absent a dismissal, the concept of an 'eto' reason strictly applied. In those circumstances the Industrial Tribunal and the Court of Appeal were entitled to find that the transfer did not constitute the reason for the variation, which was a variation of terms 'to the same extent as it could have been with regard to the transferor'.[42] Lord Slynn added that it does not follow from the proposition that the employees' rights previously existing against the transferor are enforceable against the transferee and cannot be amended by the transfer itself, that

> 'there cannot be a variation of the terms of the contract for reasons which are not due to the transfer either on or after the transfer of the undertaking. It may be difficult to decide whether the variation is due to the transfer or attributable to some separate cause. If, however, the variation is not due to the transfer it can, in my opinion, on the basis of the authorities to which I have referred, validly be made.'

41 *The Times*, October 30th, 1998.

42 *Daddy's Dance Hall*, *supra*, para 17.

Though the observations of Lord Slynn on the question of variation are strictly speaking *obiter*, they are of great authority, the only other authority directly in point on post-transfer variations being the EAT decision in *Wilson*. The decision of the House of Lords seems to open up a greater possibility that where an employer seeks to refashion the terms and conditions of the transferred workforce that a variation in terms is possible, but it will be a question of fact as to whether the variation arises from the transfer or no. The difficulty of arriving at a settled view on the facts of *Wilson* itself suggests that this will frequently be a difficult test to determine, but it seems an incontrovertible application of the decision in *Daddy's Dance Hall*.

The amended Directive[43] will, however, confer on Member States the power not to apply Articles 3 and 4 to situations of bankruptcy and other analogous insolvency proceedings which have been instituted with a view to the liquidation of assets.

What is the Current Position on Variation of Terms on a Transfer?

Daddy's Dance Hall establishes that the reason for any amendment to the terms of employment of transferred employees cannot be the transfer itself, even though the Court of Justice held that the Directive is an act of partial harmonisation which otherwise leaves the transferee with the same powers as the transferor to introduce change. At common law the transferee could agree a change in terms with the employees and this power remains unless the transfer itself is the reason for making the changes. The EAT in *Meade and Baxendale* concluded that if the transferor wishes to effect an alteration in terms, this must be done as a matter of operational policy. This issue is not simply one of time; the EAT in *Mead and Baxendale* pondered whether there was any temporal limitation to the effects of a transfer and concluded that this

> 'forensically difficult situation cannot be regarded as a continuing one. Regulation 12 cannot serve indefinitely to inhibit the parties from bringing the legal position into line with reality. The longer the period since the transfer, the easier it will be to demonstrate a variation by conduct or to justify a variation by agreement, in either event to equate the position in law with the reality. The "landmine" does not pose an indefinite threat.'[44]

43 Directive 98/50/EC, Article 4A amending Directive 77/187/EEC.

44 At para 43.

The Court of Appeal concluded that in the instant case, the purported variation of terms, including recognition of the continuity of employment of employees transferred between the transferor and transferee, finally agreed some six months after the transfer, was nonetheless connected with it. Thus, in spite of argument by the employers that the effects of the transfer must have been spent by the time of the crucial incidents, the Court of Appeal held that the 'landmine' remained active. In the *Cornwall Care* case the landmine had been de-activated by the dismissals, according to the EAT, leaving the employees to their remedy in unfair dismissal. In *Baxendale v BFL* Lord Slynn observed that 'there must, or at least may, come a time when the link with the transfer is broken or can be treated as no longer effective.' This dictum may give rise to difficulties in practice and no rule of thumb can really be proffered. However, should the transferee subsequently rationalise the whole of the pay structure within the enterprise, the amendment would not be by reason of the transfer. Any such workforce-wide change cannot easily be attributed to the transfer and would almost certainly be seen as arising from operational reasons of an 'eto' nature, even if no change in the workforce is entailed.

Red Circling

Where a transferee takes over responsibility for workers who enjoyed better terms with the transferor than they would normally enjoy with the transferee, it is possible to 'red-circle' those employees. Protecting their terms and conditions, although they create an anomaly in the pay structure of the transferee. New employees can be taken on at the transferee's normal rates, so long as the pay and conditions of the employees transferred over are not affected. Red-circling is an accepted practice when an employer attempts to re-organise a pay structure, ensuring that those whose pay would otherwise fall are not adversely affected in the short term. In the long term, such employees can be assimilated to the main pay structure by restricting increases in pay until other employees catch up. This solution is one which could deal with small-scale anomalies, though it may strain credibility if large groups are affected.

Where contractors or other transferees are spread over many sites, there is no necessity for pay at one site to be the same as pay at another. Geographical flexibility may be entirely appropriate. There is no possibility of challenge under the Equal Pay Act so long as it is clear that employees across the company are not working under circumstances in which common terms and conditions are observed as between sites.

The Collective Agreement and Variation of Terms

Collective agreements are the product of collective bargaining between employers and trade unions. Such agreements are not normally enforceable in law,[45] and since 1974 there has been a statutory presumption that such agreements are not enforceable unless otherwise specified by the parties.[46] To have legal effect collective agreements must be incorporated into the contracts of individuals. The most effective way to secure incorporation is via expressly stated terms, although that is not essential. In the absence of such a reference in the statement of terms, the relevant terms of the collective agreement may be incorporated by virtue of an implied bridging term in the contract of employment, rationalised as 'crystallised custom'[47] or as a legal incident of the contract of employment. On either analysis precise knowledge of the terms of the agreement by the worker is not necessary. Although the statutory statement of terms under ERA s.1 is not conclusive proof of the terms of the contract,[48] a reference to the terms of a collective agreement in such a statement is likely to be decisive in practice. Where the employer seeks to assert terms which are less favourable than those contained in the statutory statement, he will have to displace a 'heavy burden',[49] even though otherwise the statement is 'not even conclusive proof of the contract'.[50] For public sector workers, the statement of terms will refer to an extensive body of national and local conditions of service. Only those terms 'apt' for incorporation may be given legal effect in the collective agreement, that is to say, those terms which bear upon the position of individual workers rather than those which concern essentially collective matters.[51] Importantly, once incorporated, incorporated terms will survive the termination of a collective agreement,[52] or the withdrawal of the employer from a wider national agreement.[53]

45 *Ford Motor Co. Ltd. v AEU* [1969] 2QB 303, [1969] 2 All ER 481.

46 TULR(C)A) 1992 s.178(1).

47 Sir Otto Kahn-Freund, in *The System of Industrial Relations in Britain*, ed. Flanders and Clegg, Blackwell, London, 1954, pp.58-59.

48 *System Floors v Daniel* [1982] ICR 54, *Robertson and Jackson v British Gas Corporation* [1983] ICR 351, CA.

49 *System Floors v Daniel* [1982] ICR 54 at 58.

50 *Turrif Construction v Bryant* (1967) 2 KIR 659.

51 *NCB v NUM* [1986] IRLR 439, *Alexander v STC* [1990] ICR 291 *cf Anderson v Pringle of Scotland Ltd.*, [1998] IRLR 65.

52 *Robertson & Jackson v British Gas* [1983] ICR 351.

53 *Burroughs Machines Ltd. v Timmoney* [1977] IRLR 404, CS.

Article 3(2) of the Acquired Rights Directive provides that the transferee shall continue to observe the terms and conditions agreed in any collective agreement until the date of termination or expiry of that agreement, or the entry into force or application of another agreement, or, in the case of an indeterminate agreement, for not less than a year. This provision is based on the terms of Article 31(C)(7) of the French Code de Travail, and corresponds to the common civil law position that where there is an applicable collective agreement it constitutes a minimum from which only upward variations are possible. Regulation 6 of TUPE implements Article 3(2) by providing for the automatic transfer of any collective agreement from the transferor to the transferee, in that such an agreement shall, as regards the affected employees, have effect as if made between the transferee and the trade union. However, this provision operates in a totally different context from civil law countries, as, in the UK, the collective agreement has no legal force. A collective agreement transferred pursuant to regulation 6 may therefore be observed or broken as best suits the transferee's industrial relations situation, at least as regards the collective agreement *per se*. It is, however, a different matter as regards those terms of a collective agreement which have been incorporated into the contracts of employment of affected workers. Such terms are transferred under regulation 5 as terms of the contract and do not depend on regulation 6. Where, however, the contract of employment specifies that rates of pay and other conditions are in accordance with a collective agreement to which the transferor had adhered, the withdrawal of the transferee from that negotiating machinery does not imply that the terms of the contract of employment are thereby affected. In *Whent v Cartledge Ltd.*[54] the transferee had derecognised the union and withdrawn from the negotiating machinery, but the EAT, relying on *Robertson and Jackson v British Gas*,[55] held that the terms of the employees were unaffected and that they were therefore due to be paid the annual increase agreed in the National Joint Industrial Council for local government. The EAT noted that whereas in *Robertson and Jackson* the withdrawal of the employer from the negotiating machinery had brought about its end, with no possibility of further increases being negotiated, British Gas being the one and only employer party to that agreement, in *Whent and Cartledge* the NJC continued on, rates continuing to be negotiated between the local authorities and the relevant unions. The employees were therefore entitled to a declaration of the terms which should have been included within their statutory statement of terms and the employers found to be making unauthorised deductions from wages. Furthermore in *BET Catering Services v Ball*[56] the EAT, held that

54 [1997] IRLR 154.

55 See note 33.

56 EAT/637/96, Lexis transcript.

> 'we see no conceptual or legal difficulty in an employer agreeing (or being treated as if having agreed) a system under which he agrees to pay his own employees wages which are determined, directly or indirectly, by some third party or by a reference to the awards of third parties purporting to be directed to categories other than his own employees.'

The transferee in *BET Catering* was therefore obliged to pay the latest pay increase agreed by the NJIC for local authority workers, even though the employees in question were no longer literally local authority employees and the employer not a party to the agreement.

Whilst a collective agreement may be terminated or ignored, terms incorporated from it may enjoy continued validity, even if the transferee has withdrawn from the collective bargaining process. Any change in terms such as those incorporated in *Whent and Cartledge* would have to be made for reasons other than the transfer, if the transferee is to avoid setting off the 'landmine' referred to in *Meade and Baxendale*.

The Impact of Sex Discrimination Law on Transfer Related Variation of Terms

Compulsory competitive tendering has faced local authorities and hospital trusts with competition from private contractors paying lower wage rates for unskilled work. This has been especially marked where there is a plentiful supply of labour for any available vacancies, and local authorities which are anxious to retain the work in-house have had to consider trimming wage bills. Where the wages of part-timers have been cut, there is a risk that such policies may be held to be discriminatory, because 87% of part-timers are women. Any policy which has a disproportionate adverse impact on women opens the way to potential equal pay claims. In *North Yorkshire County Council v Ratcliffe*,[57] the County Council had organised its education provision into nine areas. When the school meals service in the first of these areas was put out to tender, the work went to a private contractor who was paying lower wages than the current local authority national rates. In order to avoid the progressive loss of the school meals service in all nine areas, the Council direct service organisation cut the wages of the existing workforce and refused to offer the normal grade rate for those jobs. Subsequently, the employees brought an action alleging unequal pay, using workers in other departments who were still earning the nationally negotiated rate for the grade in question.

57 [1995] IRLR 439 HL, [1994] IRLR 342 CA.

The County Council defended its actions under s.1(3) of the Equal Pay Act, as being due to a material factor other than sex, namely the need to compete effectively with private sector caterers. Lord Slynn, giving the judgment of the House of Lords, held, however, that the defence put forward by the County Council was tainted by sex, in that without the dinner ladies being female and working in a rural area where the possibilities for part-time work were limited, the Council would not have been able to introduce the wage cuts.

That the *North Yorkshire* case was not a one-off affair, or confined on its facts to rural areas, was demonstrated by the successful employment tribunal action taken by the dinner ladies working for Bedfordshire County Council in similar circumstances.[58] In that action the County Council had again introduced wage cuts to fend off private sector competition, opening the way for a claim under the Equal Pay Act by the workers in question, reportedly in the order of half a million pounds.

However, in *Lawrence v Regent Office Care Ltd*[58a] the EAT declined to allow such a comparison to be made between workers in a contracted-out situation and their former local authority colleagues, even though the workers were admitted to be in the same 'service' in a 'loose and non-technical sense'.

Such claims can rely on the statistical underpinning provided by research commissioned by the Equal Opportunities Commission,[59] which showed that hours in the predominantly female fields of cleaning and catering fell by 25% and 16% respectively, with consequent falls in earnings. Employment in male sectors fell by only 12% whilst that of female sectors fell by 22%. Conditions for the unskilled generally worsened with the spread of what the authors term a 'contract culture'. Thus, although the major contractors contacted in this study all had equal opportunities policies, these policies were not evidently very effective in practice.

The 1997 draft of the Directive had proposed an Article 7B which would have obliged Member States not to introduce any provisions which were discriminatory on the basis of race, sex, age, handicap, sexual orientation, colour, religion or nationality. The DTI Consultation Paper noted that this provision was not likely to be proceeded with as it was considered to be legally unsound and indeed it finds no place in the 1998 amended Directive. Article 100, the legal base of the Directive, concerned as it is with the single market, could not provide a suitable basis for such a provision, however desirable it might be in principle.

58 *The Times*, February 11th, 1998.

58a [1999] IRLR 148.

59 *The Gender Impact of CCT in Local Government*, Karen Escott & Dexter Whitfield, EOC, 1995.

INSOLVENCIES AND VARYING TERMS UNDER THE AMENDED DIRECTIVE

TUPE applies to all forms of insolvency proceedings, even though the Court of Justice has held[60] that the Directive does not apply to the transfer of an undertaking in the course of insolvency proceedings which are intended to wind up the business and realise the assets, although it does apply to insolvency proceedings where the undertaking continues to trade.[61] The 1994 and 1997 proposals for an amended Directive would have excluded bankruptcy or insolvency proceedings instituted with a view to the liquidation of the assets under competent public supervision from the operation of the Directive. The 1998 amended Directive[62] provides for a new Article 4A which will leave to Member States the option of excluding the operation of Article 3 (protection of terms) or Article 4 (dismissal rights) in cases of insolvency proceedings instituted with a view to the liquidation of the assets under the supervision of a competent public authority, which could include an authorised insolvency practitioner. In all types of insolvency proceedings to which Articles 3 and 4 will apply, (including liquidations where the Member States exercise that option) Member States may provide that the debts of the transferor in relation to contracts of employment arising and payable before the transfer or the opening of the insolvency proceedings, shall not transfer to the transferee, provided that there exists protection under national law equivalent to the provisions of the Insolvency Directive 80/987/EEC. In such situations the Member State may also provide that the transferor, or whoever is exercising the functions of the transferor (such as an administrator), the transferee and the representatives of the employees

> 'may agree alterations, insofar as current law or practice permits, to the employees' terms and conditions designed to safeguard employment opportunities by ensuring the survival of the undertaking, business or part of the undertaking or business.'

Thus the transferor or transferee and the representatives of employees may be able to agree a rescue package under this provision, but only where the undertaking is the subject of insolvency proceedings under public supervision. Such a provision touches on the fundamental conflict between the need to provide and sustain employment opportunities in a market economy and the need to protect employees from bearing the cost of economic restructuring.

60 *Abels v Bedrijfsvereniging voor de Metaalindustrie en de Electronische Industrie* [1985] ECR 469, *D'Urso v Ercole Marelli Electromeccanica Generale* C- 362/89 [1992] IRLR 136.

61 *Jules Dethier Equipment SA v Dassy and Sovram SPRL (in liquidation)* C-319/94 [1998] IRLR 266.

62 Directive 98/50/EC amending Directive 77/187/EEC.

Clearly if jobs are lost that might have been saved by the amendment of terms and conditions, then that is simply an alternative expression of the same conflict of values and interests. It may be thought that the limitation of this provision to bona fide insolvency proceedings and making it subject to other restrictions current in national law, such as, for example, a minimum wage, or the terms of a legally enforceable collective agreement where such obtains, would provide a measure of protection against the abuse of the procedure.

In the UK, where substantive collective agreements are normally only legally enforceable through their incorporation into the contract of employment, the authority of the employee representatives (especially non-union representatives in a context where collective bargaining has not hitherto been accepted) to agree such changes must be open to question. Considerable care would be needed in practice to ensure that the necessary consent had been obtained, even if the consideration was provided by the prospect of continued employment.

The possibility of judicial alteration of terms and conditions in insolvency situation, mooted in the 1994 proposals, was deleted from the 1997 proposals and does not appear in the 1998 text.

Article 4A(3) goes further, however, in permitting Member States to allow such a procedure to operate 'where the transferor is in a situation of economic crisis'. However, this is to be permitted only where such a situation can be declared to exist by a competent public authority open to judicial supervision in accord with national law. Such a national law must exist by the date of the entry into force of the Directive. The Minutes of the Council record that at this stage of the adoption of the Directive only Italy has national legislation of the kind referred to.

Article 4A(4) of the amended Directive requires Member States to take appropriate measures to ensure that insolvency proceedings are not abused in this connection, although in the Consultation Paper the Government had expressed its intention to oppose such a provision to 'ban' fraudulent insolvency proceedings which had been proposed in Article 3(5) of the 1997 draft, on the ground that it would be impracticable to distinguish the genuine from the fraudulent until after the event. The new provision would seem to go some way to meet this objection, even if it remains unclear how such 'misuse' of insolvency proceedings could be detected in advance of the event.

Conclusions

The Directive mandates the continuation of employee terms and conditions a matter of public policy that is not dependent on the will of the parties. Yet it is clear from survey evidence that employers do want the freedom to vary terms and conditions and that employees are not always resolutely opposed to a balanced package. In the 1997 Consultation Document the UK Government rehearsed the arguments for and against a greater freedom for transferees to harmonise working conditions or to make changes in terms and conditions to ensure the survival of the business but came to no definite conclusion, recognising the problematic nature of the issues. Outside of the limited proposal to give Member States the power to allow employers and the representatives of the employees to alter terms and conditions to ensure the survival of the undertaking in insolvency situations, the amended Directive will not allow for any more general alteration of terms and conditions.

Yet as Lord Slynn emphasises in the *Baxendale* and *Wilson* cases the Directive has been said to be one of approximation or partial harmonisation, under which the transferee enjoys the same freedom to vary terms and conditions as was enjoyed by the transferor, although this freedom to vary conditions is subject to the proviso that the reason for the variation of terms shall not be the transfer itself. This uncertainty in part accounts for the fear that employers have of becoming embroiled in legal proceedings as a result of transfers. It falls to the courts therefore to strike the balance between what employers might perceive as 'economic realities' and the interests of employee in continuing to enjoy the benefits of their existing terms and conditions after the transfer of the undertaking in which they are employed. The Court of Appeal in the *Meade and Baxendale* and *Wilson* cases held that an employer who has genuine 'eto' reasons for discharging employees and re-engaging them on changed terms and conditions of the workforce may do so, although the dismissal of an employee for a transfer-related reason was ineffective. That decision left unanswered the central question of the ability of an employer to retain the workforce but to vary their conditions. When the cases were heard in the House of Lords dismissals for a transfer-related reason were held to be effective but unfair. The Lords also addressed the question of the power of the employer to negotiate a variation in terms with employees in the context of a transfer and held that there can be a variation of the terms of the relevant contracts of employment that is not due to the transfer. The employer's reasons may have the character of an 'eto' reason in these circumstances, even though the 'eto' defence is only applicable in terms where there is a dismissal.

Thus the situation is now that

a. A transfer related dismissal is effective but automatically unfair.
b. A dismissal for an 'eto' reason in the context of a transfer is effective but potentially unfair.

c. A change in terms by reason of the transfer, even if agreed and on balance beneficial, is against public policy and could give rise to either rights under ERA 1996 s.13 or, if causing a fundamental breach, an automatically unfair constructive dismissal.
d. An agreed change in terms for a reason other than the transfer is possible in the same degree for the transferee as for the transferor.
e. An imposed change in terms would constitute a breach of contract. No change is lawful by reason of the transfer. If the change were for a non-transfer-related reason and was not such as to give rise to constructive dismissal, the same remedies would be applicable against the transferee as the transferor. If the change gave rise to constructive dismissal, the necessary changes in the size or composition of the workforce may well not be present, even if it could be argued that the change was being made for an economic or organisational reason.

In this context a line has to be drawn between conflicting objectives, which are recognised in the case law, namely the need to protect the continuity of employment of workers affected by the transfer of the undertaking in which they work and to safeguard their existing terms and conditions, and the need of employers to be able to adjust to changing economic circumstances in order to ensure the survival and prosperity of the enterprise. The issue of dismissals will turn upon the identification and proof of the existence of an 'eto' reason, a question partly of evidence but largely of the findings of fact which may be drawn from the evidence. Such a change must entail a change in the workforce, so that if imposed changes in terms result in constructive dismissals, the necessary changes in the size or composition of the workforce may well not be present, even if it could be argued that the change was being made for an economic or organisational reason. Where the transferee desires to take on all or a part of the transferred workforce on terms which are different from those previously enjoyed, even if on balance the terms are no worse than those which obtained previously, the courts must determine whether the reason for the change is the transfer itself, or some other reason. What is significant here is that there would be no requirement that an economic or organisational reason entailed a change in the workforce, so that variations in terms aimed at increasing the efficiency of the enterprise would appear to be possible.

What if the transferee simply desired to harmonise conditions with those of his existing workforce? Arguably, such a change arises only because of the transfer and would fall on the wrong side of the line and employees would be able to insist on their previous terms. A simple desire to cut costs by reducing fringe benefits or even wages to stay inside a limited budget or to increase or ensure profitability may be considered as being something apart from the transfer itself. Indeed an employer desiring to make such a change always will normally have some reason in mind beyond the simple fact of the transfer, outside of the special case where a transferor is preparing an undertaking for sale. Judicial opinion inclines to the view that, given time, the connection between any change in terms and the transfer must weaken and decline but a good operational reason would actually appear to be valid from the outset. Thus, post *Wilson*, what remains of the protection of employee terms, where the change does not give rise to constructive dismissal? The power to suspend the operation of Articles 3 and 4 in the new Directive 97/80 is limited to insolvency situations, so normally they will continue to operate. The development of the case law places a premium on agreeing change, for any attempt to force through change by dismissing and re-employing on inferior terms, would seem to give rise to automatic unfair dismissal, with now a much more significant level of compensation, in so far as there would be nothing about such a proposal which entailed a change in the functions of the workforce.[63] However, a major revision of terms, amounting to a withdrawal of the old contracts and a substitution of new ones, under the *Hogg v Dover College* and *Alcan Extrusions* principles, would appear to suggest that even that protection is not absolute, in that on those premises there then would be a change in the workforce. Whilst those cases may be of doubtful authority, they do suggest a yet further weakening of the protections as regards the preservation of workers existing terms and conditions of employment.

Thus the inevitable tension which exists between the pressures in a market economy for flexibility and change and the legislative protection of set terms and conditions of employment appears to be resolving itself in the direction of allowing at least agreed change for valid operational reasons. The need to reach agreement, even if under pressure, does at least ensure some balance is maintained between management imperatives and worker protections.

[63] As per *Crawford v Swinton Insurance Brokers Ltd.* [1990] IRLR42 EAT.

8. Pensions

Catherine Bailey

Prior to TUPE, an employee had a right to notice (and possibly redundancy payment if he qualified) if his employment was terminated on a transfer of the trade, business or undertaking in which he was engaged but he had no right to insist on transferring across with the business to the transferee. If he were dismissed by the first employer but took employment with the second, his continuity of employment was preserved (but he had no right to a redundancy payment) provided that the new offer of employment was made before the termination of his existing contract and the new contract took effect within four weeks of termination.[1] Where an employee refused an offer of employment with the transferee, he had no right to a redundancy payment unless his refusal was reasonable.

Of fundamental importance is that prior to the Acquired Rights Directive and the Transfer of Undertakings etc Regulations, there was no legal obligation placed upon the transferee of a business to take on the transferor's employees. In the context of Compulsory Competitive Tendering, clearly this would have given external tenderers a free rein to tender on the basis of minimum labour costs.

Prior to the coming into operation of Section 33 TURERA, it might have been open to local authorities to try to minimise potential liability for redundancy payments by securing a transfer pursuant to Section 94 Employment Protection (Consolidation) Act, which applied where there was a transfer of a business whether or not it was in the nature of a commercial venture. In such a case, paragraphs 17 and 18 of Schedule 13 to that Act made provision for the continuity of employment of transferring employees. However, Section 94 was repealed by Section 33 TURERA.

1 Paras 17(2) and 18 Schedule B Employment Protection (Consolidation) Act 1978.

THE ACQUIRED RIGHTS DIRECTIVE 77/187, TRANSFER OF UNDERTAKINGS REGULATIONS AND TURERA 1993

Articles 3.1 and 3.2 of the Directive provide that the transferor's rights and obligations arising from a Contract of Employment or from an employment relationship existing on the date of Transfer within the meaning of Article 1.1 shall be transferred to the Transferee and, further, that the Transferee shall continue to observe the terms and conditions of any collective agreement. However, Article 3.3 provides –

> 'Paragraphs 1 and 2 shall not cover employees' rights to old age, invalidity or survivors' benefits under supplementary company or inter-company pension schemes outside the statutory social security schemes in Member States.'

Additionally, Member States are to

> '...adopt the measures necessary to protect the interests of employees and of persons no longer employed in the transferor's business at the time of the transfer...in respect of rights conferring on them immediate or prospective entitlement to old-age benefits, including survivors' benefits, under supplementary schemes...'

TUPE, as originally drafted, did not follow the Directive. Regulation 7 provided that regulations 5 and 6 should not apply:

'(a) to so much of a contract of employment or collective agreement as relates to an occupational pension scheme within the meaning of the Social Security Pensions Act 1975...; or

(b) to any rights, powers, duties or liabilities under or in connection with any such contract or subsisting by virtue of any such agreement and relating to such a scheme or otherwise arising in connection with that person's employment and relating to such a scheme.'

In other words, while the Acquired Rights Directive excluded only certain parts of pension schemes from the transfer principle, TUPE excluded occupational pension schemes in the totality.

One possible justification for the exclusion may lie in the fact that, in the main, members' rights to benefits under a pension scheme lie against the trustees of the scheme rather than the employer. A business transfer, viewed from the perspective of the scheme, will create a situation where rights to preserved benefits, refunds of contributions etc may arise, so that it would be no easy matter to provide the full protection of pension rights that the Regulations are intended to provide for other terms of employment.

In the face of infraction proceedings[2] brought by the EC Commission against the United Kingdom pursuant to Article 169 of the EC Treaty, amendments to the Regulations were made by Section 33 TURERA. Among the key changes which affected transfers occurring on or after 30th August 1993 was the restriction on the exclusion of occupational pension schemes in their totality from the transfer principle - only those parts of schemes relating to old age, invalidity or survivors' benefits were to be incapable of transfer under TUPE.

The significance of the amendment is that occupational pension schemes often contain other benefits, such as provisions relating to redundancy.

The Concept of Pensions as Deferred Pay

As noted above, not all pension arrangements are excluded from the transfer provisions of ARD and TUPE. The transfer principle will not apply (under ARD) to old age, invalidity or survivors' benefits under 'supplementary company or inter-company pension schemes outside the statutory social security schemes in Member States', while TUPE now also excludes old age, invalidity and survivors' benefits under 'an occupation pension scheme within the meaning of the Social Security Pensions Act 1975...'. The application of the Directive and Regulations therefore depends upon the status of the scheme in question.

In *Defrenne v Belgian State*[3] the European Court of Justice considered the applicability of Article 119 of the Treaty of Rome to a retirement pension paid under a statutory social security scheme operated by Sabena, the Belgian Airline Company and took the view that although pay within the meaning of Article 119 could in principle include social security benefits, it did not include social security schemes or benefits, or retirement pensions which do not involve an element of agreement between the undertaking and the workforce and which are compulsorily applicable to general categories of workers. The scheme under consideration was later described in the Advocate-General's Opinion in the *Beune*[4] case as 'a classic, general government-organised pension'.

The pension scheme under consideration in *Bilka-Kaufhaus G mb H v Weber von Hartz*,[5] although adopted in accordance with the relevant German

2 *Commission of the European Communities v UK* Case C - 382/92 1994 IRLR 392, Case C - 383/92 1994 IRLR 412.

3 *Defrenne v Sabena* Case 80/70 [1971] ECR 445.

4 *Bestuur van Het Algemeen Burgerlijk Pensioenfonds v Beune* - Case C - 7/93 [1995] IRLR 103.

5 *Bilka-Kaufhaus G mb H v Weber von Hartz* 1987 ECR 100 - Case 170/84 [1986] IRLR 317.

legislation, was based on agreement between the company and its workforce and effectively supplemented the general social benefits payable under national legislation with benefits financed entirely by the company. The scheme was contractual rather than statutory in nature and this was confirmed by the fact that the scheme was regarded as an integral part of each contract of employment. The European Court therefore concluded that this was a private occupational scheme which fell within the scope of Article 119.

This line of reasoning was followed by the European Court in *Barber v GRE.*[6] In this case, the contracted-out private occupational schemes were the result of agreement between the company and the workforce or the result of a unilateral decision taken by the company, and were wholly financed by the company or jointly by the company and workforce. The schemes were only applicable to employees employed by certain undertakings and clearly derived from the employment relationship. Although the schemes conformed to national legislation, they had their own rules. Finally, the fact that the schemes were in part substitution of the statutory scheme did not preclude the application of Article 119 because the schemes gave greater benefits than the state scheme and were therefore similar to the supplementary scheme under consideration in the *Bilka* case.

A further case involving the applicability of Article 119 was that of *Griffin v London Pension Fund Authority.*[7] The facts were as follows:

Mrs. Griffin was employed as a nurse by Middlesex County Council from 1964 to 1965 and thereafter by the Greater London Council from 1965 to 1971 when she retired at the age of 44 due to ill health. She was a member of the Local Government Superannuation Scheme, a compulsory scheme established by the Local Government Superannuation Act 1937 and subject to detailed regulations made by Statutory Instrument. The scheme was contracted out and there was a fund specific to the GLC. When her pension was reduced at the age of 60, in accordance with the Regulations, the Appellant claimed that the reduction was a breach of Article 119 of the EC Treaty and the EEC Equal Pay Directive because, she argued, her local government pension would not have been reduced until she reached the age of 65 had she been a man.

The EAT, following the earlier decision of the Industrial Tribunal and taking into account the principles laid down in *Defrenne* and *Barber,* concluded that the scheme was a statutory one, governed by exhaustive rules which left no discretion for the employer, applied universally to local government staff and was not the result of an agreement between the employer and the

6 *Barber v GRE* - Case C - 262/88 [1990] IRLR 240.

7 *Griffin v London Pension Fund Authority* [1993] IRLR 248.

workforce or as a result of a unilateral decision taken by the employer. In effect, this was a statutory rather than a contractual scheme under which benefits could not be regarded as pay.

Another public sector scheme was under consideration in *Bestuur van Het Algemeen Burgerlijk Pensioenfonds v Beune,*[8] where a statutory scheme operated for the benefit of the Dutch Civil Service. In this case, the ECJ held *(inter alia)*

> 'that the only possible decisive criterion is whether the pension is paid to the worker by reason of the employment relationship between him and his former employer.'

In this instance, since the pension was paid only to a particular category of workers (albeit in this instance a very large category since the pension extended beyond the Civil Service to other categories of workers financed through public funds), related to the period of service and calculated by reference to the last salary, the Court held that the scheme broadly resembled an occupational scheme for private sector employees. It followed that this was not treated as a statutory scheme, the benefits were therefore 'pay' as in *Bilka* and *Barber*, and Article 119 therefore applied.

On the basis of previous decisions, the Court identified a list of five factors used to determine the status of the scheme. These (briefly) are as follows:

1. The degree to which the scheme is governed by statute. While statutory social security benefits are outside the scope of Article 119 the Article may apply to occupational schemes even though such scheme operates within a statutory framework.
2. An element of agreement or consensus between the employer and the workforce, or a unilateral decision by the employer, would favour a finding of an occupational rather than a statutory scheme. For example, if the scheme is regarded as being an integral part of the overall employment package, this would tend to demonstrate its consensual nature.
3. If the scheme is financed wholly by the employer, or jointly by the employer and the workforce, this tends to support the view that it is an occupational scheme. Conversely, if the fund is in receipt of public monies, the Courts will tend to view the scheme as part of the Member States social policy.
4. Occupational schemes relate to particular categories of workers, while schemes applicable to general categories of the workforce are not included within the ambit of Article 119. However, it was noted that while previous decisions referred to 'general category of workers' the concept was not defined.

8 *Bestuur Van Het Algemeen Burgerlijk Pensioenfonds v Beune* - Case C - 7/93 [1995] IRLR 103.

5. Article 119 may apply to schemes which were set up to supplement general social benefits paid under the State scheme.

Against the backdrop of the growing body of jurisprudence arising to determine which pension schemes would be classified as 'statutory' and therefore not excluded from ARD and TUPE, and which could be held to be 'occupational' and therefore excluded so far as they related to old age, invalidity or survivors' benefits, the UK Industrial Tribunals and the EAT dealt with the transfer of undertakings cases of *Walden Engineering v Warrener* and *Perry v Intec*.

In *Walden Engineering Co Ltd v Warrener*[9] the Hull Industrial Tribunal had in 1992 held that an employee who had been informed that after a business transfer he was no longer eligible for membership of his occupational pension scheme but would be contracted back into the State Earnings Related Pension Scheme ('SERPS') was entitled to claim from the transferee pension benefits equivalent to those provided to him prior to transfer. The decision was based on the proposition that since the pension scheme was contracted out of SERPS it was not an 'occupation pension scheme' for the purposes of regulation 7. The EAT overturned the tribunal's decision in the following year by holding that a contracted-out pension scheme was an occupational pension scheme within the meaning of regulation 7 and was therefore excluded from the general ambit of the regulation. The applicant lodged an appeal to the Court of Appeal, but this was subsequently withdrawn.

Between the hearing of *Walden Engineering* by the Industrial Tribunal and the EAT, the Bristol Industrial Tribunal heard *Perry v Intec Colleges*[10] where it was considered that since TUPE had failed to translate the aims of the Directive into UK law, additional wording should be implied under which the applicant was entitled to pension provision at least as beneficial as that which he enjoyed prior to transfer. The Tribunal went further to suggest that the employer could compensate the applicant in one of two ways - either by way of a lump sum in respect of loss of enhancement of accrued pension rights or by making contributions to a personal pension scheme on his behalf. This decision was criticised by the EAT in *Warrener* on the ground that the Directive was aimed at Member States and was not intended to impose any liability directly on the transferor or transferee, and that additional wording could not, in effect, be added to regulation 7 which was inconsistent with its provisions.

So far as pension provision on the transfer of staff under the CCT regime is concerned, two cases both decided in 1996 have been of assistance. Firstly, in the High Court, *Adams & Others v Lancashire County Council and BET Catering*

9 *Walden Engineering Co Ltd v Warrener* [1993] IRLR 420 EAT.

10 *Perry v Intec Colleges Ltd* [1993] IRLR 56.

Services[11] considered the transfer of employment of a number of part-time school catering staff from Lancashire County Council, under which they had been entitled to join the local government pension scheme, to an outside contractor. It was accepted that this was a TUPE transfer, but the external contractor did not offer membership of its pension scheme to transferring employees earning less than £15,000 per year - which excluded the Plaintiffs. It was accepted on behalf of the Plaintiffs (following *Beune*) that this was not a statutory scheme - in other words, it was an occupational scheme which was a 'supplementary company or inter-company scheme outside the statutory social security scheme' within the meaning of Article 3. The case turned on whether TUPE correctly implemented Article 3 of the Directive and whether the transferred staff were entitled to comparable pensions from the transferee. This was a test case supported by GMB and UNISON, its importance being one of general application to all CCT transfers.

The Plaintiffs and the Unions were to be disappointed. The Court held that in excluding the transfer of the Plaintiffs' pension rights, regulation 7 of TUPE correctly implemented Article 3(3)(limb A) of the Directive and, further, that the second limb of Article 3(3) which was directed at Member States, was limited to protecting only accrued pension rights.

The *Adams* case was heard in the High Court in January 1996. In November 1996, an Advisory Opinion was handed down from the EFTA Court, which dealt with exactly the same point (and others). The Court gives Advisory Opinions to EFTA States on matters of EC law which, while they have no legal standing within the European Union, are of considerable interest. The facts of *Eidesund v Stavanger Catering A/S*[12] are as follows:

Scandinavian Service Partner ('SSP') provided catering and cleaning services to a number of companies including the operator of a North Sea oil platform. In all, nineteen SSP staff were employed on the platform for whom SSP paid premiums into an insurance scheme on the basis of a local collective agreement.

The service was tendered and won by Stavanger Catering, who then offered work on the platform to fourteen out of the nineteen employees, but did not continue with the pension insurance premium payments. One of the transferred employees requested the Court for an Advisory Opinion as to whether, firstly, there had been a transfer within the meaning of the Directive, and secondly, if there had, whether the transferee was under a legal obligation to pay the premium for a supplementary pension scheme which was outside the mandatory state social security system.

The Court noted that there had been no previous decisions of the ECJ on the scope of the pensions exception within Article 3. Taking into consideration

11 *Adams & Others v Lancashire County Council and BET Catering Services Ltd* [1996] IRLR 154.

12 *Eidesund v Stavanger Catering A/S* Case E - 2/95 [1996] IRLR 684.

the aim of the Directive to 'ensure, as far as possible, that the employment relationship continued unchanged with the transferee' and that recognised methods of interpretation were to be used (including looking back to the preparatory work relating to the Directive), the Court concluded that all rights and obligations relating to old age, invalidity and survivors' benefits had been excluded from the general principle of transfer.

Both the High Court in the *Adams* case and the EFTA Court in the *Eidesund* case looked to the Directive's preparatory material. In *Adams*, the High Court could draw no conclusion from this work other than that the community institutions found the matter 'controversial and difficult', while the EFTA Court seems to have attached some importance to the fact that the Commission documents set out foreseen complications which might arise if the transferee were to be legally obliged to assume the transferor's obligations under supplementary pension schemes.

The *Adams*[13] case was appealed to the Court of Appeal in May 1997. Lord Justice Morritt identified the questions to be decided as follows:

1. Whether each of the transferring employees were entitled, pursuant to TUPE, to a pension from the transferee equivalent to the pension they would have enjoyed with the transferor, had the transfer not taken place. If the answer to the above question was in the negative, then it fell to the Court to decide four further matters:
2. Whether ARD required each employee to be provided with such a pension, and, if so -
3. Whether the obligations imposed by ARD were of direct vertical effect, and, if so -
4. Whether action could be taken against the Council as an emanation of the State, and, if so -
5. What remedy would be available to the Plaintiffs.

It was not disputed that the Court should adopt a purposive construction to the Directive, although such construction was to be restricted to Article 3(3) rather than to the Directive as a whole.

Significantly, the Court held that regulation 7 of TUPE correctly implemented Article 3(3) and that the Plaintiffs were therefore not entitled to comparable pension rights pursuant to the Regulations. Article 3(3) was similarly of no avail to the Plaintiffs because the first limb, excluding pension rights from the principle of automatic transfer, was unlimited. The second limb required only that Member States should protect accrued pension rights, the argument being that since there is no general obligation on the part of an

13 *Adams and Others v Lancashire County Council and BET Catering Services Ltd* [1997] IRLR 436.

employer to set up a pension scheme for its workforce, to impose this on a transfer would have placed upon a transferee a legal obligation which had never rested with the transferor. Furthermore, the Court noted that to have reached the opposite conclusion would have meant that different groups of employees with the same employer, the transferee, would have enjoyed differing benefits, which would have resulted in discrimination. In point of fact, the application of TUPE to the business of any transferee who successfully tenders for a number of local authority contracts must, of necessity, militate against the harmonisation of its workforce, at least in the short term.

The conclusion which the Court reached to question 2 above meant, of course, that questions 3, 4 and 5 did not require further consideration and it is worth mentioning that leave to appeal to the House of Lords was refused.

Entirely consistent with these decisions is Article 3 of the Commission's Directive on Supplementary Pensions,[13a] which defines a supplementary pension scheme and supplementary pension as follows:

> '"Supplementary pension scheme" means any occupational pension scheme established in conformity with national legislation and practice such as a group insurance contract or a pay-as-you-go scheme agreed by one or more branches or sectors, funded scheme or pension promise backed by book reserves, or any collective or other comparable arrangement intended to provide a supplementary pension for employed or self-employed persons.
>
> '"Supplementary pension" means retirement pensions and, where provided for by the rules of a supplementary pension scheme...invalidity and survivors' benefit, intended to supplement or replace those provided in respect of the same contingencies by statutory social security schemes.'

This puts beyond doubt that the old age, invalidity or survivor's benefits under statutory schemes, including the Local Government Pension Schemes, are excluded as TUPE transfers.

The Status of the Local Government Pension Scheme

All local government employees have automatic right to membership of the Local Government Pension Scheme, which is a 'statutory scheme' set up under Regulations made pursuant to the Superannuation Act 1972. Those not

[13a] Council Directive 98/49/EC of 29 June 1998.

wishing to join the scheme have the right to opt out. Employees contribute a percentage of their pensionable remuneration (5% currently employed manual workers and 6% non-manual workers but as from 1st April 1998 a standardised member contribution of 6% was introduced for all new members) with employers also making contributions. It is a 'contracted out scheme' for the purposes of social security legislation.

The scheme (briefly) provides the following benefits:

1. An annual pension calculated as 1/80th of the best year's pay in the last three years for each year of service, up to a maximum of 40. The pension is indexed linked.
2. A tax free lump sum payment equivalent to 3 years' pension benefit.
3. Pension provision for spouse (which no longer ceases on re-marriage) and children.
4. Life assurance from date of entry in a sum equivalent to at least 2 years' annual salary.
5. Early payment of enhanced benefit in respect of ill-health retirement, and additional benefits (depending on age and service) in respect of job loss.
6. Lump sum death grant

Additionally, there are discretions available to each participating authority - such as the discretion for individual local authorities to provide actuarially reduced pension from age *50* (but no actuarial reduction is applied if age plus service exceeds *85* - known as the 'Rule of 85').

Accepting the fact that old age, invalidity or survivors' benefits will not transfer, what then of other pension terms which provide for redundancy payments and pension enhancement on the reaching of a certain age? The EAT considered these in *Frankling v BPS Public Sector Limited.*[13b] This case involved the transfer of staff from the payroll department of an NHS Trust hospital to the private sector and their subsequent redundancy when the business was moved from Eastbourne to Glasgow.

Under Whitley Council terms, provision was made for the early payment of superannuation and compensation benefits upon redundancy, but the transferee argued that these parts of the pension scheme in fact related to old age, and were therefore excluded from transfer. The EAT agreed. Benefits related to old age did not mean benefits which were to be enjoyed at the age of 65, or indeed any specified age, but rather meant benefits to which an employee becomes entitled upon retirement, at whatever age that takes place.

[13b] *Frankling v BPS Public Sector Limited* [1999] IRLR 212 GAT.

An employee leaving the service of one authority in order to take up employment in another will have his 'reckonable service' transferred to the new employer. However, an employee who transfers to a non-local government or similar employer will have a valuation made of the 'cash equivalent' of his accrued pension rights which will then be used to purchase 'pension credits' in the new scheme. Alternatively, he may opt to retain his preserved benefits in lieu of transfer. In order to decide whether or not to transfer, it is essential for the employee to obtain full details of both schemes so that valid comparisons can be made. While, on the face of it, the scheme might have appeared a statutory one for the purposes of Article 119, as it did to the Court in the *Griffin* case and therefore outside any of the considerations of ARD and TUPE, the criteria set out in *Beune* paved the way for the acceptance by both parties in the *Adams* case that the scheme had in reality rather more in common with a private sector occupational scheme than a statutory one.

Of course, the transfer may work in reverse. Increasingly, other non-profit making bodies, notably charities, have been seeking to transfer their staff into the local government scheme. Provided certain criteria are met, including financial safeguards, the scheme is flexible enough to admit certain newcomers - for example, newly-formed housing companies having charitable status, who have taken over Council housing stock and therefore Council staff under TUPE. It is likely, in the not too distant future, that the scheme will be further extended to admit staff in joint venture and other PFI (Private Finance Initiative) Schemes.

The Second Limb of Article 3(3)

Accepting that the European Parliament did not intend a transfer of old age, invalidity or survivors' benefits under occupational pension schemes, the question then arises as to whether the UK Government has adopted sufficient measures to protect these rights for current and former employees and, if not, what remedies might be open to an aggrieved employee.

The Government's position is that the measures referred to in the second limb of Article 3(3) are adequately contained in Part IV of the Pension Schemes Act 1993 (Protection for Leavers).

The Industrial Tribunal in the *Perry* case thought that the Directive contemplated wider protection than that currently afforded by the Social Security Acts in conferring entitlement to a deferred pension. In *Adams*, the High Court considered that:

> 'A worker's right to continue to earn deferred pay is no lesser right under his employment contract than his right not to be deprived of deferred pay which he has already earned by his past service (but not yet received)'

and referred to the lack of the right to continue to earn deferred pay as 'a serious gap', but a gap which the European legislature must have intended.

On 11th March 1997, Brussels advised that a document entitled 'Memorandum on Acquired Rights of Workers in Cases of Transfers of Undertakings' had recently been adopted which set out to explain the Acquired Rights of workers. Annex 1 seeks to provide this information by way of twenty generalised questions, with short answers. Question and answer 11 read as follows:

> '11. Does the protection given by the Directive apply to benefits under non-statutory social security schemes?
>
> - No. The transfer of rights and obligations arising from an employment contract or employment relationship does not cover employees' rights to old age, invalidity or survivors' benefits under supplemental company or inter-company pension schemes outside the statutory social security schemes in Member States. However, Member States must adopt the measures necessary to protect the rights acquired *or being acquired* by employees and persons no longer employed in the business at the time of transfer'.

Clearly, the answer covers current and former employees, as does the second limb of Article 3(3), but had the intention been to demonstrate that Article 3(3) protected solely accrued rights, there would have been no need for the words 'or being acquired'. This would tend to suggest that if *Adams* had reached the ECJ or had there been a request for a preliminary ruling from the European Court, the Government's view that it had done all that was required by the second limb of Article 3(3) might well have been called into question.

The interpretation of this second limb has not been consistent across the Member States. The UK position has not been adopted in Denmark, Spain or Luxembourg, for instance, where future pension rights, occurring after transfer, are protected.

Remedies Available to Employees who transfer into Non-Pensionable Employment

In the past, the concern for local authority employers has been that a failure to secure comparable pension rights for their former employees, when these could and perhaps should have been guaranteed, may have rendered them liable for breach of contract or constructive dismissal. Since the *Adams* and *Eidesund* cases this threat must surely have receded. Similarly, the likelihood of any injunction being granted seems remote. Even prior to the 1996 cases, this had not proved an effective remedy. In *Newns v British Airways plc*[14] an employee sought an injunction restraining the company from making a business transfer until proper employees/union consultation had taken place. However, the Court rejected the argument that such a transfer would have been in breach of the contract of employment because there was nothing in TUPE or at Common Law which permitted an employee to block a transfer of the employment contract. This reasoning was followed in *Betts v Brintel Helicopters Ltd and KLM ERA Helicopters.*[15]

Proceedings pursuant to Order 14A of the Rules of the Supreme Court were brought in the case of *Kenny v South Manchester College*[16] to determine whether or not there was a transfer and, again, in *Betts* a declaration was sought by seven employees of Brintel that their employment transferred to KLM. It is not inconceivable that at some time in the future a declaration might be sought as to the status of a scheme or as to the transfer of parts of schemes which do not relate to old age, invalidity or survivors' benefits.

Judicial Review was attempted, but failed, in *NUPE v Lord Advocate,*[17] where the Regulations were challenged on the ground that they did not conform to the Directive due to the exclusion of non-commercial undertakings.

Another possibility is the reliance upon the direct effect of directives. Directives, as the name would suggest, take the form of directions to Member States which, by Article 189 of the Treaty of Rome, are binding as to the result to be achieved but leave Member States a degree of discretion as to the method of implementation. Where a Member State does not give effect to a directive, either because it fails to introduce implementing legislation at all, or because it does so imperfectly, the question then arises as to how far an aggrieved individual can rely on such a directive. Directives are capable of having vertical direct effect in a claim by an individual against an emanation of the State. The concept of 'emanation of the State' is a broad one and there is no doubt that a local authority would fall within it - *Fratelli Constanzo SpA v Comune di Milano.*[18] The need for certain criteria to be met before a community provision can be directly effective was spelled out by Mr. Advocate-General Trabucci in *Defrenne v Sabena (no. 2)*[19] :-

14 *Newns v British Airways plc* [1992] IRLR 575.

15 *Betts v Brintel Helicopters Ltd and KLM ERA Helicopters (UK) Ltd* 1996 IRLR 45.

16 *Kenny v South Manchester College* [1993] IRLR 266.

17 *NUPE v Lord Advocate, The Times,* May 5th 1993.

18 *Frateli Constanzo SpA v Comune di Milano* Case 103/88 [1989] ECR 1839.

19 *Defrenne v Sabena (No. 2)* Case 43/75 [1976] ICR 547.

> 'Under the criterion established by the case law of the European Court a community provision produces direct effects so as to confer on individuals the right to enforce it in the Courts, provided that it is clear and sufficiently precise in its content, does not contain any reservation and is complete in itself in the sense that its application by national courts does not require the adoption of any subsequent measures of implementation either by the States or the Community.'

The question of direct effect was considered at some length by the High Court in the *Adams* case, although it is submitted that since Article 3(3) requires Member State action, it is unlikely to be of direct effect. Had it been necessary for the Court to consider the effect of the second limb of Article 3(3), which requires the UK Government to take measures to protect the pension rights of the Plaintiffs, Mr. Justice Walker thought that it would have been right to make a reference to the ECJ for a preliminary ruling under Article 177 of the Treaty of Rome.

Whether or not there is to be any further attempt to directly enforce the second limb of Article 3(3) so as to eliminate the 'serious gap', and protect transferring employees' rights to continue to earn deferred pay under a comparable scheme, remains to be seen. What is clear is that the Plaintiffs may face potential problems of limitation if the UK were, at some time in the future, held not to have correctly implemented the second limb of Article 3(3) thereby resulting in the Plaintiffs' failure to make contributions after transfer which they would otherwise have made. Following *Emmott v Minister for Social Welfare and Attorney-General*[20] it was reasonably clear that a limitation period would not start to run until the State had correctly implemented the relevant Directive. Perfect implementation must, of necessity, be dealt with on a case by case basis. The scope of the *Emmott* principle was later restricted in *Steenhost-Neerings v Bestuur Van De Bedrifsvereniging Voor Detail-handel, Ambachten en Huisvrouwen*[21] in which the ECJ decided that the *Emmott* principle did not preclude reliance by the State on national rules which prevented recovery of social security benefits for a period more than one year prior to the date of the claim. In other words, the Court found a distinction between time limits on bringing a complaint which constituted a bar to the proceedings and time limits in respect of which arrears of benefit were payable.

20 *Emmott v Minister for Social Welfare and Attorney-General* [1991] IRLR 387 ECJ.

21 *Steenhorst-Neerings v Bestuur Van De Bedrij fsvereniging Voor Detail-handel, Ambachten en Huisvrouwen* Case C-338/91 [1994] IRLR 245.

A similar more recent case is that *of Johnson v Chief Adjudication Officer (No. 2)*[22] where the ECJ held that the right to a benefit, in this case a severe disablement allowance, which discriminated against women should be relied on as of December 1984 under the Directive, but that the Plaintiff was entitled to benefit only as from August 1986. Although the retroactive effect was limited, the exercise of the right was not rendered virtually impossible.

In *Rankin v British Coal Corporation*[23] the Scottish EAT considered the direct effective of Article 119 of the EC Treaty and the time limit applicable to a claim for redundancy payments in reliance upon that Article. Reversing the decision of the Industrial Tribunal, the EAT considered the claim to be 'freestanding' i.e. not arising from the Employment Protection (Consolidation) Act 1978 and the statutory time limit therefore was found to be inapplicable. The relevant time limit was a period of time 'from the date on which it was clear to any person affected that a claim could properly be made'.

More recently in *Biggs v Somerset County Council*[24] the EAT again considered the inter-relationship between a claim brought under domestic legislation and the time limits applicable thereto, and a claim brought under Article 119. In this case, the applicant presented a complaint of unfair dismissal, based on Article 119, some 18 years after the dismissal had taken place. The applicant sought to rely partly on the *ratio decidendi* of the *Emmott* case and pleaded that time limits could not run against her until such time as the relevant Community law had been properly transposed into UK law. However, *Emmott* could not apply, since directly effective Treaty Articles, unlike ARD, do not call for implementation. The EAT set out five 'General Propositions of Community Law', in which part of the ruling of the Court of Justice in *Fisscher v Voorhuis Hengelo B.V.*[25] were quoted as follows:

> '...in the absence of community rules on the matter, the national rules relating to time limits for bringing actions are also applicable to actions based on community law, provided that they are no less favourable for such actions than for similar actions of a domestic nature and that they do not render the exercise of rights conferred by community law impossible in practice...'

22 *Johnson v Chief Adjudication Officer (No.2)* [1995] IRLR 157.

23 *Rankin v British Coal Corporation* [1993] IRLR 69 EAT.

24 *Biggs v Somerset County Council* [1995] ICR 811.

25 *Fisscher v Voorhuis Hengelo B.V.* Case C-129/93 [1995] ICR 635.

The EAT went on to observe that:

> 'A similar approach has been adopted by the Court of Justice in relation to rights conferred by the direct effect of Directives.'

In dismissing the appeal, the Appeal Tribunal concluded that the statutory time limits applied to unfair dismissal claims, even where directly enforceable community rights are invoked and that because the time limits such as those laid down in the 1978 Act are not incompatible with Community law, they are not to be disregarded. The Court of Appeal similarly considered that there was no basis for disapplying the time limit when as a matter of law the claim was capable of being enforced at the moment of dismissal.

In *Magorrian and Cunningham v Eastern Health and Social Services Board and Department of Health and Social Services*[26] the European Court considered the effect of the distinction between cases involving 'access' claims and those involving 'benefit' claims. The applicants, two psychiatric nurses, had transferred from full-time to part-time employment when they had had children, as a result of which they remained within the Health and Personal Social Services Occupational Pension Scheme but without the additional benefits to which they would have been entitled had they remained working full-time (in this instance the right to retire with a full pension at age 55 instead of 60 and to count service from the age of 50 as double for the purpose of calculating benefits). The applicants successfully brought proceedings under the Equal Pay Act (Northern Ireland), a Belfast tribunal finding indirect discrimination on grounds of sex contrary to Article 119 and the Equal Pay Directive, but the question of the date from which their service should count as double for the purpose of calculating benefit rights was referred to the European Court. The applicants argued that this was an 'access' claim and that compensation was payable as from the date of the second *Defrenne* decision (8th April 1976). The respondents argued firstly that this was in effect a 'benefit' claim and that only service since the date of the *Barber* decision (17th May 1990) should be affected, and secondly that the national time limit applied - in this instance two years prior to the date of commencement of proceedings. The European Court found against the respondents on both counts - firstly, it held that the case concerned the right to belong to a scheme rather than the amount of pension to be paid because although the applicants remained entitled to a pension they were not fully admitted to the scheme during periods of part-time working, and secondly, that the respondents could not rely upon domestic law to deprive the applicants of rights to which they were entitled under Community law. To this extent, the Court distinguished between the

[26] *Magorrian and Cunningham v. Eastern Health and Social Services Board and Department of Health and Social Services* Case C - 246/96 [1998] IRLR 86.

two year limitation period imposed by the Occupational Pensions Regulations which would 'strike at the very essence of the rights conferred by the Community legal order' and the rules considered in the *Steenhorst-Neerings* and *Johnson (No. 2)* cases which simply limited the period to be taken into account prior to commencement of proceedings for the purposes of calculating the benefits which could be claimed.

Preston and Others v Wolverhampton Healthcare NHS Trust and Others and *Fletcher and Others v Midland Bank plc*[27] were test cases arising from claims by some 60,000 workers in the public and private sectors (mostly women) who had been denied access to a variety of occupational pension schemes as a result of part-time working. Again, the question of the time limit for commencing proceedings and the period for which compensation could be claimed fell to be considered. Prior to the European Court's decision in the *Magorrian* case, the Court of Appeal had unequivocally ruled that the six month time limit for commencing proceedings set down in s2(4) Equal Pay Act 1970 applied, as did the two year limit for which damages could be claimed laid down in s.2(5). However, as a result of the *Magorrian* decision, the House of Lords was not so certain that these periods of limitation were compatible with the principle of Community law that national procedural rules should not render it 'excessively difficult or impossible in practice' for a claimant to exercise rights arising out of Article 119. The House of Lords therefore referred these procedural rules (among other matters) to the European Court of Justice in the following terms:

> 'I. Is:
> a) a national procedure rule which requires that a claim for membership of an occupational pension scheme (from which the right to pension benefit flows) which is brought in the industrial tribunal be brought within six months of the end of the employment to which the claim relates,
> b) a national procedural rule which provides that a claimant's pensionable service is to be calculated only by reference to service after a date falling no earlier than two years prior to the date of her claim (irrespective of whether the date on which pension benefits become payable is before or after the date of the claim) compatible with the principle of EC law that national procedure rules for breach of Community law must not make it excessively difficult or impossible in practice for the claimant to exercise her rights under Article 119?'

27 *Preston and Others v Wolverhampton Healthcare NHS Trust and Others*) [1998] IRLR 197, *Fletcher and Others v Midland Bank plc*).

At the time of writing, the outcome is awaited, but if access to Community rights is rendered impossible there remains the possibility of an action for breach of contract (for which the usual limitation period will apply) or complaint as to an unauthorised deduction from wages pursuant to s.23 Employment Rights Act 1996. Such complaint should be presented before the end of the three month period commencing with the date of the deduction, but subsection (4) provides that where the tribunal is satisfied that it was not reasonably practicable for the complaint to be made prior to the end of the three month period, the limitation period can be extended to whatever the tribunal considers reasonable in the circumstances.

A further possibility arises from the *Francovich v Italian Republic*[28] principle which provides a remedy against the State where an individual is deprived of a right or remedy against another individual as a result of a Member State's failure to implement a Directive. In order for such an action to succeed, the Court identified three prerequisites:

1. The Directive must be calculated to confer rights on individuals;

2. The subject matter of those rights must be identifiable by reference to the provisions of the Directive, and

3. A causal link must exist between the infringement of the obligation and the damage suffered by the Plaintiff.

Article 8 of ARD provides as follows:

> '8(1) Member States shall bring into force the laws, regulations and administrative provisions needed to comply with this Directive within two years of its notification and shall forthwith inform the Commission thereof.'

The two year period expired in 1979, although clearly the deadline was not met in every respect because successful infraction proceedings were brought in 1992.

In the *Adams* case *Francovich* was briefly considered, as was the possibility of bringing such an action against a local authority as an emanation of the State in situations where a claim based on direct vertical effect was unsuccessful. However, the point did not require decision. For transferring employees, the importance of *Francovich* lies in the fact that it may provide a remedy against the State when there may be no remedy available against the transferee or

[28] *Francovich v Italian Republic* Case C-6/90 [1992] IRLR 94 ECJ.

transferor. The case of *Duke v GEC*[29] highlights this. This case was decided in 1988, i.e. prior to the *Francovich* decision. The Appellant could show that her enforced retirement before the age of 65 was discriminatory and contrary to the Equal Treatment Directive. But, the 1986 *Marshall v Southampton and South West Hampshire Area Health Authority*[30] had decided that the Directive did not possess direct effect as between individuals (GEC not being an emanation of the State). As a result, the Appellant was unable to claim damages against the Respondent for breach of the Directive. However, had this case been heard after 1991, the Appellant might have had a cause of action against the UK Government for its failure to properly implement the Directive.

The theory behind *Francovich* is that the State should not be able to take advantage of its own misfeasance or non-feasance. In the context of the second limb of Article 3(3), liability would rest with the Government, which alone is in a position to introduce relevant legislation. While local authorities are clearly emanations of the State for the purposes of directives, they are not in a position to implement Article 3(3) without secondary legislation.

The ECJ's radical *Francovich* ruling in 1991 may well have been tantamount to the opening of Pandora's Box. There is a body of opinion, supported by Advocate-General Leger, that the doctrine in *Francovich* should not be limited to the incorrect implementation of directives, but should extend to all breaches of directly effective community law. Certainly, in a 1995 case backed by the Equal Opportunities Commission for Northern Ireland, the Treasury was obliged to settle a *Francovich* claim for £34,000 which arose due to the Government's failure to implement the EC Equal Treatment Directive in Northern Ireland until 1989. Currently, it is understood that there are many Union-backed *Francovich* claims, principally relating to the non-implementation of ARD, currently awaiting determination.

The Practical Application of Pension Provision to Staff Transfers

If the case law is now reasonably clear, in practical terms dealing with staff pensions in the context of CCT, the Local Government Act 1988 and the statutory definition of anti-competitive behaviour remains far from straightforward.

The Local Government Act 1988 introduced the requirement to avoid anti-competitive behaviour and gave the Secretary of State powers to prevent authorities behaving in a manner 'having the effect or intended or likely to have the effect of restricting, distorting or preventing competition' (Local Government Act S.7(7)). Section 17(1) of the Act provides:

29 *Duke v GEC Reliance* [1988] AC 618.

30 *Marshall v Southampton and South West Hampshire Area Health Authority* [1986] QB401.

> 'It is the duty of every public authority to which this Section applies, in exercising, in relation to its public supply or works contracts, any proposed or any subsisting such contract, as the case may be, any function regulated by this Section to exercise that function without reference to matters which are non-commercial for the purposes of this Section.'

The contracts to which the section relates are 'contracts for the supply of goods or materials, for the supply of services or for the execution of works' (ss 3) - in other words, all the various functions carried out by County and District Councils subjected to CCT.

Sub-section 5 sets out a list of the non-commercial matters to be disregarded, at the head of which is –

> '(5)(a) The terms and conditions of employment by contractors of their workers or the composition of the arrangements for the promotion, transfer or training of or the other opportunities afforded to, their workforces.'

It is the conflict between the combined effect of ARD, TUPE, European and domestic case law and TURERA, on the one hand, and the UK Government's CCT and privatisation strategies on the other, which have led to much debate and the issuing of Circulars and Papers by the DOE in recent years.

On 11th March 1993 two sets of Guidance were issued by two separate Departments. There was a marked difference between the Guidance issued by the then Secretary of State for the Environment, Michael Howard MP, which appeared to discourage local authorities from involving TUPE and reiterated the Secretary of State's powers to take action for anti-competitive conduct, and that issued by the Chancellor of the Duchy of Lancaster, William Waldegrave MP. The latter Guidance on the relevance of the Regulations went into some depth as to when TUPE might apply and included a statement at paragraph 13 under the heading 'What the Regulations Require' to the effect that when an employer (i.e. a transferee) unilaterally alters an employees terms and conditions of employment '*including pensions*' that employee would have remedies in constructive dismissal and/or breach of contract. The view that it was the Regulations, rather than the Employment Protection (Consolidation) Act, that protected pension rights ran directly contrary to what the Solicitor General, Sir Nicholas Lyell, had told a Standing Committee on 18th January 1990[31] -

[31] Hansard, PSA and Crown Supplies Bill - Standing Committee D. 18.1.90 Col 502.

> 'Rights and obligations relating to Civil Servants' pension benefits, while not protected by the Directive or TUPE, are protected by United Kingdom employment laws. Broadly, the position is that a person's contractual benefit cannot be changed...substantially to his detriment without giving rise either to a claim for constructive dismissal or for compensation... In other words, in the case of a person transferred under TUPE the transferor and the transferee must so arrange things that the pension rights enjoyed by staff after the transfer are broadly comparable with those enjoyed before.'

On this understanding of the law, the Cabinet Office had issued Government Departments with Guidance on the market testing process, which included advice that private sector contractors should provide broadly comparable pension rights for transferring Civil Servants.

So far as local authorities were concerned, the Guidance previously given by the Department of the Environment was replaced in June 1993 by Circular 10/93 in which authorities were advised that the Government's view upon the application of TUPE to CCT was as set out by Michael Howard MP on the 11th March 1993. Furthermore, local authorities were to refer to TUPE 'in neutral terms' but to provide contractors sufficient employee details to enable them to prepare TUPE tenders. In practice, this meant that on top of the usual tenderer evaluation exercise, local authorities were obliged to consider TUPE and non-TUPE bids for the same work.

The local authority associations sought to exert pressure upon the Secretary of State to give further Guidance with particular reference to the applicability of TUPE, indemnities, the disclosure of employee information and pensions. A request was also made for a Government indemnity against any costs falling on local authorities arising from the UK Government's failure to properly implement ARD.

In September 1993, the Department of the Environment informed representatives of the local authority of associations that a further Guidance or 'Issues Paper' would be issued as a sequel to Circular 10/93. In the version of the 'Issues Paper' sent to the press, 'Issue 11' dealt with future pension arrangements for transferring employees. However, following a meeting with contractors' organisations 'Issue 11' was deleted in its entirety. The Minister, however, made it clear in paragraph 11 of a letter to Chief Executives dated 21st January 1994 that the Government's view on pension rights in relation to transfers continued to be that set out in the Government's Guide to Market Testing paragraph 5.18 -

> 'Occupational pension rights are not transferred by TUPE. Pension rights accrued before the transfer are protected by social security legislation. But if pensions rights overall in the new employment are to be worse there may be grounds for claims of constructive dismissal against the Department or Agency. To avoid the risk of this, pensions in the new employment should be broadly comparable...'

On 15th March 1995 further Guidance was published which supplemented the January 1994 Issues Paper. This did not constitute Statutory Guidance within the meaning of S.9 Local Government Act 1992 and the Guidance was careful to point out that:

> 'In relation to CCT contracts it is for individual local authorities to take their own legal advice and individual authorities may as a result take different views from those expressed by the Department. The purpose of this letter is not to give legal advice but to indicate on the basis of the advice available to him the way in which the Secretary of State will exercise his powers in relation to anti-competitive behaviour in circumstances where there are complaints about the handling of pension issues.'

DOE Circular No.5/96[32] followed on 2nd April 1996, entitled 'Guidance on the Conduct of Compulsory Competitive Tendering' which replaced Circular 10/93. It contains no new provisions as to pension matters but refers local authorities back to the advice on TUPE issued on 21st January 1994 and in the 15th March 1995 Guidance.

The Underlying Legal Problems

1. The Government's view was and still is based upon the notion that transferring employees whose pension rights are reduced are entitled to claim constructive dismissal/breach of contract against the transferor authority. It is suggested that this is misconceived because the transferor has committed no anticipatory breach; nor is it likely to have breached the implied term of mutual trust and confidence. In effect, an employee would be seeking to claim breach of contract by the transferor arising from its failure to secure benefits which the Directive and Regulations had deliberately not transferred.

[32] Department of the Environment Circular No.5/96: 2 April 1996 Guidance on the Conduct of Compulsory Competitive Tender.

To date, the most helpful case is that of *Sita (GB) Ltd v Burton & Others,*[33] where it was held that an employee's fears for his terms and conditions of service on an impending transfer did not amount to a breach of the implied term of trust because those terms and conditions were protected by TUPE. By implication, it could be argued that if the employee's fears related to an employment matter which was not protected by TUPE e.g. future pension rights, then the result may well have been rather different.

Equally, it is difficult to foresee how a transferee would become liable since by virtue of ARD and TUPE he is under no obligation to provide a pension scheme in any event.

2. It has been the Government's view that the insertion of clauses in tender documents requiring comparable pensions will not offend Section 17 Local Government Act 1988 because the avoidance of claims of unfair dismissal/ breach of contract is a legitimate commercial consideration. This rests on the presumption set out at (1) above. However, while the Guidance merely confirms that the Secretary of State will not judge a requirement for comparable pension arrangements as anti-competitive, this does not of itself render such tender provision lawful. In this context, the Guidance states:

> 'Section 17 should not be construed as derogating from an authority's duty under the Acquired Rights Directive to protect the employee.'

It is not altogether clear what is meant by this, since ARD patently excludes from the transfer principle the most important parts of occupational pension schemes. The only sensible conclusion is that the draftsman may have had in mind the general duty imposed by the second limb of Article 3(3) and claims arising from the direct vertical effect of the Directive and *Francovich* principle.

One argument open to the Government lawyers would be that Section 17(5)(a) relates to 'conditions of employment by contractors of their workers...' i.e. the terms and conditions of contractor's existing workforce, as opposed to the terms and conditions under which the authority's workers would be employed if they were transferred to that contractor. This point does not seem to have been taken.

33 *Sita (GB) Ltd v Burton & Others. The Times,* December 5th 1996

3. An authority requiring the successful tenderer to provide broadly comparable pensions or other compensation can only effectively do so by setting out the requirement in the tender documents. Thereafter interested tenderers will be supplied with 'workforce information', the contents of which are set out as Annex A to the Guidance and include pension arrangements. Ultimately, all being well, a binding contract is entered into embodying the authority's specification and conditions of contract as well as ancillary matters such as future pension arrangements, indemnities, bonds etc. One of the problems which has come to light on re-tendering is the lack of statutory provision requiring contractors not to act anti-competitively. Effectively, a local authority has no redress against a contractor who refuses to provide workforce information or, rather worse, against a contractor who provides the information, unsuccessfully tenders the second time round and, finally, in anticipation of the pending transfer of the workforce to a rival, gives a substantial paid award to take effect shortly before the date of transfer.

   If a contractual requirement for comparable pensions were found to be unlawful, this might put in jeopardy the whole contract. Whilst an unlawful term might not of itself render the contract unlawful, a contract entered into pursuant to a mistake might be void or voidable at the instance of the contractor.

4. If it is accepted that local authorities can legitimately require transferees to make pension provision for transferring staff, what is the extent of the obligation and how is it assessed to have been met?

   Dr. P. Elias' advice to the Local Government Management Board in April 1993 referred to 'equivalent' pension rights. The Government's Guidance and the Government's Actuary Department's advice consistently refers to 'comparable' pensions. The two words are given different meanings in this context. The Guidance is explicit:

   > 'Equivalence or replication of pension terms should not be required, and contractors should be free to put forward such proposals as they wish, provided they first consider whether they can offer broadly comparable pensions and secondly, so far as a pension is not available, to offer to compensate employees.'

   Compensation may take the form of increased pay, or improvements in other benefits.

   The evaluation of comparable pensions is a matter for the authority, although the assessment of comparability should be based on professional advice - either from an independent actuary or the Government Actuary's Department (GAD). In either case, an assessment based on such advice would provide a defence against claims that the authority may have acted anti-competitively.

GAD provides a particularly helpful 'Passport' system. This enables a contractor to approach GAD in advance of a particular tender submission to enable its scheme to be compared with the relevant public sector scheme. Under the Passport system, GAD issues a certificate to the effect that, in its opinion, the tenderer's scheme meets the broad comparability requirement in respect of overall benefit for a defined part of the workforce. It is now possible for contractors to obtain Passports for schemes which substantially mirror all the public sector schemes, including the Local Government Pension Scheme.

In the event of the lead tenderer being unable to provide a comparable scheme, the tender is not necessarily automatically to be rejected. The Guidance suggests that it is open to authorities to 'explore with an otherwise lead tenderer how, if at all, he intends to deal with any lack of comparability e.g. by submitting revised pensions proposals or offering additional cash compensation to the transferred staff'. Other tenderers whose schemes are not comparable must similarly be given the opportunity to put forward alternative proposals. This suggestion is not without difficulty. Leading Counsel has advised the Local Government Management Board that contractors should be required to provide broadly comparable pension schemes in any event and, further, that the DOE is in error in stating that a contractor can 'buy-out' pension benefits which cannot be offered under its own scheme. Provision is also made in the Guidance for an adjustment of the tender price, upwards or downwards, in accordance with the number of employees opting in or out of the contractor's scheme during the contract period.

Finally, local authorities have no statutory powers under which detriment payments can be made to employees transferring on less favourable terms. It is therefore all the more important for the authority to correctly specify its requirements in the tender documents at the outset and to base its assessment of comparability on professional advice.

5. There is the issue of indemnities. As an alternative to seeking broadly comparable pensions, some authorities inserted indemnity clauses into their contract documents. Because there were fears that liability for failure to provide broadly comparable pensions did not transfer to the contractor and the question of broad comparability could only authoritatively be determined by a Court (i.e. long after the contract had been sealed) local authority associations urged the Secretary of State to permit authorities to seek indemnities where they believed that the proposed pension

arrangements were not comparable. The DOE originally took the view that it was inappropriate for local authorities to seek indemnities in respect of any CCT matter. *Circular 10/93*[34] therefore made no mention of indemnities. The January 1994 Issues Paper did however concede that there may be occasions when it would be legitimate for local authorities to seek indemnities - where the contract had been entered into on the basis that TUPE did not apply but was found at a later date to be subject to the Regulations (Issue 1) it was considered reasonable for an authority to seek an indemnity against claims based on failure to consult staff.

The Guidance of 15th March 1995 extended the concept to claims based on failure to provide comparable pensions. While the DOE is of the view that limited indemnities can lawfully be required (and the Local Government Management Board provide a draft indemnity clause) it is at least arguable that this is not in fact the case. The *Local Government (Direct Service Organisations) (Competition) Regulations 1993*[35] prescribe the financial costs which can be taken into account in the evaluation of tenders. Arguably, they exclude the validity of evaluating other financial factors, i.e. they are a complete code for the purpose of carrying out the evaluation - *c.f Hazell v London Borough of Hammersmith & Fulham.*[36]

Against this argument, it could be said firstly that it is wrong to maintain that the 1993 Regulations exclude the possibility of other factors being taken into account - local authorities fiduciary duties to their taxpayers require that other features tending to affect the value of a bid should not be ignored. Secondly, if the 1993 Regulations are exclusive of other financial factors, authorities are nevertheless entitled to take into account the provision of an indemnity as a non-financial factor in the evaluation of the bid.

Assuming that authorities have the power to require indemnities, particularly in relation to pension provision, the DOE's view is that any attempt to obtain excessive indemnities would be anti-competitive and fall foul of S.9(4) Local Government, Planning & Land Act 1980 and S.7(7) Local Government Act 1988 because it may discourage potential contractors from bidding. Additionally, the seeking of excessive indemnities

34 Local Government Act 1972, Section 9: Competition in the Provision of Local Authority Services. DOE Circular No.10/93 issued 14th June 1993.

35 The Local Government (Direct Service Organisations)(Competition) Regulations 1993 SI 1993 No.848 (as amended).

36 *Hazell v London Borough of Hammersmith and Fulham* [1992] AC1.

or any indemnity as a matter of course might be capable of challenge on account of its failure to meet standards of *Wednesbury*[37] reasonableness.

In practice, many authorities restrict their indemnity requirements to paragraph 4 of the January 1994 Issues Paper and to those referred to in the March 1995 Guidance. The draft indemnity clause provided by the Local Government Management Board is widely drafted and certainly more comprehensive than that envisaged by the March 1995 Guidance.

The Current Position

Since the March 1995 Guidance, as far as it is possible to tell, the prevailing tendency in local government circles seems to have been to adopt the line of least resistance and follow DOE advice. Incoming contractors have therefore been required to make broadly comparable pension arrangements for transferring staff.

In June 1995 however the former Solicitor to the Audit Commission whose opinions have, in the past, carried considerable weight, issued advice to all District Auditors in England and Wales in the following terms:

> 'A decision by a local authority not to accept the lowest tender on the ground that the tenderer is not proposing to make broadly comparable pension provision for employees of the local authority...would be likely to be regarded by the Courts (although not, it appears, by the Secretary of State) as anti-competitive.[38]'

The Audit Commission sought to distance itself from this advice and the DOE immediately wrote to all Chief Executives, on 28th June 1995, reiterating the Department's views. Circular *5/96* has since been published which has again confirmed the advice previously given by the Department, by reference to the previous Guidance and the 1993 Regulations.

Two further cases, reported in 1997, have both shaken certain commonly held assumptions about the applicability of ARD and TUPE to transfers of staff engaged on local authority work either as part of the Direct Service Organisation or employed by outside contractors. In *Ayse Suzen v Zehnaeker*

[37] *Associated Provincial Picture Houses Ltd v Wednesbury Corporation* [1948] IKB 224.

[38] 'New advice wrecks DOE pension rules' Local Government Chronicle 23 June 1995 EMAP Business Publications.

Gebaudereingung GmbH Krankenhausservice and Lefahrt GmbH[39] the European Court of Justice held that ARD did not apply where on the termination of a cleaning contract with the first undertaking and renewal with a second there had been no ancillary transfer of significant tangible or intangible assets and no taking over of the major part of the workforce assigned to the performance of the contract by the first contractor.

Shortly thereafter in *Betts and Others v Brintel Helicopters Ltd*[40], the Court of Appeal held that there was no relevant transfer from Brintel to KLM because the second contract operated in a different way from the first, and there was no transfer of assets or employees. The only similarity lay in the nature of the work.

As a result of these cases, comprehensive enquiries will have to be carried out to ascertain whether TUPE will apply, particularly where white-collar work is contracted out. In such circumstances, it is unlikely that physical assets will be transferred, and it may be no easy matter to identify staff assigned to the work to be contracted, so that although the *Spijkers* test will still hold good, in many instances the only certainty will be the transfer of customer base. As more white-collar work is tendered for the first time, and as more predominantly blue-collar work is re-tendered, it becomes all the more imperative to ascertain whether the insistence on comparable pensions rests on a contractual basis or whether it arises from the Directive.

The Immediate Future

In 1994, the European Commission proposed a replacement Directive, the legal basis for which was again Article 100 of the Treaty of Rome. However, ARD has remained substantially intact, subject only to the minor amendment of Article 3 paragraph 3 (renumbered paragraph 4) by Council Directive 99/50/EC [40a] and to construction by the European Court and the domestic courts of Member States.

Paragraph 4 provides that 'unless Member States provide otherwise' supplementary company scheme benefits continue to be excluded from transfer. In practical terms, the amendment in not significant because Article 7 already allowed Member States to introduce laws and administrative provisions more favourable to employees.

[39] *Ayse Suzen v Zehnaeker Gebaudereingung GmbH Krankenhausservice and Lefarth GmbH* [1997] IRLR 255.

[40] *Betts and Others v. Brintel Helicopters,* Times Law Reports 1 April 1997.

[40a] Council Directive 98/50/EC dated 29 June 1998.

Mention has already been made of the *Memorandum*[41] issued by the European Commission early in 1997 which gives guidelines on the application of the Directive. This has the laudable aim of attempting to enlighten both employers and employees, and the general public, as to the provisions of the Directive in the light of twenty years of decisions handed down by the Court of Justice. However, it is submitted that the reference to 'rights acquired or being acquired', referred to in the answer to Question 11, serves to confuse rather than to explain the obligations of Member States. The Directive itself does not use these words.

The Memorandum was set out in full in a Public Consultation document issued by the Department of Trade and Industry and dated December 1997.[42] This document sought to obtain views on the approach to be adopted by the Government on the Commission's proposal for amending the Directive. So far as Article 3 is concerned, the proposal suggested that the wording should remain unchanged. Paragraphs 36-39 of the text of the Consultation Document dealt with the exclusion of certain occupational pension rights and set out very succinctly the nub of the problem, particularly insofar as it affects public sector employees. The conclusion, set out in paragraph 39, is worth quoting in full:

> 'The Government intends to consider responses to this consultation document before deciding whether or not to seek an amendment to the Directive to end the current exclusion of certain occupational pension rights, but to allow transferee employers in this instance to make only comparable rather than necessarily identical provision; and would welcome views as to how the technical problems raised by such an amendment might be solved.'

41 Memorandum from the Commission on acquired rights of workers in cases of transfers of undertakings. Guidelines on the Application of Council Directive 77/187/EEC of 14 February 1977 based on the case law of the Court of Justice of the European Communities.

42 European Acquired Rights Directive and Transfer of Undertakings (Protection of Employment) Regulations 1981 (The TUPE Regulations) Public Consultation Issued by Department of Trade and Industry Employment Rights Directorate December 1997 URN 98/513.

9. Information and Consultation

Pascale Lorber

INTRODUCTION

In a context of continuing European market integration and increased world competition, companies have reacted by re-structuring, re-locating their establishments or have been privatised or have contracted out some of their services in order to adapt to the new economic environment. One of the consequences of such trends over the last thirty years has been a call for labour flexibility in order to facilitate such changes. The risk of such a process could be a 'backlash of social and political resistance' as described by Shanks in the 1970s, leading to the enactment of the Social Action Programme.[1] Such a concern is still present today, as evidenced by the strong social as well as political reaction towards the decision by the French group Renault to close down its Belgian factory, making more than 3,000 workers redundant, so as to re-locate in Spain.[2]

In order to avoid the process of economic integration being hindered by such reactions, the idea already present in the 1974 European Social Action Programme, was to include elements of industrial democracy within the larger context of 'humanising the process of industrial change'.[3] Participation of employees would allow a certain degree of involvement of workers in the process of decision-making, thus increasing the legitimacy of management actions. However, participation is a rather vague and wide term which covers various realities. Before further analysing how participation of workers entered the European social field and by extension the United Kingdom, a pause is

1 As quoted in More G. 'The Acquired Rights Directive: Frustrating or Facilitating the Labour Market Flexibility' in *New Legal Dynamics of the European Union*, OUP, 1995 at 131.

2 See European Works Council Review April 1997 and EIRI April 1997 at 3 and 33.

3 *supra* 1 at 130.

required in order to define and delimit this notion. Several aspects of participation have been identified. It divides mainly into two forms. First, *direct participation* consists of management initiatives to inform and consult, and/or to delegate authority and responsibility to individual or groups of employees in relation to immediate work organisation and conditions.[4] This type of participation covers techniques such as one-way communication, where information is communicated down the hierarchy to employees directly by newsletters, briefings, etc. or two-way communication system, where employees are given the opportunity to comment and ask questions about the information communicated. Further, and more developed, this form of participation includes also direct consultation of employees at the workplace or delegation of tasks to individuals and teams - in the shape of quality circles for example.[5] The purpose of such practices also generally termed *employee involvement*, which seem to have developed in the last few years,[6] is to improve employee motivation and commitment directly at the workplace level. Complementary forms of participation which are aimed to achieve the same objective are financial participation, in the form of profit-sharing schemes for example.

The second form of participation is referred to as *indirect participation* or *representational participation*. The employees do not participate directly, but it is their representatives who are involved, whether they are trade unions or works councillors, generally at a higher level in the structure of the undertaking. Again here the patterns of participation are varied. The workers' representatives can be informed, consulted or both, or at the end of the scale can actively play a role in the decision-making process. Information is considered as 'the weakest form of participation',[7] since it simply consists of management providing information to workers' representatives. Consultation, on the other hand, goes a step further since workers' representatives will be expected to give an opinion on the information provided by the employer. Whether this opinion is taken into account or not, or to what extent the workers' representatives' view alters the management decision is a practical issue. As to the more integrated form of collective participation, workers' representatives are members of works councils or sit on the company's board. When these structures exist, an opportunity is given to representatives of the workforce to positively 'participate' in the decision-making process of the

4 Greaty J. and Sisson K. *Conceptualising Direct Participation in Organisational Change. The EPOC project.* European Foundation for the Improvement of Living and Working Conditions (1994).

5 See Gold M. *Direct Communication in European Multinationals: A Case Study Approach.* European Foundation for the Improvement of Living and Working Conditions (1994).

6 Millward N. [et al.] *Workplace Industrial Relations in Transition. The ED/ ESRC/PSI/ACAS Surveys* Dartmouth 1992 at 175-180.

7 Barnard C. *EC Employment Law.* Wiley 1996 at 8.3.

company at a formative stage. This constitutes a more sophisticated form of involvement that is not common to all Member States in the European Union. The purpose of indirect participation is the collective representation of the workforce, through the workers' representatives, who will assess the policies and decisions of the management in terms of their potential impact on the workforce as a whole. The function of indirect participation has thus been described as 'democratic',[8] the idea being that workers' representatives should be informed, consulted and their views should be taken into account when decisions affecting employees' interests are made. This is particularly the case when companies' strategies relate to acquisitions, mergers, or other restructuring programmes.

In this context, one of the rights protected by the Acquired Rights Directive[9] is for employees' representatives to be informed and consulted when a transfer occurs.[10] The aim of this paper is thus to concentrate on this particular form of indirect employees' participation by examining briefly in a first part, how these concepts were introduced at European level and how they were implemented in the United Kingdom, considering the general background in this field. The focus will then shift onto the duty to inform and consult in the event of a transfer of undertaking, in order to assess the effectiveness of such mechanisms. This is of particular interest when one scrutinises the recent developments at European level, attempting to promote further information and consultation in the wider context of economic integration and companies' restructuring.

Information and consultation : the European background

The general idea of indirect participation of employees in undertakings has been promoted at European level since voices were raised about the necessity to create a 'Social Community'. In order to realise this idea, a Social Action Programme was adopted in 1972-74.[11] One of the three main objectives set out in this programme was the participation of workers in the life of

8 *Supra* 5.

9 Council Directive of 14 February 1977 on the Approximation of the Laws of the Member States Relating to the Safeguarding of Employees Rights in the Event of Transfers of Undertakings, Business or Parts of Businesses (77/187/EEC) [OJ 1977, No L61/27], amended by Council Directive 98/50/EC of 29 June 1998 [1998]OJ L20/88.

10 Article 6. This article remains principally the same in the 1998 Directive.

11 Council Resolution concerning a Social Action Programme for the European Communities. 1 January 1974. 74/C 13/1 OJ.

undertakings.[12] On this basis, new projects of Directives were considered, but the Commission adopted a twofold approach to promote this objective.[13] On the one hand, the participation of workers was envisaged through a 'company-law' approach, attempting to promote involvement of workers' representatives on company boards while, on the other hand, proposals were considered in the field of social policy, promoting information and consultation of employees' representatives in advance of important decisions in the life of the undertaking.[14] The first approach proved to be rather unsuccessful despite numerous attempts, translated through two main proposals which never became binding law. The first proposal was the European Company Statute.[15] The idea was to allow European companies, referred to as *Societa Europea*, to release themselves from national legislation, thus being regulated by Community Law. This draft provided as a second main purpose for employees' representation either on supervisory boards or through European Works Councils. The second proposal was the Fifth Directive[16] which concerned only public limited companies. It required the setting up of a two-tier board structure where employees would be represented on the supervisory board. The primary obstacle to the adoption of such instruments was the diversity or absence of models adopted in the Member States[17].

On the 'social' front, proposals were also made at the beginning of the 1980s to adopt a general regime for information and consultation of workers' representatives. The main proposal was the 'Vredeling' draft Directive[18]. The purpose was for the central management of a complex-structured undertaking to provide substantial information to workers' representatives via local management. Consultation of workers' representatives would take place when the employer's decision would affect employees' interests.[19] The outcome was similar to the one for involvement of workers' representatives on companies'

[12] See also Politique Sociale de la Communauté. Marché Intérieur. Situation au 1er Juillet 1994. Commission Européenne, vol 6 Juillet 1994.

[13] Hall M. *Legislation for Employee Participation: a Case Study of the EWC Directive*. Warwick Papers in Industrial Relations , No 39, March 1992.

[14] A model with a 'more modest objective' as described by Docksey C. in *Information and Consultation of Employees: the United Kingdom and the Vredeling Directive* (1986) MLR vol. 49 No.3 at 281.

[15] OJ 1970 C124, amended in 1975 COM(75) 150 final.

[16] Originally proposed in 1972 (OJ C131/72) and revised in 1975 and 1983 (OJ 1983 C240/2).

[17] For a detailed account of the proposed Directives, their content, and the opposition encountered see Barnard C. *EC Employment Law,* Wiley 1996 from 8.11; Rood M. *Workers' Participation: New Initiatives at European Level* (1992) 8 Int.J.Comp.L.L.I.R 320. As to the revival of the European Company Statute, see below .

[18] Originally proposed in 1980 (OJ C297/80) and reviewed in 1983 (OJ C317, Supplement 3/80 EC Bull).

[19] For a detailed account of the proposals see *supra* 17 and Docksey C *supra* 14.

boards: it met a great deal of criticism and consequently was never adopted.

In view of the opposition to a general regime, the Commission altered its strategy and decided to introduce information and consultation requirements in specific fields. Thus, two Directives were adopted: the 1975 Directive on Collective Redundancies[20] and the Directive on Transfer of Undertakings.[21] These two European instruments were transposed into United Kingdom law.

The United Kingdom background

As described by Neal,[22] the United Kingdom system of industrial relations presents unique characteristics when compared to other European countries. In terms of collective labour law, it has traditionally been a voluntary system of collective bargaining with strong independent trade unions. The State refrains from intervening in the sphere of labour law, leaving to the main industrial actors to deal with the regulation of the workplace. This feature, described as 'collective laissez-faire'[23] constituted one of the prides of the United Kingdom system of industrial relations.[24] In such a system, workers had their interests represented and protected by trade unions who negotiated with management their terms and conditions of employment within the framework of collective bargaining. In the UK public sector trade union density is generally higher than in the private sector. The long history of national bargaining in the public sector has resulted in complex sets of agreements in central and local government and the NHS. However, as a result of CCT and now 'best value' policies, much traditionally public sector work has been transferred to the private sector, where union recognition is less well developed, both as regards the coverage and scope of agreements.

However, in the wider sense of industrial democracy, no system of institutionalised participation existed whereby workers' representatives would be informed or consulted on a regular basis when corporate decisions were

20 Council Directive of 17 February 1975 on the Approximation of the Laws of the Member States relating to Collective Redundancies (75/129/EEC) [OJ 1975, No L48/29] (as amended by Council Directive of 24 June 1992 (92/56/EEC) [OJ 1992, L245/3] and now consolidated by Council Directive 98/50/EC of June 29 1998 [1998] OJ L225116.

21 Directive 77/187/EEC [OJ 1977, No L61/27] amended by Council Directive 98/50/EC of June 29 1998 [1998] OJ L201188.

22 Neal A.C *The European Framework Directive on the Health and Safety of Workers: Challenges for the United Kingdom* (1990) 6 Int.J.Comp.L.L.I.R 90.

23 Kahn-Freund O. *Labour and the Law* First Edition. 1972. London; and Davies P. and Freedland M. *Labour Law and Public Policy*. Chapter 1. Clarendon Press. 1993.

24 Report of the Royal Commission on Trade Unions and Employers' Associations. Cmnd 3523. May 1968.(Referred to as the Donovan Report).

made through the institution of works councils, as in Germany or France,[25] for example, or whereby employees' representatives would sit on the companies' boards, thereby directly influencing the policy of the undertaking. As to the latter form of participation, an attempt was made in the mid-1970s to remedy this situation as part of the 'Social Contract' between the Labour Government and the trade union movement.[26] A committee was established to consider the issue of introducing workers' participation in the management of undertakings in order to promote industrial democracy. The report of the so-called Bullock Committee[27] produced some radical proposals with regard to employees' representation on company boards some of which were translated in a Government White Paper[28] the following year, but in a somewhat weaker form. However, these proposals were never implemented, since the Labour Government lost the general election in 1979, ceding their place to a long-standing Conservative administration which took a rather different view of the whole system of industrial relations. The Thatcher years brought a new climate to the field of labour law. One way of promoting de-regulation and competitiveness was to progressively dismantle the power of the trade unions and to encourage individual relationships between employees and employers. The idea of worker participation in management was raised again following earlier reverses in the 1989 Community Charter of Fundamental Social Rights of Workers,[29] but, consistently with overall United Kingdom policy, the Conservative government did not sign. In the same year, the Department of Employment issued a document entitled 'People and Companies. Employee Involvement in Britain'[30] where it made clear that it was fully committed to promote and encourage what it called voluntary employee involvement, in other words, direct participation[31] given that it increases prosperity, flexibility and productivity of companies. However, the government reiterated that it was firmly opposed to European Community proposals for compulsory legislation on worker participation, on the basis that compulsion was not adapted to the United Kingdom voluntary tradition of industrial relations. Such European requirements meant delay, inflexibility, and extra costs for businesses, and would generally disrupt the existing system.

[25] See Pichot E. *Employee Representatives in Europe and their Economic Prerogatives*. Report conducted for the European Commission. January 1995.

[26] For a complete account on the 'Social Contract', see Davies P. and Freedland M. *Labour Law and Public Policy*. Chapter 8. Clarendon Press. 1993.

[27] Report of the Committee of Inquiry on Industrial Democracy (Chairman Lord Bullock), Cmnd. 6706. 1977.

[28] *Industrial Democracy* Cmnd. 7231 (HMSO 1978).

[29] Articles 17-18. Reported in Social Europe 1/90 at 45.

[30] Department of Employment. 1989. London HMSO.

[31] As defined in the introduction, see *supra*.

The question that one may consequently ask is: can a picture be drawn of what is the current situation in terms of workers' participation in the United Kingdom? As indicated, a complex and growing system of direct participation is in place[32] in terms of information and consultation *directly* with workers or groups of workers through newsletters, briefings, joint consultative committees, or quality circles for example. Furthermore, companies employing more than 250 employees are required to include in their annual reports a 'statement describing the action that has been taken during the financial year to introduce, maintain or develop arrangements aimed at' involving employees through information and consultation.[33]

In terms of indirect participation, defined as consisting of information and consultation of workers' representatives on the one hand, and participation on company board on the other hand, the current system presents two characteristics. First, there are no provisions providing for the presence of employees or their representatives on supervisory or unitary boards of companies as proposed in the Bullock Committee Report or as promoted in the European proposals.[34] Second, the existing provisions relate to information and consultation. As to the former, it has been part of United Kingdom industrial relations as an element of collective bargaining. According to TULR(C)A 1992 s.181, there is a general duty for the employer to disclose information to recognised trade unions for the purpose of collective bargaining. It consists of all information relating to the employer's undertaking, which it would be in accordance with good industrial relations to disclose and without which trade union representatives would be impeded from carrying on collective bargaining. However, this duty is somewhat weakened, first because s.182 lists categories of information which need not be disclosed[35]

32 For an account of the nature of employee involvement see Marchington M., Goodman J., Wilkinson A. and Ackers P. *New Developments in Employee Involvement,* Employment Department. Research Series No.2 May 1992 (the main findings of this survey are summarised in Hibbert A. *Employee Involvement : A Recent Survey.* Employment Gazette. December 1991 at 659).

As to the importance of employee involvement see Millward N. [et al.] *Workplace Industrial Relations in Transition. The ED/ ESRC/PSI/ACAS Surveys.* Dartmouth 1992 at 151-180.

Examining the reactions of the Social Partners towards this form of participation see Geary J., Rees C., Sisson K. *Management-Initiated Direct Participation. United Kingdom.* European Foundation for the Improvement of Living and Working Conditions. Working Paper No: WP/95/03/EN. 1995.

33 Sch 7 para 11 Companies Act 1985.

34 See Fifth Directive and the European Company Statute *supra* 15, 16 and 17.

35 In essence, an employer is not required to disclose information when such a disclosure would be against the interests of national security, could contravene a prohibition imposed by or under an enactment, would cause substantial injury to his undertaking; when the information has been communicated to him in confidence, when it relates specifically to an individual, and when the information is obtained for the purpose of bringing, prosecuting or defending any legal proceedings.

and second, because the remedy available in case of failure to disclose has been criticised for being relatively ineffective.[36]

Consultation, however, is a duty which was imposed upon employers, essentially by European Directives transposed into national law. Employers are under statutory obligation to inform and consult in four areas. The first obligation is the only one established nationally without European 'interference' and is a requirement for the employer who decides to opt-out of the state pension scheme - in order to operate an occupational company pension scheme- to consult any independent trade union recognised by him in respect of the employees concerned.[37] There is also an obligation to disclose certain information to the recognised trade union once the new pension scheme is established.[38] The second duty to inform and consult relates to health and safety matters. There is a general obligation for the employer to consult safety representatives[39] on arrangements for co-operating with employees in promoting and developing health and safety measures and in checking their effectiveness[40], while an additional obligation to consult 'in good time' on specific matters was introduced by the Management of Health and Safety at Work Regulations in 1992.[41] In order to carry out their functions, safety representatives should be provided with the adequate information.[42]

The two remaining occasions where an employer is required to inform and consult are linked to situations of restructuring or reorganisation which have considerable impact upon employees. The duty arises where an employer is proposing to make employees redundant and where an employer is proposing either to dispose of or to acquire an undertaking or part of an undertaking.

36 See Dickens L and Bain G.S *A Duty to Bargain? Union Recognition and Information Disclosure* in Lewis R. *Labour Law in Britain* at 99. Blackwell 1986; and Morris G.S. and Archer T.J. *Trade Unions, Employers and the Law* at 185. Butterworths 1993.

37 SI 1996/1172. *The Occupational Pension Schemes (Contracting Out) Regulations 1996.*

38 See Pension Schemes Act 1993 s.113 and Occupational Pension Schemes (Disclosure of Information) Regulations, SI 1996/ 1655.

39 Safety Representatives were originally people appointed by recognised trade unions. Since the Health and Safety (Consultation with Employees) Regulations ASI 1996/ 1513, when there is no recognised trade unions, the employer can consult employees directly or safety representatives elected directly by the employees.

40 Health and Safety at Work Act 1974, s.2(6) and see Safety Representatives and Safety Committee Regulations 1977, SI 1977/500.

41 See Regulation 4 as amended by SI 1992/2051. This is the result of the European 'Framework Directive' on Health and Safety (89/391/EC).

42 Ibid. Regulation 7.

The requirement to inform and consult for collective redundancies was the first of the two European Directive implemented into United Kingdom Law by the Labour Government in 1975.[43] The procedural requirements are now to be found in TULR(C)A 1992 s.188-189.[44] In essence, the employer is to engage in consultation with the workers' representatives with a view to reaching an agreement on ways and means of avoiding or reducing redundancies or mitigating their effects when 20 or more redundancies are proposed within a period of 90 days in the same establishment. He must consult in good time in order to try to reach an agreement. A time-scale is provided, requiring the employer to begin consultation at least 30 days in advance of the first dismissal, or 90 days in advance when 100 or more employees are proposed to be dismissed within 90 days. In order to adequately consult and attempt to reach an agreement, the employer must provide written information as to principally, the reasons for the redundancies, their numbers, the method of selection and timing, to the workers' representatives.

Despite the fact that the Acquired Rights Directive was enacted only two years after the Collective Redundancies Directive, the task to transpose it into domestic law was passed on to the new Conservative Government which implemented reluctantly the European legislation in TUPE 1981.[45]

The duty to inform and consult in TUPE

According to the preamble of the Acquired Rights Directive 'it is necessary to provide for the protection of employees in the event of a change of employer, in particular, to ensure that their rights are safeguarded'. In order to achieve this goal, the Directive protects employees in three ways[46]. It provides for contracts of employment to be safeguarded given that, first they are automatically transferred from one employer to another, and two, that employees cannot be dismissed by reason of a transfer. Collective rights are protected by way of imposing a duty upon transferor and transferee to inform and consult workers' representatives. In comparison with the Collective Redundancies Directive, such a duty does not seem to be carrying the same importance. While information and more significantly consultation is the primary obligation imposed on the employer where he envisages to dismiss a group of employees, when a transfer occurs, the employer is submitted to a broad duty to inform but a narrow duty to consult.[47] This difference of primary

43 Employment Protection Act 1975, s.99.

44 as amended by TURERA 1993 and the Collective Redundancies and Transfer of Undertakings (Protection of Employment) (Amended) Regulations 1995 (SI 1995 No 2587).

45 Transfer of Undertakings (Protection of Employment) Regulations 1981, SI 1981/1794.

46 Barnard C. *EC Employment Law* 1996 Wiley at 355.

47 Hepple B. *The Transfer of Undertakings (Protection of Employment) Regulations* (1982) 11 ILJ at 38.

objective is translated in the Act and the Regulations which transposed the European Directives into United Kingdom law, with regard to the nature and timing of the information and consultation, as well as the amount of compensation awarded if the employer fails to comply with his duty. This is why it is of interest to consider in details the TUPE regulations that impose the duty to inform and consult upon the employer[48] and the ones that contain enforcement provisions,[49] in the light of similar obligations existing in the event of collective redundancies.

Information

When a relevant transfer occurs, the employer must inform appropriate representatives in respect of any affected employees. Affected employees being defined as either employees of the transferor or of the transferee,[50] it appears that both employers are concerned by such a duty. Adopting such a wide definition implies that the relevant employer could have to inform workers' representatives of employees who are not to be transferred but who will be affected by such a transfer. In some circumstances, all the employees of the two undertakings concerned by the transfer may thus be considered as being *affected*.

As to the content of the duty, the information to be provided falls into four categories.[51] The employer will inform the appropriate representatives of:

> a) the fact that the relevant transfer is to take place, when and the reasons for such a transfer;
> b) the legal, economic and social implications of the transfer for the affected employees;
> c) the measures that the employer envisages taking in connection with the transfer, in relation to the employees, or the fact that he will not take any measures;
> d) if the employer is the transferor, the measures which the transferee envisages to take in connection with the transfer, in relation to the transferred employees, or if he envisages that no measures will be taken.

In this last case, the transferee has to communicate to the transferor the relevant information in order for the latter to fulfil adequately his obligations.[52]

48 Regulation 10.

49 Regulation 11.

50 Regulation 10(1).

51 Regulation 10(2).

52 Regulation 10(3).

The first category of information to be provided is unambiguous. Questions arise, however, as to what is meant by 'legal, economic and social implications of the transfer'. TUPE reproduced literally the text of the Directive for this second type of information, and consequently no help for the purpose of interpretation can be found in the European instrument. The task to determine what is expected from the employer was thus left to the tribunals and courts. In *Institution of Professional Civil Servants and others v Secretary of State for Defence,*[53] the High Court judge Millett J attempted to define such notions. This case concerned the privatisation of the two remaining Royal dockyards under the Dockyard Services Act 1986, which contained equivalent provisions to the one contained in regulation 10 of TUPE. It required the Minister responsible for the dockyards to inform and consult with the recognised trade unions on the transfer of the Royal Dockyards to commercial companies. The trade unions took an action against the Minister, alleging that he had not fulfilled this duty. One of the questions identified by the judge in this instance was what the extent of the obligation imposed upon the Secretary of State was. In this context he construed 'legal, economic and social implications' as meaning 'consequences of the transfer for the employees'.[54] Without indicating further what kind of information should be covered in general terms, the judge referred to categories of information disclosed by the defendant in that particular instance. A wide range of issues were covered, including the general terms and conditions of employment such as pay, hours of work or holidays, but also pensions, redundancy arrangements, and finally various procedures for disciplinary hearings, etc.

One can thus draw from this description that an employer should refer to the effect of the Regulations[55] in terms of consequences for the contract of employment, which should be continued and remained unchanged -with the exception of pension arrangements which do not come under the scope of the Regulations and notify employees of that situation. The question then remains whether this category of information covers the 'legal' implications, and whether further information should be provided to come in the 'economic and social' category. The argument could be put forward that as long as the employer demonstrates a reasonable effort to be as complete as possible in the amount and categories of information he provides, a court or tribunal would be satisfied that he had fulfilled his obligation under Regulation 10(2)(b). This was certainly the position adopted by the judge in *Institution of Professional Civil Servants and others v Secretary of State for Defence* who concluded that the

53 [1987] 3 CMLR 35, [1987] IRLR 373.

54 Ibid. at [31].

55 Schofield P. *Protection of Employment on Transfer of Undertakings* (1983), Journal of Business Law at 30.

employer in this instance the Secretary of State 'had taken all reasonable steps to inform the workforce' and that 'he had fulfilled and more than fulfilled his statutory duties'.[56]

As far as the two remaining categories of information are concerned, they relate to the measures envisaged in connection with the transfer, taken either by the transferor or by the transferee. Both transferor and transferee have to inform workers' representatives either of the fact that they will not take any measures or if such measures are considered necessary by one or the two employers concerned by the transfer, they are not only under the obligation to inform the workers' representatives of these measures, but they also have to consult them on these issues.[57]

There is no express provision in the Regulations that the information provided to workers' representatives should be in writing, whereas this is the case in the event of collective redundancies.[58] It could be implied that such information should be in writing, given that under regulation 10(4) the information must be delivered or posted to an address notified by the appropriate representative to the employer.[59] However, the appropriate representatives cannot 'dictate the form in which the information is provided', whether the documents should be the originals or copies.[60]

The final question in relation to the delivery of information relates to its timing. According to the Regulations, the employer should deliver information '*long enough before a relevant transfer to enable the employer* of any affected employees *to consult* all the persons who are appropriate representatives of any of those affected employees'.[61] By comparison, Article 6 of the Directive refers to information being provided in 'good time', a phraseology also found in the provisions concerning collective redundancies.[62] This drafting is rather

[56] [1987] 3 CMLR 35.

[57] For further discussion on what constitute 'measures', see below.

[58] TULR(C)A 1992 s.188(4) : '[T]he employer shall disclose in writing to the appropriate representatives'.

[59] McMullen J. *Business Transfers and Employee Rights,* Butterworths 1992 (2nd Edition) at 243. He also refers to the industrial decision of *NALGO v British Waterways Board* COIT 11548/88/LN/A where the tribunal decided that the information must be in writing.

[60] See *Institution of Professional Civil Servants and others v Secretary of State for Defence* [1987] 3 CMLR 35 at [28].

[61] Regulation 10(2). Emphasis added.

[62] At least these were the words used in the Collective Redundancies Directive while originally TULR(A) 1992 s.188 transposing the Directive, stated the information should be provided 'at the earliest opportunity'. This was amended by the Collective Redundancies and Transfer of Undertakings (Protection of Employment) (Amendment) Regulations 1995, SI 1995/2587 which then reproduced the terms used in the Directive.

surprising considering that consultation does not necessarily take place when a transfer occurs. This will be the case only in the event of measures being envisaged by one or both the employers concerned by the transfer. One might then wonder whether an employer could disclose information just before the transfer materialises because no measures will be taken? This would not seem to be the adequate attitude to adopt for the employer considering the spirit of the Directive. Nevertheless, scrutinising the text of the Directive and of TUPE, one can note that the first category of information relates to the fact that the transfer is to take place, implying that information is not required at the stage of proposal for a transfer.[63] Consequently, adopting a literal approach would mean that an employer could give information at a short notice to the appropriate representatives when no measures are envisaged. One could then wonder what would be the purpose of the whole exercise? Surely the intention of the drafters of the Directive were not to allow such a situation to happen when requiring the information to be delivered 'in good time'. When facing the issue of interpreting such a provision, as found in TUPE, the courts and tribunals would certainly be expected to adopt Millett J's attitude in *IPCS v Secretary of State for Defence*, where he stated that:

> 'The Regulations ... were introduced in pursuance of a Directive of the EEC..., and in case of ambiguity must be construed if possible in conformity with the Directive.'[64]

The same point of view was put forward by Hepple. Looking at the two Directives referring to information being provided in 'good time' and, at collective redundancies provisions when United Kingdom law required for the information to be disclosed 'at the earliest opportunity', he considered that the TUPE obligation should be interpreted as meaning 'as soon as the transferor and transferee have formed a definite intention to transfer, whether or not measures are envisaged'.[65]

Consultation

Having given the specified information, the second step for the employer consists in consulting appropriate representatives if he envisages taking measures in relation to the transfer.[66] Consequently, if no measures are taken,

63 Hepple *supra* n.47.

64 [1987] 3 CMLR 35 at [9]; (1987) IRLR 373.

65 Supra n.47.

66 Regulation 10(5).

consultation is not an obligation.[67] Similarly, it was considered that consultation is not required for the two other categories of information.[68]

The process of consultation is thus triggered when the transferor and/or transferee envisage they will take measures in connection with the transfer. This provision is defined neither by the Regulations nor by the Directive. Millett J in *IPCS v Secretary of State for Defence* construed this provision in the context of the Dockyard Services Act 1986, and considered that 'measures is a word of the widest import, and includes any action, step or arrangement'.[69] This rather general statement does not specify what in practice may be considered as being 'measures'. These could include any changes in the working environment or practices, such as pensions, modified disciplinary procedures or policy for mobility or promotion, or potential reduction of the workforce -in which case the collective redundancies provisions would apply in addition to the ones provided in TUPE. Considering such a 'wide' concept, any transfer would almost certainly entail changes which would constitute 'measures', whenever in a context of or in situations of contracting out where the advantages or security found in the public sector would not necessarily be afforded by private contractors.[70]

Once it is acknowledged that whatever constitutes 'measures' are envisaged, the process of consultation can begin. Under Regulation 10(6), it is for the employer concerned to consider any representation made by the workers' representatives, to reply to these representations, and if he rejects any of them, state his reasons. The scope of the duty to consult was thus originally defined in TUPE. The obligation enacted in the Directive was, however, somehow wider since according to Article 6(2), the employer should consult on the measures envisaged 'with a view to seeking an agreement'. This provision did not appear in the United Kingdom transposing instrument and there was therefore a discrepancy between the two pieces of legislation. This was one of the heads under which the European Commission threatened infringements proceedings against the United Kingdom for non-compliance

[67] As stated by an unreported industrial tribunal case *NATTKE v Rank Leisure Ltd* COIT 1388/134 discussed in Bowers J. *Transfer of Undertakings Regulations: the Unresolved Problems* (1984) New Law Journal at 209-210. This was also confirmed by Millett J in *Institution of Professional Civil Servants and others v Secretary of State for Defence* [1987] 3 CMLR 35 at [13].

[68] Ibid. See also McMullen J. *Business Transfers and Employee Rights,* Butterworths 1992 (2nd Edition) at 248.

[69] *Institution of Professional Civil Servants and others v Secretary of State for Defence* [1987] 3 CMLR 35 at [12]; (1987) IRLR 373.

[70] This might particularly be the case in terms of pensions. See previous chapter by Bailey C.

with the Directive.[71] In order to rectify this deficiency, the United Kingdom Government added to regulation 10(5) via TURERA 1993 s.33 that consultation should take place with a view to reaching an agreement. This amendment should provide for a more meaningful process of consultation, given that the employer would have to demonstrate a genuine attempt to discuss the measures and their consequences and to take into consideration the representations made by the appropriate representatives in order to reach an agreement. However, in the context of the Collective Redundancies Directive, the European Court of Justice considered that consultation 'with a view to seeking an agreement' is not an obligation with regard to results.[71a]

As to the time when consultation must begin, the Regulations are silent. This might appear as an oddity considering that the provision found in the Directive reads: '[the employer] shall consult... in *good time* on such measures with a view to seeking an agreement'.[72] One could have expected that when the United Kingdom Government rectified the aforementioned discrepancy, it would have reproduced the whole sentence of the Directive, and not only a part of it. According to Hepple,[73] the moment at which consultation should start must therefore be interpreted in the light of the provision found in the Directive. The question remains as to what does *in good time* mean. One can assume that considering that the Regulations enact that information should be provided long enough before the transfer so that consultation can take place and considering that the employer is under a duty to consider representations made by the workers' representatives and reply to them, a rather long period should be given. This was not necessarily the opinion of Millett J in the *IPCS* case. He considered that measures could be altered and envisaged at a rather late stage, but a company could not be blamed for then consulting at such a later stage when it is for reasons beyond its control. He consequently concluded

71 Which eventually took place, see *Commission v United Kingdom* Cases C-382/92 and C-383/92 [1994] IRLR 392 (for Transfer of Undertakings), 412 (for Collective Redundancies). The proceedings were brought against the United Kingdom for non-compliance with both the Acquired Rights Directive and the Collective Redundancies Directive because of several discrepancies arising between the two Directives and the two national provisions. Most of the deficiencies were dealt with by TURERA 1993, amending the existing provisions to be in conformity with the European obligations. The only issue which was not resolved and which constituted an infringement for both Directives related to the designation of employees' representatives. See Davies P. *A Challenge to the Single Channel* (1994) 23 ILJ 272; and O'Hara J. *Community Law and British Industrial Relations* 1996. Institute of Employment Rights. Chapter 3.

71a Case 284/83 *Dansk Metalarbej der forbund and Specialarbej der forbundet i Denmark v H. Nielsen and Son, Meskinfebrik A/S* [1985] ECR 553 in Comission Memorandum on Acquired Rights of Workers in Cases of Transfers of Undertakings, COM(97) 85.

72 Article 6(2). The new Article 6(2) has replaced the word 'seeking' by 'reaching' in line with the terminology of the Collective Redundancies Directive.

73 *Supra* n.47.

that consultation should take place: 'as soon as measures are envisaged and if possible long enough before the transfer', and not: 'as soon as measures are envisaged and in any event long before the transfer'.[74]

In order to assess when consultation should begin in order to be meaningful, some insight is needed into the nature of such consultation. According to the Regulations, an employer must consult when he *envisages* that he *will* be taking measures.[75] The use of such a word as 'envisage' could have given the idea that consultation would take place at a formative stage. However, Millett J in the *IPCS* case gave a rather narrower definition of those terms and considered that:

> 'In my view, it is not enough that there should be some possibility in contemplation; the company must have formulated some definite plan or proposal which it has in mind to implement...'[76]

Defining the timing and nature of the duty to consult in such a narrow way limits the potential role and intervention of the workers' representatives. Clearly they have no say in the decision concerning whether the transfer should take place at all, as reminded by the judge:

> 'Parliament can hardly have intended to compel the employer in the private sector to consult the unions on the desirability of the transfer itself or the sufficiency of the reasons for it. These are matters of business policy for the transferring employer to decide, and the unions cannot expect to participate in the decision.'[77]

Further, their sole role seems to be confined to help with the implementations of measures already decided by the employer. This interpretation seems to be difficult to reconcile with the word 'envisage' which was directly reproduced from the Directive. By contrast, the Collective Redundancies Directive requires the employer to consult workers' representatives when he 'contemplates'

[74] *Institution of Professional Civil Servants and others v Secretary of State for Defence* [1987] 3 CMLR 35 at [11]; (1987) IRLR 373.

[75] Regulation 10(5).

[76] *Institution of Professional Civil Servants and others v Secretary of State for Defence* [1987] 3 CMLR 35 at [12]; (1987) IRLR 373.

[77] Ibid. at [13].

[78] Article 2(1) of Council Directive of 17 February 1975 on the Approximation of the Laws of the Member States relating to Collective Redundancies (75/129/EEC) [OJ 1975, No L48/29] as amended by Council Directive of 24 June 1992 (92/56/EEC) [OJ 1992, L245/3] and consolidated by Council Directive 98/59/EC of 20 July 1998 [1998] OJ L225116.

collective dismissals.[78] Consequently, consultation seems to be sought at a much earlier or formative stage, in other words, before the employer has formed any definite views on the need for redundancies. This is confirmed by the content of the consultation process given that according to Article 2(2), it should cover 'ways and means of *avoiding collective redundancies* or reducing the number of workers affected, and of mitigating the consequences by recourse to accompanying social measures aimed, inter alia, at aid for redeploying retaining workers made redundant'. Nevertheless, the equivalent duty reproduced in the United Kingdom domestic law refers to consultation when redundancies are *proposed*, and originally did not transpose Article 2(2) of the Directive. The question which arises is whether such a wording reduces the scope of the obligation, given that 'proposing' could be interpreted as meaning that the employer has already made a decision as to the occurrence of the redundancies. Thus the consultation would take place at a later stage and ultimately, there was a potential discrepancy between United Kingdom law and the Directive depending upon how 'proposing' was construed. English courts were asked to answer that question. Before turning to the position of the courts, it has to be noted that TURERA 1993 amended the provisions on Collective Redundancies. Before 1993, the obligation to consult for the employer consisted of considering any representation made by the representatives, and reply to those representations and if he rejected any of them, state his reasons.[79] Here again the European Commission threatened to take actions deeming that this provision was a poor transposition of the European obligation. TURERA consequently altered the Act and widened the scope of the obligation to consult since the new TULR(C)A 1992 s.188(2) reads:

> 'The consultation shall include consultation about ways of-
> a) avoiding the dismissals,
> b) reducing the number of employees to be dismissed, and
> c) mitigating the consequences of the dismissals,
> and shall be undertaken by the employer with a view to reaching agreement with the appropriate representatives'.

Nevertheless, the word 'proposed' remained. When the courts had to interpret this term in the light of the Directive's wording, they remained rather shy until the famous Divisional Court case of *R v British Coal Corpn and Secretary of State for Trade, ex p Vardy*[80] where it was found that the duty to consult in the Directive was wider than the one under United Kingdom law. According to Glidewell LJ:

79 TULR(C)A 1992 s.188(6).

80 [1993] IRLR 104. Case decided before the amendments made by TURERA 1993.

> 'The verb 'proposes' in its ordinary usage relates to a state of mind which is much more certain and further along the decision-making process than the verb 'contemplate'; in other words, the directive envisages consultation at an early stage, when the employer is first envisaging the possibility that he may have to make employees redundant. Section 188 applies when he has decided that, whether because he has had to close a plant or for some other reason, it is his intention, however reluctant to make employees redundant.

This interpretation was, however, not accepted by Blackburne J. in the subsequent case of *Griffin v South West Water Services Ltd*[81] and the question thus remains open.

Returning to the issue of determining the timing of consultation, another feature differentiates the collective redundancies provisions from the transfer of undertakings regulations. TULR(C)A provides for a time-scale within which to consult the appropriate representatives. The employer should consult at least 30 days before the first dismissal takes effect or 90 days when 100 or more employees are planned to be dismissed.[82] Such provisions do not exist for a transfer of undertaking situation. This might be explained by the relative speed at which such decision can be made.

In conclusion, the process of consultation provided for by the transfer of undertakings regulations appears weak and ill-fitted to such situation. Indeed, when one imagines that practically most of the measures which are likely to be taken will be at the transferee level, and that it will be the transferor's task to consult and discuss these measures with his employees' representatives, one can only wonder how efficient such a process can be.[83] The terms and conditions of transferring employees are protected as a matter of public policy, according to the ECJ in *Daddy's Dance Hall*.[83a] In that case the Court held that the transferee can agree changes with the representatives of his workforce to the same extent as the transferor, provided that the transfer itself is not the reason for the changes. It follows, as Lord Slynn held in a significant *obiter dicta* in the *Wilson*[83b] case, that a transferee can only reach agreement on

81 [1995] IRLR 15, and for comments see Eady J *Collective Dismissals, Consultation and Remedies. Griffen* v *South West Water Services Ltd* (1994) 24 ILJ 350.

82 TULR(C)A 1992 s.188(1A).

83 See Hepple B. *The Transfer of Undertakings (Protection of Employment) Regulations* (1982) 11 ILJ at 38.

83a Case C-324/86, [1988] ECR 739, [1989] 2CMLR 517, [1988] IRLR 315.

83b [1998] IRLR 706.

changes which are for non-transfer reasons, i.e. operational reasons of an economic, technical or organisational character. Thus even though the transferor or transferee consults with the representatives of the workforce with a view to seeking agreement on any measures which it may be proposed to take in relation to the affected workforce, such an agreement will only be valid if the measures taken are not by reason of the transfer, whether or not they are, on balance, beneficial to the employees. Such a result is disappointing considering the maybe more elaborate and more meaningful mechanisms existing in the event of collective redundancies. This lack of effectiveness is unfortunately confirmed by the nature of remedies available where the requirements to inform and consult are not fulfilled. Before considering such sanctions, a brief comment should be made with regard to 'workers'' or 'employees' representatives'.

Who is to be informed and consulted?

According to TUPE, the employer should inform and consult 'appropriate representatives'. This formula was introduced by the 1995 Statutory Instrument which amended the existing legislation for transfer of undertakings and collective redundancies situations.[84] This new instrument was the response by the United Kingdom government to the 1994 ECJ judgement condemning the United Kingdom for not having adequately implemented the two Directives[85] with respect to employees' representatives. According to the two Directives, workers' representatives meant the workers' representatives provided for by the laws or practices of the Member States.[86] In the United Kingdom, trade unions were the only channel available to represent employees, and both the United Kingdom instruments implementing the Directives referred to recognised trade unions to be informed and consulted in such situations. However, they could only be informed and/or consulted when they were recognised by the employer. Such recognition was not automatic and indeed left to the discretion of the employer, who could even 'de-recognise' a union without any justification.[86a] The result was a gap in the legislation, given that there would be no information or

[84] Collective Redundancies and Transfer of Undertakings (Protection of Employment) (Amendment) Regulations 1995, SI 1995/2587.

[85] *Commission* v *United Kingdom* Cases C-382/92 and C-383/92 [1994] IRLR 392 (for Transfer of Undertakings), 412 (for Collective Redundancies).

[86] Article 1(b) of the Collective Redundancies Directive and Article 2(c) of the Acquired Rights Directive.

[86a] This situation should be changed by following Fairness at Work and the adoption of the Employment Relations Bill - first section on trade unions.

consultation process taking place in workplaces where trade unions were not recognised, thus effectively allowing employers to evade their obligations. Such lacuna in the United Kingdom domestic law constituted the main ground for the infringements proceedings initiated by the European Commission. In order to put an end to this declared breach of Community Law, the Government amended TUPE and TULR(C)A via the 1995 Statutory Instrument. Subsequently, the duty imposed upon employers is to inform and consult 'appropriate representatives' who are defined as either recognised trade unions or existing elected representatives whom it is appropriate to inform and consult in the circumstances, or specifically elected employees' representatives.[87] The employer is left with a choice to consult one or the other category, even where unions are recognised, thus putting even further in danger the traditional channel of workers' representation.[88] Furthermore, the statutory instrument introducing these changes does not give any indications as to how the employees' representatives should be elected. The new regulations were generally criticised for failing to ensure that employees were properly represented. A few trade unions subsequently challenged, unsuccessfully, the 1995 instrument through judicial review proceedings.[89] Such complex and uncertain situation might change, as the current Labour government issued in February 1998 a consultative document on employees' information and consultation rights on transfers of undertakings and collective redundancies, aimed at reforming the 1995 statutory instrument on several accounts.[90] The bulk of the proposed changes relates to employees' representatives. First, the rights of recognised trade unions are safeguarded in so far as it would be their representatives who would have to be consulted in the two situations envisaged if they are already recognised, thus not leaving a choice to the employer.[91] Second, if no trade union is recognised, representatives will have to be elected. However, such elected employees will have to be both independent and capable, whilst clarification and precision are provided with regard to how elections should be conducted.[92] The mention of capable and *independent* representatives might be linked to the 1997

[87] TUPE Regulation 10 (2A).

[88] See Davies P. *A Challenge to the Single Channel* (1994) 23 ILJ 272; and O'Hara J. *Community Law and British Industrial Relations* 1996. Institute of Employment Rights. Chapter 3.

[89] *R v Secretary of State for Trade and Industry ex parte UNISON* (1996) IRLR 438 (Divisional Court). See for an account of this decision Skidmore P. *Worker Rights – A Euro litigation Strategy?* (1996) 25 ILJ at 225.

[90] Employees' information and consultation rights on transfers of undertakings and collective redundancies. Public consultation. Department of Trade and Industry. Employment Relations Directorate. February 1998. URN 97/988.

[91] Ibid, paragraph 19.

[92] Ibid, paragraph 26.

proposals for an amended Acquired Rights Directive,[93] in so far as the text included an additional article in the section dealing with information and consultation.

According to the proposed Article 6A,

> 'For the purposes of the information and consultation requirements laid down in this Directive, the Member States shall provide for employee representatives who enjoy the *necessary independence* to carry out the function assigned to them.'

However, this provision was not incorporated in the new revised Directive.

Finally, should a dispute arise in this context, the burden will be on the employer to prove that representatives are independent and capable, and that the election conditions were met.[94]

FAILURE TO INFORM AND CONSULT

If an employer fails to inform and/or consult the appropriate representatives, he can escape any sanctions by putting forward a special defence available in the Regulations. If this defence is not successful, or if such a defence is not available to him, meagre remedies can be obtained by the workers' representatives through an action before an industrial tribunal.

THE SPECIAL DEFENCE

According to Regulation 10(7), an employer is excused from the duty to inform and consult if there are *special circumstances*. The employer can use this defence only if he proves first that there were 'special circumstances which rendered it not reasonably practicable' for him to perform the duty, and second, that 'he took all such steps towards its performance as were reasonably practicable in those circumstances'.[95] The burden of proof rests upon the employer. Such a defence was 'created' by the United Kingdom government since there is no equivalent in the Directive. Consequently, the consensus amongst commentators[96] and in courts appears to be that such provision should be interpreted narrowly. According to McMullen:

93 COM (97), 60 final 24th February 1997. OJ No C124, 21/04/1997, p.48.

94 *Supra* 90 paragraph 23 and 26.

95 Regulation 11(2).

96 See Hepple *supra* L83 and McMullen *supra* C68.

> 'The purposive approach to the Transfer Regulations... should require the courts to treat the defence with some circumspection as it clearly diminishes the rights envisaged by the Directive.'[97]

The courts did indeed take the same view, as evidenced by the case-law in the context of collective redundancies where the same defence is available to employers.[98] Considering first the meaning of 'special circumstances', the courts found that it would be a question of facts to be scrutinised in each case in order to determine whether such circumstances were present. However, it was established that for an employer to successfully show that there were special circumstances, he would have to prove that he was constrained by some event or occurrence beyond, or substantially beyond his control. This event must be unforeseen or unexpected.[99] Thus, it was held that insolvency does not constitute in itself special circumstances. If unforeseeable events lead to insolvency, it could constitute special circumstances, while if it is the result of a gradual run-down which was expected, the employer could not rely on it as a defence.[100]

Returning to the specific context of transfer, one might wonder what could constitute 'special circumstances'. Speed or urgency to transfer an undertaking or part of an undertaking seems to have been accepted as a valid defence in *NATTKE v Rank Leisure Ltd,*[101] which was the first case to be brought before a tribunal for failure to consult. In this instance, a cinema was sold within a few days upon the insistence of the buyer who wanted to show a film that had just won a prize at a festival, and the tribunal found that the need for speed for the take-over was a 'special circumstance'.

Another potential defence which could be put forward by an employer, according to McMullen,[102] is secrecy. In a context of information disclosed to employees by the employer, it is not unusual to see the issue of confidentiality being raised.[103] Consequently, an employer might attempt to argue that due to the secrecy surrounding the transaction he could not reasonably inform

97 Ibid. McMullen at 246.

98 TULR(C)A s.188(7) and s.189(6).

99 *Clarks of Hove Ltd v Bakers' Union* [1978] ICR 1076, [1978] IRLR 366, CA.

100 Ibid.

101 Unreported decision COIT 1388/134. This case is commented by Bowers J. *Transfer of Undertakings Regulations: the Unresolved Problems* (1984) 134 NLJ at 209-210.

102 *Supra* N68 at 245.

103 See the defence available to employers for disclosure of information for collective bargaining purposes, *supra* n35 and in the European Works Council Directive (Council Directive 94/45/EC of 22 September 1994) on the establishment of a European Works Council or a procedure in Community-scale undertakings and Community-scale groups of undertakings for the purpose of informing and consulting employees. OJ L254/64) Article 8. *Infra.*

the workers' representatives. Nevertheless, the judge, in the *IPCS*[104] case, appears reluctant to accept such an argument. The transferee could not pass the information to the transferor 'under cover of commercial confidentiality', given that it would effectively amount to a breach of the duty to inform.

Even where the employer can prove that 'special circumstances' occurred, he has to establish that he did all he could, as far as was reasonably practicable in those circumstances, to perform his duty. Depending upon the circumstances, this could spread from doing nothing to attempting to inform and consult at a very short time before the transfer occurs. This will clearly be a matter for the courts to decide in the view of the facts of each individual case. The judge in *NATTKE*[105] did accept that the 'special circumstances' were present but found that the employer had not taken the reasonable steps to comply. He sent the information to the workers' representative two days after the sale agreement, knowing that completion of the transfer took place five days after such agreement. Consequently, the information was received two days after the transfer had taken place. It was suggested that to have taken reasonable practical steps towards compliance, the employer could have given or delivered the information to the workers' representative, as opposed to sending it by post.[106]

Finally, the transferor cannot be excused if he relies on the argument that it was not reasonably practicable for him to perform his duty because the transferee did not provide him with the relevant information. However, he can issue a notice to the transferee that he will establish that he was not given the adequate information in court and such notice makes the transferee party to the proceedings.[107] As a result, he might be ordered to pay the compensation awarded by the tribunal to the employees transferred if it is proved that he was responsible for the non-compliance with the Regulations.[108]

The existence of the 'special circumstances' defence in the Regulations does not seem at first to be in line with the spirit of the Directive, given that it is yet another tool available to employers to reduce the scope of an obligation already weak. The courts, fortunately, have construed this provision as narrowly as possible, and it has proved difficult for the employers to rely upon this defence. This is not, however, supplemented by deterrent sanctions in the event of failure to perform the duty to inform and consult.

104 *Institution of Professional Civil Servants and others v Secretary of State for Defence* [1987] 3 CMLR 35 at [11]; (1987) IRLR 373.

105 COIT 1388/134. See Bowers J. *Transfer of Undertakings Regulations: the Unresolved Problems* (1984) 134 NLJ at 209-210.

106 Ibid. at 210.

107 Regulation 11(3).

108 Regulation 11(4).

Remedies

In the event of a failure to inform and/or consult, the first step consists for the appropriate representatives in seeking a declaration, and possibly compensation, through a complaint before an industrial tribunal. If an award is made by the tribunal in this first instance, and the employer fails to pay the compensation, the second step must be taken by the aggrieved employee who would seek an order for payment. An appeal on a point of law is possible before the EAT.[109]

As to the first step, the workers' representatives must bring an action before an industrial tribunal within three months of the date on which the transfer was completed.[110] Nevertheless, this time limit is not strictly defined, given that first the Regulation itself allows the industrial tribunal a certain discretion to extend this period when it is proved that it was not practically reasonable to present the complaint within the three months.[111] Second, it was established that not only the complaint can be brought before the transfer takes place[112], but also if it does not occur at all.[113]

If it is demonstrated that there has been a breach of the relevant duty, the industrial tribunal must make a declaration to this effect, and order the relevant employer to pay 'appropriate compensation' to the employees affected.[114] Such an award cannot exceed four weeks' pay and the amount is determined by the tribunal considering what is just and equitable in the light of the seriousness of the employer's failure to comply with his duty.[115] The maximum of four weeks' pay was introduced by TURERA 1993, once again as a consequence of the threat of infringement proceedings by the European Commission against the United Kingdom Government. Before this amendment, the award could only amount to a maximum of two weeks' pay, and additionally the award could be reduced under certain circumstances to avoid cumulative awards.[116] The Directive is silent on the issue of remedy

[109] Regulation 11(10).

[110] Regulation 11(8)(a).

[111] Ibid.

[112] *BIFU v Barclays Bank plc* [1987] ICR 495; *South Durham Health Authority v UNISON* [1995] ICR 495; (1995) IRLR 507 (EAT).

[113] *BIFU v Barclays Bank plc* [1987] ICR 495.

[114] Regulation 11(4). The relevant employer is generally the transferor, but it could also be the transferee if he fails to give the necessary information to the transferor.

[115] Regulation 11(11).

[116] Under the old Regulations, there was a set-off system of any amount received for breach of contract or money payable under Collective Redundancies. See McMullen, *supra* N.68 at 249.

available to the workers' representatives for non-compliance with its provisions. However, as a matter of Community law, it is well established that 'when a Community regulation does not provide any specific penalty in case of breach, ... the Member States retain a discretion as to the choice of sanctions'.[117] This choice is not a 'carte blanche' for the Member States, given that they must respect the obligation laid down in Article 5 of the EC Treaty according to which the penalty must be 'effective, proportionate and dissuasive'.[118] The United Kingdom Government was reminded of such an obligation, since it was considered at European level that the remedies provided by the United Kingdom legislation in the event of failure to inform and consult when a transfer takes place were insufficiently deterrent and effective,[119] and consequently, the Regulations did not comply with the requirements of Article 5 of the Treaty.

As a result, TURERA 1993 amended the Regulations, increasing the maximum from two to four weeks' pay, and abolished the system whereby deductions could be made to the protective award.

Nevertheless, one might wonder whether the comment made by Hepple in 1982 that 'the sanctions for breach are derisory'[120] is still valid, and more specifically whether the amended version of the Regulations comply with the Community obligation under Article 5 of the Treaty. By comparison, if one looks at the penalties imposed for failure to inform and consult in the event of collective redundancies, the remedies available are also financial compensation,[121] but the maximum for the award is 90 days when 100 or more employees are made redundant or 30 days when the number of employees is less than 100. The current government is proposing in its recent consultative document to scrap this discrepancy and to simplify the present provisions. If there was a breach of the duty to inform and consult, an industrial tribunal could award up to ninety days' pay to each employee in the affected workforce, whether that breach arises in the event of transfer of undertakings or collective redundancies, whether there are fewer than 100 redundancies

117 Case C7-90 Vandevenne and others [1991] ECR I-4371, as quoted in the opinion of Advocate General Van Gerven in case C382/92 and C383/92 *Commission v United Kingdom* [1994] ECR I-2345 and [1994] ECR I-2479.

118 The first case in which the court raised the issue of effective penalties was *Sabine Von Colson and Elizabeth Kamann v Land Nordrhein-Westfalen* [1984] ECR 1891.

119 See *Commission v United Kingdom* [1994] ECR I-2345 paras 52-59.

120 Hepple B. *The Transfer of Undertakings (Protection of Employment) Regulations* (1982) 11 ILJ at 38.

121 TULR(C)A 1992 s.189(2).

or more.[122] According to the government, this proposed remedy would be appropriate and in line with the European requirements.

In this context, we have seen that, according to European Law, the remedy must be effective, proportionate and *dissuasive*. Currently, one could wonder whether a *maximum* of four weeks' pay, or even ninety days, falls within this description when the English courts have found that such a remedy is a compensation to employees and *not* a penal remedy, in other words it must not constitute a punishment to employers who did not comply with their duties.[123] One could generally consider that financial remedies do not constitute a dissuasive or deterrent sanction in such cases. When considering that consultation should take place with a view to reaching an agreement, it has been stated that 'the absence of a pre-emptive remedy … is a major flaw'.[124] Alternative remedies were envisaged in the event of collective redundancies. At European level, the first draft of the Collective Redundancies Directive put forward the idea that, should the duty to inform and consult not be complied with, the whole procedure would be null and void. This proposal did not appear in the final draft. At United Kingdom level, the question was raised whether an injunction could be used as a remedy when the employer breaches his obligation, thus forcing him to inform and consult, but the court rejected this idea due to the difficulties to police the injunction.[125] Finally, as far as the 1997 proposal for amendment of the Acquired Rights Directive was concerned,[126] a new Article 7a requires expressly that 'Member States shall take the necessary measures to ensure that the sanctions in the event of failure to comply with the national provisions adopted under this Directive… are enforced', and that 'the sanctions shall be effective, proportionate and dissuasive'. The 1998 Directive retained this spirit but watered down the provision, since Article 7a now states:

> 'Member States shall introduce into their national legal systems such measures as are necessary to enable all employees who consider themselves wronged by failure to comply with the obligations arising from this Directive to pursue their claims by

[122] Employees' information and consultation rights on transfers of undertakings and collective redundancies. Public consultation. Department of Trade and Industry. Employment Relations Directorate. February 1998. URN 97/988. Paragraph 34.

[123] See *NATTKE v Rank Leisure Ltd.* COIT 1388/134. This case was decided before the amendments made by TURERA 1993.

[124] Cavalier S. *Transfer rights: TUPE in Perspective,* Institute of Employment Rights. December 1997.

[125] See *Griffen v South Water Services Ltd.* commented in Eady J. *Collective Dismissals, Consultation and Remedies* (1994) 23 ILJ 350.

[126] COM (97), 60 final 24th February 1997. OJ No C124, 21/04/1997, p.48.

judicial process after possible recourse to other competent authorities'[126a]

As a result, one can doubt whether the remedy available in the event of transfer is adequate, even if the financial penalty was increased, and might be further adjusted.

Where an industrial tribunal takes the view that compensation should be awarded which is not always the case, even if there has been a breach of the obligation,[127] and the employer fails to pay the protective award, a second action can be brought before the industrial tribunal, but this time, by the individual employee or employees who have not been paid. This complaint should be made within three months of the original tribunal's order.[128]

Scrutinising the duty to inform and consult in the context of transfer of undertakings seems to lead to the conclusion that it remains a weak obligation despite the improvements made by TURERA 1993 to the original text adopted by the Conservatives in 1981, given that such changes were included under pressure of the European Commission or as a result of the European Court ruling. As noted, the remedies available in the event of failure to inform and consult are weak, but the nature of the consultation process shares the same characteristic. Such an obligation is only a pale shadow of what is required in the context of collective redundancies. First, while the consultation process is the primary obligation imposed upon the employer or the primary right for the employees in the Collective Redundancies Directive, it constitutes *one* of the protected rights in the Acquired Rights Directive. Second, consultation takes place at a formative stage and the primary purpose is to avoid the dismissals. In a transfer situation, the process is triggered when measures which will affect employees are envisaged. There is no consultation as to whether the transfer should take place at all since it is considered that such a decision remains within the ambit of the managerial prerogative.[129] The process of consultation did improve in the United Kingdom when the requirement to consult 'with a view to reaching an agreement' was added, since there must be a genuine attempt to take into consideration the

126a Council Directive 98/50/EC of 29 June 1998 amending Directive 77/187/EFC on the approximation of the laws of the Member States relating to the safeguarding of employees' rights in the event of transfers of undertakings, businesses or parts of business [1998[OJ L 201/88.

127 See *NATTKE v Rank Leisure Ltd.* COIT 1388/134, where the tribunal found that a declaration was here sufficient considering that there had been a default to inform and consult, but consultation was not required since there was no measures envisaged on the part of the employer.

128 Regulation 11(5) and 11(8).

129 See Millett J in *Institution of Professional Civil Servants and others v Secretary of State for Defence* [1987] 3 CMLR 35 at [13], *supra*.

representation of the workers and to negotiate, but the aim is to implement as smoothly as possible a *fait accompli*.

However, the difference in the regime and nature of consultation could be explained by the inherent purpose of the two regulations, in other words what is at stake when a collective redundancy occurs or when a transfer takes place. The obligations found in these two regulations are imposed where the situations of the employees are threatened. In one case, the employee could find himself without work, whereas in the case of transfer, this should not happen because the employee's contract of employment is transferred to the new employer, and thus his employment should be protected.[130] Therefore, the issue at stake is somehow less vital, at least in the short-term, for the employees affected by the transfer. If one of the measures envisaged by the transferee is to dismiss part of the workforce because he could not take on all the employees, then the collective redundancies provisions would apply.

One could nonetheless argue that for the kind of decisions made by management concerning a transfer or restructuring in general, employees' representatives should be allowed to express their views since such decisions are bound to affect their interests. In a context of fundamental changes in the labour market and of increased competitiveness something more might be required than an ad hoc system of information and consultation when such fundamental events occur. This has been the view for more than 20 years at Community level where there have been attempts to promote participation of employees at board level or a general system of information and consultation, mainly through works councils. These ideas have been revived recently as concerns are growing about the need for a stronger Social Europe in the context of an economy driven by market forces. The weakest of these two forms of participation has already met some success through the European Works Council Directive while other ideas are flourishing at European level. Such concepts are foreign to the United Kingdom system, but one could reasonably hope that these developments would have some impact on the United Kingdom system of industrial relations.

A STEP FURTHER: PARTICIPATION OF EMPLOYEES IN THE GENERAL CONTEXT OF RESTRUCTURING

The first success at European level to generalise information and consultation was realised by the European Works Council Directive.[131] It was adopted in

[130] See TUPE Regulation 5 for the transfer of the contract of employment from the transferor to the transferee and Regulation 8 providing that an employee cannot be dismissed by reason of a transfer.

[131] Directive on the establishment of a European Works Council or a procedure in Community-scale undertakings or Community-scale groups of undertakings for the purpose of informing and consulting employees. 94/45/EC, 1994 O.J (L254/64) 30.09.1994.

September 1994 and gave two years to Member States to implement it into their national law. This instrument provides that large multinational enterprises operating in more than one European country have to introduce a new body at European level: a 'European Works Council',[132] or at least a procedure for the purpose of informing and consulting employees. This new body is intended to constitute an information-sharing and consultation forum for management and employees. Therefore, the purpose of the Directive is for employees of complex-structured undertakings to gather and form an organised group to which management, dealing frequently with transnational operations such as mergers or take-overs for example, will have to report. This European legislation was the first product of the Protocol and Agreement on Social Policy of the Maastricht Treaty. As a result it applies to all European Union Member States and by extension to the Member States of the European Economic Area with the exception of the United Kingdom, due to its so-called 'opt-out'. The direct consequences of such a situation is first, that the United Kingdom does not have to implement the Directive into its domestic law. Second, in terms of companies affected by this new obligation, the Directive applies to Community-scale undertakings and Community-scale groups of undertakings. They are defined in Article 2 of the Directive as being undertakings that employ at least 1,000 employees on the territory of the Member States and at least 150 employees in each of at least two Member States. The UK 'opt-out' consequently means that Community-scale undertakings or groups of undertakings do not have to take into account their United Kingdom workforce when determining the number of employees in the Member States, as the United Kingdom does not belong to the club of Member States for the purpose of this particular Directive.

However, United Kingdom companies are not left untouched by this Directive. The second aspect of innovation of this instrument is its transnational effect. In other words if United Kingdom-owned companies employ enough workers on the Continent i.e. on the territory of the Member States as defined in the Directive to meet the threshold indicated in the Directive,[133] they have to establish this new forum.[134] As to United Kingdom subsidiaries or branches of Community-scale undertakings headquartered in another Member State, technically they should not be counted in the total workforce and consequently

132 Thereafter referred as to EWC.

133 See Article 2 of the Directive.

134 For an account of the problems caused by such mechanism, see Lorber P. *An Attempt to Assess the Curious Impact of European Works Council Directive on the United Kingdom System of Industrial Relation and Labour Law,* Jagiell. U.Yearbook L.L.S.P, (9), Cracow (1997) 95; and Neal A.C *United Kingdom Point of View,* in Blanpain R. and Hanami T. *European Works Council. The Implementation of the Directive in the Member States of the European Union,* Euro-Japan Institute for Law and Business. Peters 1995 at 306.

workers' representatives employed in such subsidiaries could not sit at the table of this new forum. However, the experience shows that this situation has not materialised and United Kingdom employees are treated as their European counterparts.[135]

Once it is established which companies are affected by the EWC Directive, such undertakings are given a certain amount of leeway to establish the new forum. The 'social partners' were encouraged to create it by agreement, thus being able to adapt this new structure to their own circumstances[136] in 'a spirit of co-operation'.[137] If however, no agreement is reached, or if the parties so decide, a mandatory Works Council is provided for in the Annex of the Directive.[138]

These 'subsidiary requirements' indicate what is expected from this new forum. The EWC should meet with the management once a year, to be informed and consulted on the progress and prospects of the business. The kind of subject matters upon which the EWC could be informed and consulted are listed in the Annex and include 'substantial changes... concerning transfers of production, mergers, cut-backs, or closure of undertakings' etc.[139] Furthermore, such meetings should similarly take place when a crisis or unusual situation occurs which would affect the workers' interests 'to a considerable extent'.[140] These 'exceptional circumstances' could include the sudden decision to transfer part of the undertaking. In this case, information and consultation should take place as soon as possible on the basis of a report drawn up by the management and on which an opinion might be delivered by the EWC.

At first, such a system appears as a clear improvement since the information and consultation process is organised on a regular basis and on a wide range of issues, probably entitling the workers' representatives to have a larger

135 This is rendered possible by Article 1(4) of the Directive which states that the EWC is to cover all the establishments located within the Member States unless a wider scope is provided for in the agreement creating the European Works Council. Furthermore, existing agreements have included their United Kingdom personnel. See Lorber P. ibid. at 103.

136 Article 6 of the Directive is the mechanism provided for establishing the EWC by agreement since September 1996. During the period of two years given to Member States for implementation between September 1994 and 1996 companies were given the opportunity to create an EWC by what amounted to a 'private opt-out'. According to Article 13, the provisions of the Directive would not apply to companies which have reached an agreement providing for transnational information and consultation with employees and covering the entire workforce. Thus, if an enterprise managed to negotiate such an agreement, fulfilling these two conditions, the Directive's obligation would not apply.

137 Article 9.

138 Article 7 indicates in what circumstances these 'subsidiary requirements' apply.

139 Paragraph 2 of the Annex.

140 Paragraph 3 of the Annex.

picture of the company's situation and to learn about the policy prospects. Such awareness might entitle them to express concerns at a much earlier stage and discuss alternatives with the management. But a closer scrutiny of the provisions shows that the nature of the process is even weaker compared to the one found in the Collective Redundancies and Acquired Rights Directives. The information is indeed wider, but consultation is defined as 'the exchange of views and establishments of dialogue between employees' representatives and central management'[141] . If one takes a sceptical view of this definition, consultation could amount to a simple dialogue where employees' representatives are listened to but not heard. This seems to be confirmed by the subsidiary requirements which even though providing for an emergency meeting with detailed provisions as to how consultation should take place, the final sentence states that '[t]his meeting shall not affect the prerogatives of the central management'.[142] Furthermore, there is no reference to consultation *with a view to reaching an agreement* in the EWC Directive in comparison to the requirements found in the Collective Redundancies and Acquired Rights Directive, thus weakening further the role of the European body.

Such weakness is demonstrated by the first case which put the EWC Directive to the test.[143] The French car manufacturer Renault announced without warning, in February 1997 -in the context of re-structuring- its decision to close down its Belgian factory in order to re-locate in Spain, thus leading to the potential collective dismissals of more than 3,000 employees. The management neither informed nor consulted its European Works Council of this decision and was thus in breach of the agreement establishing and laying down the powers of that body.[144] The EWC decided subsequently to take legal action to prevent management from acting on its decision. The competent French judge ruled in favour of the plaintiffs, finding that the EWC should have been informed and 'consulted' meaning given an opportunity to express their observations in a context of dialogue with management before the announcement of the decision to close down the

141 Article 2(1)(f).

142 *Supra* N140. This statement does thus confirms the view taken by Millett J. in *Institution of Professional Civil Servants and others v Secretary of State for Defence* [1987] 3 CMLR 35 at [13]. *Supra.*

143 Lorber P. *The Renault case: the European Works Council put to the test* (1997) 13 Int.J.Comp.L.L.I.R at 135.

144 Renault signed an agreement establishing its European Works Council with the relevant trade unions originally in May 1993, and this was renewed in May 1995 thus an Article 13 Agreement. The full text of this agreement can be found in Social Europe *Agreements on Information and Consultation in European Multinationals* Supplement 5-95 at 111.

factory. The judge also prescribed that the decision could not be made until the information and consultation process had taken place. This decision sent a clear message that such obligation should be taken seriously. Renault did subsequently inform and 'exchange views' with the EWC, but the final outcome remained the decision to close the factory.[145]

Other criticisms were raised with regard to the scope of the EWC Directive. First, the obligation to inform and consult a body composed of employees' representatives was limited to multinationals. Considering that workers are now entitled, through their representatives sitting in a new body, to receive information and express their views when they are employed by an undertaking within the threshold of the Directive, one could wonder if employees of smaller or non-international firms could not benefit from the same treatment. In most European Union countries, institutions, equivalent to national works councils, exist, and even if the powers of the employees' representatives within these differ from one state to another, the general aim is to provide for information and consultation. There are, however, exceptions as not all Member States, in particular the UK and Ireland, are familiar with such a concept. As a consequence of this lack of 'uniformity', but also by reaction to the Renault incident, and in the light of what is considered as a successful EWC Directive so far, in 1997 the European Commission put forward a proposal for information and consultation at national level to add to transnational information and consultation.[146] The objective is to ensure that workers' representatives would be informed and consulted at national level whenever a decision is made which is likely to affect their interests. The European Commission started by consulting the European Social Partners asking whether a case could be made for a coherent European framework with common principles and obligations for employee information and consultation in a national context. The response was somewhat mixed. Whilst the European Trade Union Congress was largely in favour of the initiative, the employers' organisation felt that this issue should be determined at national level, and there was no room for European intervention, especially as statutory and negotiated procedures were already in existence in most countries. Nevertheless, the Commission entered the second round of consultation, submitting to the social partners a proposal, and asking them whether they wished to enter negotiations on the basis of such draft, considering that should they decide not to start such negotiations, such draft would become a Directive.[147] Following the European Employers Association's refusal to

[145] EIRI July 1997 at 20.

[146] EIRI June 1997 at 9.

[147] European Works Councils Bulletin. Issue 12, November / December 1997 p.11 *National consultation rules: Commission presses on,* EIRI November 1997 at 10.

negotiate on this issue,[147a] the Commission promptly adopted a draft directive in November 1998.[147b] Two innovative aspects emerge from this proposal in terms of information and consultation. First, the notions of information and consultation are explained in greater details. The text emphasises the need for a meaningful and effective process of information and consultation in terms of timing, content and method.[147c] The proposal is also more prescriptive with regard to the type of information which should be communicated and to the subject matters on which consultation should take place.[147d]

Second, the idea that sanctions should be more effective and constitute a substantial deterrent in case of failure to inform and consult is clearly included in Article 7 entitled 'Protection of Rights'. In effect, not only does the proposal require Member States to provide for 'effective, proportionate and dissuasive' penalties 'in the event of infringement of the directive',[147e] it also provides that in case of a 'serious breach' by the employer of the information and consultation obligation, the employer's decision will be effectively null and void[147f]. This prescriptive provision which represents a positive step, is likely to be controversial in the light of these innovative aspects, some doubts have been expressed as to the likelihood of adoption of this proposal.[148]

The scope of the EWC Directive was secondly limited geographically, as the United Kingdom had 'opted-out' of this social provision. Thus, originally, UK employees were not to benefit from such European Works Councils and were deprived of the right to be informed and consulted. However, since December 1997, the UK has re-entered the club of the Member States for the purpose of the EWC Directive, thus re-adjusting the situation for the UK employees. Following its electoral manifesto, the Labour government, elected in May 1997, 'opted-in' what is referred as to the 'Social Chapter'. As a consequence, not only did the Government agree to be part of and participate in the future social provisions discussed at European level, it also confirmed that it will apply and implement the two Directives which were adopted under the Social Protocol and from which they were formerly excluded. One of these two Directives was the European Works Councils, whilst the other piece

[147a] EIRI November 1998 of 1.

[147b] Proposal for a Council Directive establishing a general framework for informing and consulting employees in the European Community COM (1998) 612 final (1999) OJ C 2/3.

[147c] Article 2 (1) (d) and (e).

[147d] Article 4(1).

[147e] Article 7(2).

[147f] Article 7(3).

[148] EWC Bulletin, Issue 19, January/February 1999 at 8 and EIRR 299, December 1998 at 13.

of legislation concerns Parental Leave.[149] Thus, on 15th December 1997, the European Union Council of Labour and Social Affairs Ministers gave final approval to a Directive applying the provisions of the existing European Works Councils to the UK, putting an end to the UK opt-out from its requirements. The UK have now two years to implement the provisions of the new Directive[150] which is the same period which was given to the other Member States in September 1994, and companies newly affected by this Directive will be able to use the same options to set up their European Works Councils, including the equivalent of Article 13 agreement.

It thus appears that if one wants to promote the idea of participation, in the sense of strengthening the process whereby the position of employees is more influential, the only form still available is the participation at board level. As indicated previously, the European Commission has never been successful on this territory, meeting constant criticisms either because the systems proposed rendered the national systems unattractive because they could then be seen as too rigid, or because other domestic systems were not familiar at all with the representation of employees at board level. Nevertheless, the European authorities never gave up and in November 1995, the Commission tried to re-launch the issue by reviewing the long-standing proposals in this field and by proposing new options, and seeking the opinion of the relevant other authorities.[151] This led to the commissioning of a group of experts to suggest ways of breaking the 20 year deadlock over the issue of worker participation in the management of companies. The emphasis was put on a new proposal for the European Company Statute,[152] and the experts advocated flexibility as opposed to imposing a set model of participation, an option which was also favoured in the EWC Directive. Thus, the Report encourages the social partners to seek an agreement on the best way to involve employees at management level, but in the event of failure to reach such an agreement, the new proposal would provide for a set of reference rules to apply.[153] Despite these new encouraging proposals, which have still not yet materialised, the new rules would only apply to companies which decide voluntarily to register as *Societa Europea,* thus opting out of national legal

[149] See European Works Councils Bulletin. Issue 11 September / October 1997 at 1 and Issue 12, November / December 1997 at 5: *EWCs 'extension' Directive to end UK opt-out.*

[150] Council Directive 97/74/EC of 15 December 1997 extending, to the United Kingdom of Great Britain and Northern Ireland, Directive 94/45/EC on the establishment of a European Works Council or a procedure in Community-scale undertakings and Community-scale groups of undertakings for the purposes of informing and consulting employees. OJ (L10/22) 16.1.98.

[151] Communication from the Commission on Workers' Information and Consultation, COM(95) 547 Final, Brussels, 14.11.1995 in (1996) Int.J.Comp.L.L.I.R. 176.

[152] *Supra* n.15.

[153] See the Davignon Report in EIRI June 1997 at 28.

systems and being regulated by Community law. One could then wonder how popular would these proposals be, and principally how United Kingdom undertakings would consider such a new system, coming from an environment where this form of worker participation does not exist at all.

These new initiatives clearly demonstrate that, at least at European level, some form of workers' involvement is considered fundamental in an economic environment that is quickly changing and which consequently considerably affects workers' interests. This topic has re-emerged on the agenda with a clear willingness to adopt new legislation. What remains unclear is how these new proposals will link up with the existing legislation and whether the governments of the Member States and social partners are ready to follow.

Conclusion. The United Kingdom and workers' participation: prospects

As we have seen, within the context of the United Kingdom industrial relations system, the general concept of workers' indirect or institutional participation is neither well known, nor wide spread. These characteristics make the United Kingdom stand in a rather unique position amongst the other Members States perhaps with the exception of Ireland. The difficulties in adapting to the systems promoted at European level through the Collective Redundancies and Transfer of Undertakings regulations have been evidenced by the resulting implementing legislation, which provides for relatively weak obligations to inform and consult imposed upon employers, despite the progressive improvements brought to the United Kingdom texts bearing in mind that they were adopted under pressure of the European institutions.

Consequently, the plethora of new European initiatives and proposals in the same direction of workers' participation do not seem suitable to the United Kingdom pattern, at first glance. Nevertheless, the EWC Directive seems to have been accepted positively by United Kingdom undertakings, and the general concept of leaving the social partners to deal with 'implementation' of these measures suits the general United Kingdom background and traditions.[154]

These ideas are of considerable importance in a context where, in all European countries, patterns of work have changed. The need for flexibility in the labour market has become the new credo and downsizing, outsourcing, subcontracting and restructuring bring new dimensions to the world of work. Within such

[154] In this context, it is of interest to note that the TUC found that United Kingdom companies have set up EWC agreements under Article 13 faster than any other European countries, since it appears that one in three companies affected have concluded such agreements, while in Germany the ratio was one in seven, and one in eight in France. See TUC News, 23rd September 1996.

environment, employees found themselves in a precarious situation and in order to avoid a social backlash,[155] because employees feel that they are paying the price of the market integration and the completion of the Monetary Union, a form of partnership should be developed between the workforce and management.

'The role of workers in decision making and the need to review and strengthen the existing arrangements for workers' involvement in their companies will also become essential issues'.[156]

When decisions are made at management level which affect the employees, they should be heard and given the opportunity to see their representations being taken into account, knowing that they can rely on effective sanctions if these obligations are not fully respected. Indeed, as Cavalier points out: 'A change of employer caused by a transfer or merger may be economically desirable, but the rights of employees cannot be sacrificed to economic considerations. Changes must be handled in a consensual manner'.[157]

After nearly 20 years of Conservative governments accompanied by fundamental changes in the labour market, even the United Kingdom system of industrial relations seems to have evolved towards the willingness to increase partnership at work.[158] This trend is certainly noticeable in terms of the increased *direct* participation[159] in United Kingdom undertakings. The promotion at European level of *indirect*, more sophisticated, workers' participation, combined with the willingness of the social partners in the United Kingdom to adapt to the new environment and a new Government more open to these European developments, might open the way to the establishment of a complementary institutionalised or centralised participation of workers in the United Kingdom. Such changes seem necessary and would certainly help to open the door to industrial democracy.

155 See the trade unions reactions triggered by the Renault case throughout Europe in EWC Report March and April 1997.

156 *Partnership for a new Organisation of Work,* EU Green Paper published in EIRI May 1997 at 26.

157 Cavalier S. *Transfer rights: TUPE in Perspective,* Institute of Employment Rights. December 1997. 49.

158 See the reactions of the trade unions and the employers towards the EWC Directive in Lorber P. *An Attempt to Assess the Curious Impact of European Works Council Directive on the United Kingdom System of Industrial Relation and Labour Law* Jagiell. U.Yearbook L.L.S.P, (9), Cracow (1997) 95; and the recent speech of the TUC General Secretary at the CBI conference on the issue of recognition in EIRI July, 1997 at 3.

159 *Supra.*

10. The Amendment of the Acquired Rights Directive

Dr Stephen Hardy

Following the agreement at the Brussels Summit in 1993 amongst the EU Member States to amend the Acquired Rights Directive (ARD) the EU Commission in September 1994 presented its proposals[1] to amend the existing Directive. This announcement gave rise to controversy, as evidenced in previous chapters, resulting in the European Parliament's (EP) rejection of the 1994 revisions and in another set of proposals[2] being put forward in 1997. Even then, many EU Member States had second thoughts about any future revision of the ARD, so that the political agreement reached in June 1998 was somewhat unexpected. In this chapter, we will seek to assess the effects of the final amended Directive,[3] as well as the views of the EU Member States governments towards a revised Directive and the impact which the amended ARD will have on the public sector.

The Proposed Revisions

In this era of EU social dialogue, any proposed or revised social legislation must receive some consultation amongst the EU social partners, which includes the Union des Confederations de l'Industrie et des Employeurs d'Europe (UNICE), Centre Europeen des Entreprises a Participation Publique (CEEP) and European Trade Union Confederation (ETUC). Such consultations about the revised ARD took place, but no agreement, other than the fact that the ARD needed revising, could be reached. It emerged that the main area of contention lay with contracting-out. Apart from the EU social partners, the other EU institutions have also been very active in analysing the EU

[1] COM(94) 300 Final.

[2] COM(97) 60 Final.

[3] Directive 77/187/EEC as amended by Directive 98/50/EC.

Commission's proposals. Such scrutiny has been so critical, that the EU Commission has been forced to review and redraft its amendments twice since 1994. Most notably, the EP on 13th November 1996 delivered its Opinion on the EU Commission's original 1994 proposed revised ARD.[4] Consequently, the EU Commissioner announced on 21st May 1997 at the Social Affairs Council his withdrawal of the revised ARD and presented a second draft revised ARD.[5] This version, drafted in March 1997, took a more radical approach, adopting all of the amendments raised in the EP's Opinion. The most major revisions proposed by the EP, and accepted by the EU Commission, were: the removal of the distinction in terms between the transfer of 'an economic entity' and 'an economic activity'; the introduction of joint liability; and the inclusion of insolvency proceedings under the ambit of the ARD, but subject to the exclusion of the rights in Articles 3 and 4 where the proceedings are aimed at the liquidation of the assets and in other circumstances giving EU Member States an option to derogate in respect of the rights contained in Articles 3 and 4.

Finally, in June 1998 agreement was reached at the Cardiff Council on an amended Directive. The British Government had produced a national consultation paper at the end of 1997 and the differences between the 1997 draft and the agreed 1998 text partly reflect the concerns expressed in that paper. Directive 98/50/EC amends the definition of a transfer, by making implicit reference to *Suzen* and *Henke*, permits Member States to allow negotiated change to terms and conditions in some insolvency situations, introduces joint and several liability but restricts the transfer of debts in insolvency situations, requires the transferor to provide the transferee with adequate information and includes occupational pensions within the bundle of rights which pass on transfer.

Note that the 1998 amended ARD is based on Article 100 and required to be unanimously approved by the Council of Ministers. For this reason the particular priorities of the EU Member States needed to be respected in searching for an agreement which could be acceptable to all.

4 EP Opinion of the Committee on Social Affairs and Employment (Rapporteur, Hugh Kerr MEP), 13 November 1996, A4-0367/96). See also, Hardy & Painter (1996) 25 ILJ 160 for further commentary.

5 COM (97) 60 Final. See also for further elaboration IDS Brief, Issue 425, May 1997, p. 19.

THE SCOPE OF THE DIRECTIVE

The jurisprudence of the European Court of Justice (ECJ) since 1985 has caused much tension amongst those EU Member States who have initiated contracting out exercises.[6] In fact, it was the ECJ's seemingly conflicting rulings on the applicability of the ARD that engendered these calls for reform. The EU Commission's proposed revisions since 1994 have therefore primarily sought to redefine the scope of the ARD. In particular, in its original revised Article 1 in 1994, the EU Commission proposed that the ARD be applied to transfers of economic entities which retain their identities. This distinction between the transfer of *economic entities* and *activities* has been understood to mean that most of the business transfers which occurred throughout the 1980s would be excluded from the protection afforded under the revised ARD. The EU Commission believed that it was this anomaly, alongside the controversial implications of the *Schmidt* and *Suzen* rulings, as already discussed in previous chapters, which was causing the stumbling block towards agreement between the EU social partners and the reason for the delay in revising the ARD, prior to 1998.

In view of this distinction, where the EU Commission intended to draw the line between transfers and non-transfers for a while remained unclear. Ostensibly, the EU Commission's original proposal seemed to affirm the ECJ's tests in the *Spijkers*[7] and *Redmond*[8] rulings. The ECJ in its judgments in these cases drew a distinction between the transfer of 'economic entities' and a mere 'activity transfer'. However, this distinction was later blurred in the case of *Schmidt,*[9] where the ECJ held that the contracting-out of cleaning involving one person amounted to a transfer protected under the directive. The *Schmidt* ruling in fact narrowed the semantic distinction between 'activity' and 'economic entity' business transfers.Given both the growing case law on the scope of the ARD, the EU Commission's proposed redefinition of Article 1 attracted much criticism from all EU Member States. For example, the British Department of Employment's 1995 Consultation Paper stated that: 'the present text does not appear to provide the certainty and clarity needed'. The British Business Services Association, the contractors' interest group, argued that: 'it would open up a new phase of commercially damaging

6 See the EU Commission's Report, 'Contracting Out of Services', 1993.

7 [1986] 2 CMLR 296 ECJ.

8 [1992] IRLR 366 ECJ.

9 [1994] IRLR 302 ECJ.

uncertainty and costly litigation'.[10] Also, the UK's TUC observed that the revision was 'inconsistent with the case law of the ECJ and would lead to great confusion and uncertainty if implemented. It creates a distinction between 'economic entity' and 'activity' which is difficult to sustain'.[11] Furthermore, the EU Commission's 1994 revised ARD failed to include sea-going vessels, thus permitting business transfers to take place on the high seas, so as to avoid legal liability.

Furthermore, adding to the uncertainty surrounding the scope of the ARD was the ECJ's ruling in the '*Rygaard*' case.[12] This case concerned a firm of carpenters who were contracted to construct a canteen. Following the bankruptcy of the main contractor, the carpenters, who had been made redundant as a consequence, were transferred to the sub-contractor to complete the work. Ole Rygaard, one of the carpenters affected, sought damages for wrongful dismissal. Disagreeing with the Advocate-General, the ECJ held that there was no transfer where one undertaking merely made available to another certain workers and materials for carrying out particular works. The ECJ's reasoned that the making available of workers and materials did not constitute a stable economic activity.

Consequently, distinguishing its decision in *Schmidt*, the ECJ ruled that a reliance on such authority presupposed the existence of an economic entity capable of transfer. Evidently since no assets had been transferred, enabling certain activities formerly undertaken by the transferor to be transferred, then the purpose of ARD had not been satisfied. This ruling did very little, except to suggest that the ECJ might have been retreating from its earlier position in *Schmidt*. In any event, confusion surrounding the scope of the ARD and its applicability to contracting-out exercises remained.

Similarly, the ECJ in *Suzen* argued that a cleaning contract to clean a church-run secondary school in Bonn, which was terminated by one contractor and awarded to another, giving rise to eight dismissals on the grounds of redundancy, did not by the mere fact that the service provided by the old and new contractor was similar support the conclusion that a business transfer had taken place. The ECJ held that a transfer of activities was insufficient to amount to a transfer of an undertaking. Thus, no relationship need exist between the transferor and transferee prior to the transfer for the ARD to apply, but the passing of tangible assets or the taking over of a workforce remain as prerequisites for meeting the *Spijkers* test. Had the ECJ followed the Advocate-General's advice, the *Suzen* decision would have impacted on

10 *The Municipal Journal*, 22nd December 1994.

11 See the TUC's evidence to the House of Lords Select Committee on the European Communities, Sub-Committee E (Law and Institutions) 5th Report, Session 1995-96, HL paper 38, 13 February 1996, p. 40, para. 2.2.

12 C-48/94, [1996] IRLR 51 ECJ.

all contracted labour-only services, but at present a legal distinction now exists between labour-intensive and activities-based business transfers. It is expected that other forthcoming cases might clarify what constitutes a transfer further. In the meantime, the EU Commission withdrew[13] its proposal to narrow the scope of the ARD, thus, retaining the existing definition, provided by the 1977 Directive. Yet, the EU Commission's desire was kept alive by the *Suzen* ruling.

In the event, the final text, as agreed at the Cardiff Summit, clarifies the scope of the Directive. It provides that the test for a business transfer is 'where there is a transfer of an economic entity which retains its identity, meaning an organised grouping of resources which has the objective of pursuing an economic activity, whether or not that activity is central or ancillary' (amended Article 1(1)(b)). This is a clear and brief alternative to the suggestion of the House of Lords Select Committee in its April 1998 Report, Acquired Rights Revisited,[14] that the Directive included a non-exhaustive list of factors drawn from the Spjikers case. As such it is to be welcomed, since it resolves much of the controversy already discussed, but will still leave the national courts with much work to do in applying the new definition to the many possible transfer-type situations which can occur in reality.

Insolvency transfers

Up until now the Directive has been silent on the position as regards business transfers caused by insolvency, but the ECJ has twice ruled that the ARD does not apply to transfers in the context of liquidation proceedings, although it can apply to proceedings short of liquidation.[15] It was this distinction which was incorporated in the amendments proposed to the Directive in 1994 and again in 1997. EU Member States were to be given a discretion as to whether to apply the individual employment protection provisions of the ARD to business transfers which take place in the context of insolvency proceedings, instituted with a view to the liquidation of the assets of the transferor under the supervision of a competent judicial authority.[16]

The 1994 and 1997 drafts provided that in the context of proceedings short of liquidation, such as administration or judicial arrangements, often termed 'pre-insolvency matters', instituted with a view to securing the survival of the undertaking, the revised ARD would apply in the normal way subject

13 COM(97) 85 Final.

14 22nd Report of the House of Lords Select Committee on the EC, *Acquired Rights Revisited*, April 1998.

15 See *Abels* [1985] ECR 479 ECJ and *D'Urso* [1992] IRLR 136 ECJ.

16 Article 1(5) of the 1994 and 1997 drafts of the Directive.

to a number of qualifications. Firstly, EU Member States would have had the discretion to provide that the transferor's debts, either in the form of arrears of payments, damages, or other liabilities, due before the business transfer or prior to the opening of insolvency proceedings, did not transfer to the transferee. This provision could be relied upon only if the affected employees are afforded the protection required by EC 'Insolvency' Directive 80/897/EEC. Secondly, EU Member States could allow the employer and employee representatives 'to change the terms and conditions of employment by an agreement concluded as a means of ensuring the survival of the undertaking'. Where such an agreement was reached, it would be presumed, unless the contrary was proven, that the alteration took place to ensure the undertaking's survival, and that any resultant dismissals were for 'economic, technical or organisational' reasons, entailing changes in the workforce. Finally, EU Member States could empower competent judicial authorities to alter or terminate contracts of employment or employment relationships existing at the date of the business transfer. The EU Commission proposed a related amendment in 1977 to 'ban the use of fraudulent insolvency proceedings'.[17] The UK Government, in its 1997 consultation paper, was opposed to the proposal to ban the use of fraudulent insolvency proceedings on the ground that it would be difficult in practice to distinguish between the fraudulent and the genuine and then only after the event.

These proposals attracted criticism, the second report of the House of Lords Select Committee on the EC (*Acquired Rights Revisited*) commenting that the distinction established in *Abels* and incorporated into the 1997 draft did not take account of the distinction drawn in *Dethier*,[18] between insolvency proceedings in which the entity concerned continued to trade and to which the Directive applied and other forms of insolvency proceedings in which this is not the case. Where the business continues to trade there could be no justification for depriving the employees of the protection of the Directive. Similarly, the 1997 DTI Consultation Paper on the proposed amendments to the Directive concluded that it would be difficult to draw a clear distinction in practice between the two types of regime. Moreover, the British TUC has pointed out that, '*the reality is that it will not always be clear at the outset of the procedure whether it will lead to a continuation of the business or its termination*'.[19] It would be difficult to control the strategic choice of insolvency proceedings by

[17] COM 97(60) Article 3(5).

[18] *Jules Dethier Equipment SA v Dassy and Sovram* SPRL C-319/94 [1998] IRLR 266.

[19] TUC evidence to the House of Lords Select Committee on the European Communities, Sub-Committee E (Law and Institutions) 5th Report, Session 1995-96, HL paper 38, 13th February 1996, p.41.

insolvency practitioners or to condemn as fraudulent a choice which had employment advantages, according to Davies and Hepple.[20] However, the 1998 amended Directive does provide in Article 4a(4) that 'Member states shall take appropriate measures with a view to preventing the misuse of insolvency proceedings in such a way as to deprive employees of the rights provided for in this Directive'.[21]

A new Article 4a(1) of the 1998 amended Directive provides that Articles 3 (preservation of employment rights) and 4 (dismissal rights) do not apply to bankruptcy and analogous insolvency proceedings, unless the EU Member States provide otherwise. This gives to EU Member States such as the UK the option to apply the Directive to all forms of bankruptcy and insolvency proceedings and to avoid the type of difficulties adverted to by the House of Lords Select Committee. Thus the Member States can apply Articles 3 and 4 to liquidation and to other forms of insolvency proceedings, but where such proceedings fall within the scope of the Directive, Article 4a(2) then provides that where these are conducted under competent public supervision (which may be an insolvency practitioner determined by national law) an EU Member State may provide that pre-transfer debts arising under the contract of employment and payable before the transfer or the opening of the insolvency proceedings shall not be transferred to the transferee. This is providing that the employees enjoy protection at least equivalent to that provided under the Insolvency Directive 80/987/EEC.

Changes in Terms and Conditions

The 1998 text also allows EU Member States to provide in applicable insolvency proceedings that the transferee, transferor, or a person exercising the transferor's functions, may agree changes in the employees' terms and conditions with the representatives of the employees, insofar as national law or practice permits, designed to safeguard employment opportunities by ensuring the survival of the business.[22] A crucial difference between this and

20 Evidence to the House of Lords Select Committee on the EC, 22nd Report, April 1998.

21 In evidence to the House of Lords Committee the DTI showed an awareness of the need to distinguish between the substance and the technical form of a rescue but offered no specific prescription as to how abuse was too be avoided in this context. (Minutes of Evidence p. 6.)

22 Article 4a (2)(b) There is a further provision that where Member State legislation defines, at the date of the entry into force of the Directive, a situation whereby a competent public authority under judicial supervision may declare that an enterprise is in a situation of serious economic crisis, the above derogations on debts and the adjustment of terms and conditions of employment may apply. As the Directive enters into force on the date of its publication in the Official Journal and the Council Minutes are recorded in the text of the Directive as noting that only Italy currently has such legislation, this provision acts only to protect the particular Italian position.

the 1994 and 1997 proposals is that the reference in those proposals to the capacity of the parties to such an agreement to determine whether and to what extent dismissals were to take place for an 'eto' reason has been deleted. This excision removes one of the more regressive features of this admittedly difficult compromise between different approaches to protecting employment.

The UK Government is clearly alive to the need to ensure that such representatives, especially when not drawn from a recognised independent trade union, are properly independent and equipped to fulfil this and other functions under the Collective Dismissal Directive, as evidenced by the proposals contained in the 1998 Consultation Paper on Employees' Information and Consultation Rights.[23]

Apart from the provisions of the 1977 Directive, UK law puts few obstacles in the way of such agreed changes, although it is not self-evident how an agreement reached by ad hoc employee representatives to change terms and conditions would become incorporated in the contracts of employment of the affected employees.

Joint Liability

The existing 1977 ARD gives EU Member States the option to provide for joint liability in respect of obligations to dismissed employees. Currently, ten out of the fifteen EU Member States already have some form of joint liability whereas Belgium, Denmark, Ireland, Luxembourg and the UK do not. The 1994 proposal was to make joint and several liability of the transferor and transferee compulsory in respect of obligations that fall due after the business transfer, but the transferor would be liable only to 'the extent corresponding to the portion of the relevant period, which expired on the date of the transfer'. EU Member States could limit the transferor's joint liability to those obligations which arose before the date of the business transfer, and which fall due within the first year following that date.

In a UK context, many parties, including *inter alia* the Confederation of British Industry (CBI), Forum for Small Businesses, the Local Government Management Board and the Law Society, objected to the original proposal. This opposition might explain why the EU Commission in its 1997 draft limited its proposal to obligations falling before the date of the transfer. This change was viewed by the EU Commission as advantageous insofar as it would have removed the confusion which presently faces applicants regarding which party to name as respondent to any action which they might initiate.

[23] URN 97/988.

Irrespective of this significant shift in policy by the EU Commission, in the 1997 consultation document the British government did not support this revision on the grounds of national law and practice. In particular, the UK government noted that a liquidator of an insolvent transfer might not be able to settle claims from employees, until he was sure there was no residual liability arising from the transfer. The House of Lords Select Committee was against the change on the ground that questions of the disposition of liability could be dealt with on a commercial basis, the apportionment of liabilities and the provision of indemnities being well established practice. In any event, the final amended version of the new Directive,[24] as agreed at the EU Cardiff Summit, now provides for the option of joint and several liability 'in respect of obligations which arose before the date of transfer from a contract of employment or an employment relationship existing on the date of the transfer.' There is therefore no requirement on the UK to deviate from the present situation as regards the distribution of liability.

Pensions

The amended Article 3(4)(a) allows EU Member States to apply the provisions of the Directive to old-age, invalidity and survivors' occupational pensions, rather than excluding them as has been the case in the original 1977 Directive and as was the case in the 1994 and 1997 drafts. The House of Lords Select Committee in its first report had recommended that the exclusion be ended and replaced with a requirement for comparable pensions. The British Government's consultation paper recognised both the value of such an amendment in protecting employee interests and the difficulty of ensuring that comparable pensions would in practice be provided. The promise of further consultation on the issue has now been overtaken by the terms of the revised Directive, but consultation will still be necessary on the implementation of such an option. It would be difficult to ensure the transfer of identical pension rights, which are linked to particular pension schemes, especially where those schemes are limited to the transferor's employees. However, comparable defined benefits or contributions to money purchase schemes would arguably be sufficient to transfer the pension rights of employees under the terms of the Directive. The implementation of the amended Directive would encounter the problem of ensuring that pensions are comparable in circumstances outside the remit of the Government Actuary's Department, if the UK decides to exercise the option which is open to it.

24 Article 3(1).

CONSULTATION AND INFORMATION

The provisions on information and consultation in Article 6 of the amended directive render the text more easily understandable but make some substantive changes. The new Article 6(5) gives EU Member States the option of limiting the obligation to consult to undertakings above the national minimum size for the election of a works council. Most EU Member States, other than the UK and Ireland, have exemptions in line with their works councils' exemption, some at five and others at twenty employees, but it follows that there is no minimum threshold for information and consultation in those EU Member States (the UK and Ireland) which have no procedures for national works councils of any kind.

The Government conceded in its 1997 consultation paper that the minimum threshold of 50 employees originally mooted by the House of Lords Select Committee in its first report on transfers had not attracted support elsewhere in the Community and it was not supported by the Select Committee in its second report of April 1998 and does not appear in the revised text of the Directive.

The proposed revised ARD recognises that questions of restructuring are often taken at a group level and Article 6(4) therefore recognises that the relevant decision may be taken by a controlling undertaking or employer, as does the Collective Dismissals Directive.

The EU Commission proposed a new Article 6A in 1997 under which EU Member States had to provide for employee representatives who enjoy the necessary independence to carry out the functions assigned to them. This reflected the EU Commission's concerns that the UK arrangements for elected employee representatives do not provide satisfactory guarantees of independence. Clearly, with or without the EU Commission's proposals in this area, the British transposition of the information and consultation provisions contained in the 1995 Regulations has been criticised as being inadequate and imprecise.[25] The February 1998 consultation document on 'Employees Information and Consultation Rights on Transfers of Undertakings and Collective Redundancies' attempts to address the defects apparent in the 1995 Consultation Regulations by elaborating the conditions under which employee representatives, to be consulted in the absence of a recognised independent union, are elected and the facilities which are to be afforded to them. The 1998 Fairness at Work White Paper promised action in this regard.[26] The result is that the final 1998 amendment to the Directive

[25] As was argued on behalf of the applicant unions in *R.v Secretary of State for Trade and Industry ex p. Unison and others* [1996] IRLR 438.

[26] See chapter 5.

does not contain any requirement on the independence of employees' representatives.

The 1997 requirement that information be given 'when' the transferor and the transferee envisage a transfer was criticised as impracticable and contributing little to the scheme of protection and has been dropped, although amongst the information which must be provided will be the date of the transfer. It remains the case that it is only the transferee who needs to consult his employees when he envisages measures in relation to his employees. In other respects the obligation to inform and consult remains substantially unchanged.

Provision of workforce Information to Contractors

The UK Government proposed in the 1997 consultation document, that relevant workforce information to be given by transferors to prospective transferees.[27] The EU Commission has observed that in a contracting-out situation, prospective contractors need comprehensive and accurate information about the size and terms and conditions of employment of the existing workforce. The government believes that such accurate information would lead to more realistic bids for contracts, as, in the past, sitting contractors, who are also re-tendering for the contracts which they control, have failed to share information or have provided inaccurate information in any case.[27a] Article 3(2) of the amended Directive gives an option to EU Member States to require that the transferor notifies the transferee of all obligations which will be transferred under the Directive, so far as those rights are or ought to have been known to the transferor at the time of the transfer. However, a failure to give appropriate notification shall not affect the transfer of the rights. It must be right that though the obligation to notify will clearly need to be supported by adequate sanctions, these should fall upon the transferor and not upon the employees.

Sanctions for Non-Compliance

A new Article 7a, first proposed in 1997, introduced an obligation on EU Member States to provide for sanctions which are 'effective, proportionate and dissuasive', where employers fail to comply with the relevant national

[27] See Hardy, Adnett and Painter, *TUPE and CCT Business Transfers: UK Labour Market Views*, Staffordshire University Institute of Industrial and Commercial Law, 1997, for further evidence of UK contractors' experiences and practices of consultation under CCT.

[27a] See Employment Relations Bill 1999, Part II.

implementing legislation, although no such amendment appears in the text of Directive 98/50. The amendments introduced by the 1993 Trade Union Reform and Employment Rights Act increased the value of the remedy where the employer fails to inform and consult as required from two weeks' to four weeks' pay per employee.

ANTI-DISCRIMINATION

In the 1997 proposals a new Article 7b would have provided that Member States may under no circumstances introduce discrimination on the basis of sex, race, age, handicap, sexual orientation, colour, religion or nationality in applying the Directive. As the UK Government observes in its consultation document this wide provision was legally unsound and was unlikely to be implemented. In particular, the proposed Article 7b would have gone beyond the legislative basis of the Directive in Article 100, which provides only for measures which directly affect the functioning of the EU single market. Whilst it is established[28] that contracting out of work can have an adverse impact on women, this provision seems also to go beyond the aims of the Directive set out in its 1977 Preamble and has been dropped from the 1998 amended Directive. These objectives are better able to be pursued under the rubric of equal opportunities than under Article 100 measures of this kind.

Finally, the EU Commission did not include take-overs by way of share transfers, nor do sea-going vessels fall within the scope of the amended Directive.

EU POLITICAL CONTROVERSY

At both EU and British domestic levels there has been a fierce political debate surrounding the proposed revision of the ARD, which has been conducted behind closed doors. It is understood that the French government disliked the EU Commission's original 1994 redraft, as did the German government, who have displayed some hesitation following the ECJ's decision in *Schmidt*. Other EU Member States' governments either indicated their satisfaction with the suggested reforms or decided to remain silent at the time.

Open political battles were fought in the EP, where Parliamentarians were seeking to delay, if not defeat, the EU Commission's 1994 proposals.[29] Notably,

[28] Escott and Whitfield, 'The Gender Impact of CCT in Local Government', 1995, EOC Discussion Series, No. 12. And *Ratcliffe v North Yorkshire County Council* [1995] IRLR 439 HL.

[29] See the oral questions by: Stephen Hughes MEP, B4-1442/95-0-0254/95, in the Minutes of the EP Plenary Session, 16.1.1996, pp. 16-17; and, Mme. van Dijk MEP, B4-0002/96-0-00003/96, in the Minutes of the EP Plenary Session, 16.1.1996, pp.17-18.

both the Legal Affairs and Women's Committees of the EP produced Reports criticising the EU Commission's revised Directive. Of importance, is the call by the EP's Women's Committee that the exclusion of contracting-out from the scope of the Directive would be indirectly discriminatory, since most of the workers affected by such a proposal would be women. Some 78.2% of the EU female workforce are contracted in public services.[30] These arguments were given further substance by the British Equal Opportunities Commission's (EOC) survey into the discriminatory effects of contracting-out[31]. As a result of such arguments, the EP called for the withdrawal of the EU Commission's 1994 proposals. In harmony with EP's opposition, the Opinion of the Economic and Social Committee (ESC),[32] also highlighted the flaws in the EU Commission's original proposal

As a result of this EU controversy, the EU Commissioner for Social Affairs withdrew the EU Commission's 1994 proposals. Subsequently, following this withdrawal, the EP approved the EU Commission's 1997[33] draft, subject to amendments. Most importantly, the EP retained its objection to the narrowing of the scope of the ARD and therefore deleted amendments 2-4. Consequently, the EU Commissioner agreed with the EP, and upheld the EP's suggested final amendments and deletions.[34]

UK Responses and Reaction

The House of Lords Select Committee on the European Communities, Sub-Committee 'E' on 'EU Law and Institutions', in March 1996 published its report on the EU Commission's 1994 proposed revised text.[35] After hearing evidence from academics, representatives from both the unions and business, legal practitioners and others,[36] it emerged that the main areas of controversy related to the scope of the ARD; the inclusions of share transfers, pensions, sea-going vessels and insolvency situations; mandatory introduction of joint liability for a minimum of twelve months after the transfer; and the rights to information and consultation. Other matters which proved to be almost as

30 See the EU Commission's 'Employment in Europe', 1995, Annexe, at p. 187, HMSO.

31 See Escott and Whitfield's study, ibid., EOC Research Discussion Series, No. 12, 1995.

32 See CES 317/95 - SOC/256, 29-30 March 1995.

33 COM(97) 60 Final.

34 COM(97) 85 Final.

35 See House of Lords Select Committee on the European Communities, Sub-Committee 'E' (Law and Institutions) Paper 38, 5th Report, Session 1995-96, 13 February 1996, HMSO.

36 House of Lords Select Committee on the European Community, Sub-Committee 'E' (EU Law and Institutions) Public Oral Evidence Proceedings, 1 & 22 November, and 6 December 1995.

equally contentious concerned whether or not judicial authorities should be permitted to change terms and conditions and the setting of the threshold for applicability at the level of fifty employees. Two major concerns within the Committee were whether to maintain the exclusion of pension provision protection in the ARD and to reinforce the consultation rights, despite ECJ rulings on both these issues.[37]

Professor Hepple in his written submission to the UK House of Lord's Committee outlined the general shortcomings of the existing 1977 ARD,[38] namely the unclear scope of the directive. In his evidence to the Committee,[39] Professor Hepple suggested that the revised article 1 was 'wrong in principle' and did not achieve the clarity desired. As Lord Slynn later summarised the position in a debate on the report: 'Representatives of both employers and employees thought that this was not a helpful distinction to introduce between 'activity' and 'economic entity' particularly as it was thought that some activities could themselves constitute an economic entity'.[40] CBI concerns centred upon the inclusion of contracting-out under the scope of the Directive, which the case law had already achieved. In seeking some moderation in this blanket application, the CBI submitted that: '...the current situation damages contracting-out',[41] resulting in delays in tendering and higher administrative costs and distorted competition. They also vehemently opposed the inclusion of pensions rights under the directive.[42]

The TUC, whilst welcoming the EU Commission's attempts to clarify the law, were sceptical of its intentions should the proposed revisions seek to distort the ECJ's rulings. The TUC contended, like ETUC, that the ARD provided: '...minimum floor of protection for workers in situations of business transfers'[43] and consequently they did not want to see any proposed narrowing of the scope of the Directive to exclude contracting-out or any other type of business transfers.

UK legal practitioners were represented by the Law Society and the Employment Lawyers Association. The Law Society advocated that the threshold of employees to which the ARD applied should be lowered to 20, in common with other recently enacted UK legislation, such as the Disability Discrimination Act, 1995. Whilst the Employment Law Association (ELA)

37 See *Barber v GRE* [1990] I ECR 1889 ECJ.

38 See House of Lords Report, ibid, pp. 6-12.

39 Oral evidence of 1 November 1995, 1600-1800, transcribed in the House of Lords Report, ibid., pp. 12-23.

40 See Hansard HL 4 June 1996, col. 1192.

41 See Report, ibid. , p. 26, para. 10.

42 Ibid, pp. 28-29.

43 Ibid, p. 43.

desired more differentiation between an economic entity and activity. They suggested that if the purpose of revised article 1(1) is to exclude such cases as *Schmidt*, then it had failed to do so.[44] The ELA considered the implications of joint liability unfavourable, particularly in terms of equal pay, and were concerned that the inclusion of share transfers would alter the directive, as it no longer protects acquired rights, but creates 'new' ones.[45]

The Society of Practitioners of Insolvency sought to highlight the distinction between the different objectives of bankruptcy law and employment law, they advocated greater clarity and were supportive of the rescue culture where business transfers were taking place due to liquidation. The argument in favour of the status quo was that an exclusion was based on the desire not to lower the number of potential rescuers of insolvent businesses due to the costs that would be incurred should they have to comply with the pre-existing terms and conditions. The previous UK Government's Industrial Relations Division of the DTI, maintained that the application of the Directive to contracting-out, would restrict 'entrepreneurial freedom'. Such, the DTI argued, might inhibit, even distort, competition in the British labour market.

Having heard all of the evidence their Lordships' Committee, consisting of eminent practitioners, experts and academics, made the following main recommendations:

i) To reject the EU Commission's proposed 1994 amendment to Article 1;
ii) Share transfers should be included under the Directive;
iii) Non-liquidation proceedings should be included under the Directive;
iv) To reject the Commission's joint liability proposal;
v) An EU definition of the term 'employee'[46] should be provided for the ARD;
vi) To support the proposed changes bringing the text of Article 6 into line with the equivalent provisions of the Collective Redundancies Directive. But that the 50 employees threshold should be lowered to 20;
vii) To extend the scope of the Directive to include sea-going vessels; and,
viii) The Commission should consider the inclusion of 'comparable' pension rights.

It was clear that the UK Parliament recommended that the EU Commission's 1994 proposed revised ARD should not be accepted, as it fundamentally departed from the law already established by the ECJ on the 1977 ARD. This

44 Ibid, p. 55, para. 7.

45 Ibid, pp. 75-76, paras. 192-194.

46 See the *Levin* case [1982] ECR 1035 ECJ and *Mikkelson v Danmols Inventar A/S* [1985] ECR 2639 ECJ. Also, see McMullen [1996] ILJ Vol. 25, No. 4, December, p. 286 at pp.295-298.

stance it confirmed in 1997, when the House of Lords Committee heard further evidence. Their Lordships' conclusions drew little attention, the previous UK government's response was solely limited to their Lordships' recommendation to include 'comparable' pension rights within the scope of the ARD. Like the EU Commission, their Lordships failed to take the opportunity provided by the revision process, to define what is meant by the 'economic', 'technical' and 'organisational' for the purposes of the 'eto' defences. Nevertheless, the robustly critical view adopted by their Lordships ensured that the new UK Government refused to accept the EU Commission's 1994 proposals.

However, their Lordships' findings put pressure on both the EU and the new British Government to reconsider the revision of the Directive. As Lord Slynn aptly put it when he addressed the House of Lords on the Committee's Report: 'The report with which this debate is concerned, if not dealing with a subject which attracts the headlines, is one which deals with issues of considerable importance to employees and of considerable importance in difficult economic times to employers'.[47] The House of Lords Select Committee second report, entitled Acquired Rights Revisited, canvassed the options with regard to the scope of transfers, joint liability, insolvency situations and information and consultation and clearly contributed to the thinking of the UK Government in its role as then President of the EU under which agreement was reached at the Cardiff Council on an amended Directive.

The current UK Government undertook a consultation exercise on the EU Commission's final proposals. In response to the consultation document on a revised ARD, the TUC reiterated its opposition to any move to narrow the scope of the ARD and outlined its commitment to reversing the *Suzen* decision. Furthermore, the TUC[48] sought to extend the ARD to share transfers, 'comparable' pensions, and insolvency situations and to support the mandatory introduction of joint liability. However, the TUC remained concerned that consultation with workers' representatives should take place when a business transfer is envisaged. Also, the TUC contended that the ARD should cross-refer to the European Works Councils Directive, in terms of consultation, in order for consultation to be facilitated at multinational levels. Moreover, the TUC vigorously argued that the possibility of dismissals for 'eto' reasons should only be available to an employer following agreement with workers' representatives. Similarly and as to be expected the

47 See Hansard HL 4 June 1996, cols. 1191 - 1206, at 1191.

48 TUC Response to the DTI Public Consultation on the proposed revision of the ARD and TUPE Regulations, 12/2/98.

Confederation of British Industry (CBI) retained its opposition to any reversal of the ECJ's ruling in *Suzen* and continues to seek the exclusion of contracting-out from the ambit of the ARD.

The Amended Directive

The text of the amended Directive is interesting in that it can be seen both as bringing the text into line with the case law of the Court of Justice and as an attempt to address the diverse concerns of the EU Member States about the transfers regime. The Directive remains one of partial harmonisation, which provides EU Member States with an option both to increase employee protection directly, as, for example, in regard to occupational pensions, and with options to facilitate the preservation of employment opportunities indirectly by providing a facility to adapt terms and conditions in cases of insolvency, or providing that the transferor's outstanding debts do not transfer to the transferee. The revisions to the Directive are therefore consistent with the principle of subsidiarity and respect for national practices. The crucial new definition of the scope of transfers is clearer than the previous version, respects the case law of the Court and the diversity of views of the EU Member States. Even if the UK Government would have wished to return to a pre-*Suzen* definition of transfers, such would not have been politically possible in a situation which required unanimity in the Council.

Francovich Claims

With the newly elected UK Government facing 188 writs, so-called '*Francovich* claims' (initiated by British unions for the alleged partial and ineffective transposition of the ARD), a new dimension is added to the debate surrounding the future revision of the Directive. The *Francovich* doctrine[49] is a legal means by which an EU Member State can be sued for its failure to implement a directive. The *locus standi* for such a claim relies upon the fact that the aggrieved EU citizen has suffered detrimental loss and the loss is attributable to the EU Member State's failure to implement a directive comprehensively. The existence of this new EU remedy linked the jurisdiction of domestic legal systems more closely to that of the ECJ and marks a clear departure from the EU's previous stance of no EU remedies being available in national law. Similarly, the ECJ in *Brasserie du Pecheur,*[50] has elaborated upon the criteria

49 *Francovich v Italian Republic* [1992] IRLR 84 ECJ.

50 [1996] IRLR 267 ECJ.

for State liability established by the *Francovich* ruling. Whilst reinforcing the ECJ's general rule that Community law confers rights of redress on individual EU citizens for losses caused by EU Member States' breaches of Community law, the key determinant of a 'serious' breach is now determined by considering whether the EU Member State disregarded its discretion to enact the legislation as it sees best to fulfil its EU legislative obligations.

The legal outcome of these rulings is that to present a successful *Francovich* action in the context of the ARD, four conditions have to be met: firstly, the applicant must show that the relevant directive grants rights to individuals; secondly, those 'rights' are identifiable on the basis of the directive's provisions; thirdly, there is some causal link between the breach of the EU Member State's obligation and the detrimental damage incurred; and fourthly, following *Brasserie*, that the EU Member State concerned did 'manifestly and gravely' disregard the limits on its discretion to implement the ARD. Above all the *Francovich* ruling exemplifies the development of a significant right to make a claim for damages for failure to comply with an EU legislative measure which is not directly effective.

The implications of these *Francovich* claims in relation to the law governing business transfers is that there is no longer any sole reliance on the ARD being directly effective, in order to initiate a claim for losses incurred following a business transfer. The *Francovich* doctrine is certainly more generous than direct effect which should widen the number of applicants available to initiate proceedings when they incur a detriment in their terms and conditions following a business transfer. Further opportunity for *Francovich* claims to succeed has been given by the ECJ in its ruling in the *Dillenkofer* case.[51]

In any event, the *Francovich* claims have already been recognised in UK law, with the EAT's judgment in *Secretary of State for Employment v Mann*.[52] The President of the EAT acknowledged the EU remedies available in the High Court. This ruling shows that an Employment Tribunal has no jurisdiction to hear a *Francovich* action, as following the *Francovich* ruling domestic law jurisdiction was conferred by Community law to EU Member States' courts only. This position was later confirmed in *Potter v Secretary of State for Employment*,[53] holding that an ET does not have the jurisdiction to entertain a *Francovich* action claim against the State for damages. Thus, stipulating that all *Francovich* claims must be pursued in the ordinary courts, as the matter concerned damages. In terms of business transfers the domestic remedies

51 [1997] IRLR 60 ECJ.

52 [1996] IRLR 4 EAT.

53 [1997] IRLR 21 CA.

available are probably a more potentially successful route to pursue than EU remedies.

Clearly, now a final amended ARD is agreed, a full and correct implementation is the key to its success, although the substantial extent of the discretion afforded to the Member States makes this an easier matter than would otherwise have been the case. Otherwise, future *Francovich* claims have the potential to undermine any future ARD. As was the British experience of the existing 1977 ARD after infraction proceedings in 1992, initiated by the EU Commission.

THE LEGALITY OF A REVISED TUPE

Whilst claims against EU governments exist under the *Francovich* doctrine, any EU Member State government could potentially have its transposition of these newly revised measures challenged in their domestic courts. Subject to s.2(2) of the European Communities Act 1972, in a UK context, the British government's implementation of a revised ARD, in terms of a new set of TUPE Regulations, could be challenged in the courts on the grounds of *ultra vires*. Under Article 7 of the ARD, EU Member States are reminded that the ARD provides only a minimum floor of rights and that EU Member States can provide employees with more favourable rights should they so desire. The amended Directive incorporates several options under which EU Member States are clearly empowered to introduce provisions which are more favourable to employees, as with pensions, but others, such as the capacity to vary terms and conditions in insolvency situations, which could be construed as antithetical to the short-term interests of employees, whatever their longer-term impact upon employment prospects. However, any provision which could be considered as a reinterpretation of the minimum standards established under the Directive could open up the possibilities of litigation. For example, should the UK Government seek to reconstitute the scope of the ARD towards a pre-*Suzen* definition, such might be construed by the courts as *ultra vires*[54] and resort may be made to primary legislation.

[54] See *R. v Bedfordshire CC ex parte GMB*, unreported [1997] and *R. v UNISON* [1996] IRLR 438 HC, for examples of judicial review proceedings on the ARD.

Conclusions

Even with further rulings the approach adopted in *Suzen* and *Henke* to delimiting a business transfer has been maintained and is now incorporated in the revised Directive. The amended Directive is much clearer, especially as regards the definition of a transfer but it will still leave questions as to what constitutes an 'organised grouping of resources' in both capital and labour intensive industries for the national courts. The number of options left open by the 1998 amended Directive for national implementation means that policy debate on the transfers regime cannot and will not stop.

Select Bibliography

Atkinson, J. (1984), 'Manpower Strategies for Flexible Organisations', *Personnel Management*, 16.

Barnard, C. (1996), *EC Employment Law,* Wiley.

Bourn, C. (1998), 'When does the transfer of a service contract constitute the transfer of an undertaking?', *European Law Review*, 23, 1.

Bowers, J. (1984), 'Transfer of Undertakings Regulations: the Unresolved Problems', *New Law Journal* 134.

Cappelli, P. (1995), 'Rethinking Employment', *British Journal of Industrial Relations*, 33, 4.

Cavalier, S. (1997), *Transfer rights: TUPE in Perspective,* Institute of Employment Rights.

Collins, H., (1996), 'Market Power and Bureaucratic Power', *ILJ*, 15,1.

Collins, H., Independent Contractors and the Challenge of Vertical Disintegration for Employment Protection Laws, 10 *Oxford Journal of Legal Studies*.

Commission Européenne, Politique Sociale de la Communauté. Marché Intérieur. Situation au 1er Juillet 1994., vol 6 Juillet 1994.

Council Resolution concerning a Social Action Programme for the European Communities. 1 January 1974. 74/C 13/1 OJ.

Daniels, W.W., *The Impact of the Employment Protection Laws*, PSI.

Davies, P. L. (1992), 'The Emergence of European Labour Law', in McCarthy, W. (ed.) *Legal Interventions in Industrial Relations, Gains and Losses*, Oxford: Blackwell.

Davies, P.L. (1994), 'A Challenge to the Single Channel', *Industrial Law Journal, 23,1, 272-285.*

Davies, P.L. (1995), 'Market Integration and Social Policy', *Industrial Law Journal*, 24,1, 49-77.

Davies, P.L. (1996) 'Opting out of Transfers', *Industrial Law Journal,* 25, No. 3.

Davies, P.L. (1997), 'Taken to the Cleaners? Contracting Out of services Yet Again', *Industrial Law Journal,* 26,2,193-197.

Davies, P.L. and Freedland, M., (1982) *Transfer of Employment*, Sweet and Maxwell.

Davies, P.L. and Freedland, M. (1993), *Labour Law and Public Policy,* Clarendon Press.

Department of Employment, *People and Companies. Employee Involvement in Britain*, 1989. London HMSO.

Department of the Environment Circular No.5/96: 2 April 1996 Guidance on the Conduct of Compulsory Competitive Tender.

Dickens, L. and Bain, G.S. (1986), 'A Duty to Bargain? Union Recognition and Information Disclosure', in Lewis, R. *Labour Law in Britain,* Blackwell.

Docksey, C. (1986), *Information and Consultation of Employees: the United Kingdom and the Vredeling Directive,* MLR vol. 49 No.3 at 281.

Eady, J. (1994), 'Collective Dismissals, Consultation and Remedies. Griffen v South West Water Services Ltd', *23,4 Industrial Law Journal, 350-354.*

Elias P. and Bowyers J, *Transfer of Undertakings, the Legal Pitfalls*, FT Law and Tax, 1996.

Elias, P. (1982),'The Transfer of Undertakings: A Reluctantly Acquired Right', *Company Lawyer*, 147.

Escott K. & Whitfield D. (1995), *The Gender Impact of CCT in Local Government, EOC Discussion Series*, No. 12.

European Commission, *Growth, Competitiveness and Employment, the Challenges and Ways Forward into the 21st Century*, Bulletin of the EC, Supplement 6/93.

European Commission, *Contracting Out of Services*, 1993.

European Commission, White Paper, *Growth, Competitiveness and Employment*, 1994.

European Commission, *Employment in Europe*, HMSO, 1995.

European Commission, Green Paper, *Partnership for a new Organisation of Work*, EU Green Paper 1997.

European Parliament, *Opinion of the Committee on Social Affairs and Employment* (Rapporteur, Hugh Kerr MEP), 13 November 1996, A4-0367/96.

European Works Councils Bulletin. Issue 12, November / December 1997 p.11 *National consultation rules: Commission presses on;* EIRI November 1997 at 10.

European Works Councils Bulletin. Issue 15 May / June 1998 at 7.

Freedland, Mark (1996), 'Employment Policy', in *European Community Labour Law, Principles and Perspectives*, (Ed.) Davis, Lyon-Caen, Sciara and Simitis, Clarendon Press.

Geary J., Rees C., Sisson K. (1995), *Management-Initiated Direct Participation. United Kingdom,* European Foundation for the Improvement of Living and Working Conditions. Working Paper No: WP/95/03/EN.

Gold, M. (1994), *Direct Communication in European Multinationals: A Case Study Approach,* European Foundation for the Improvement of Living and Working Conditions.

Greaty, J. & Sisson, K. (1994), *Conceptualising Direct Participation in Organisational Change. The EPOC project,* European Foundation for the Improvement of Living and Working Conditions.

Hall, M. (1992), 'Legislation for Employee Participation: a Case Study of the EWC Directive', Warwick Papers in Industrial Relations, No 39, March.

Hardy & Painter (1996), 'Revising the Acquired Rights Directive', *Industrial Law Journal*, 25,2, 160-168.

Hardy, Adnett & Painter (1997), *TUPE and CCT Business Transfers: UK Labour Market Views*, Staffordshire University Institute of Industrial and Commercial Law.

Hepple B. (1976) 'Workers Rights in Mergers and Takeovers: The EEC Proposals', *Industrial Law Journal*, 197.

Hepple, B. (1982), 'The Transfer of Undertakings (Protection of Employment) Regulations', *Industrial Law Journal* ,11, *29*.

Hepple, B. (1987), 'The Crisis in E.C. Labour Law', *Industrial Law Journal*, 16, 1, 77.

Hepple, B. & Byre, A. (1989), 'EEC Labour Law in the UK – A New Approach', *Industrial Law Journal*, 18, 129.

Hepple, R., 'Labour Law and Public Employees in Britain', in Lord Wedderburn and Murphy, W. T. (eds) *Labour Law and the Community: Perspectives for the 1980's*.

Hibbert, A. (1991), 'Employee Involvement : A Recent Survey', *Employment Gazette* 659.

House of Lords Select Committee on the European Communities, Sub-Committee 'E' (Law and Institutions) Paper 38, 5th Report, Session 1995-96, 13 February 1996, HMSO.

House of Lords Select Committee on the European Community, Sub-Committee 'E' (EU Law and Institutions) Public Oral Evidence Proceedings, 1 & 22 November, and 6 December 1995.

House of Lords Select Committee on the EC, 22nd Report, *Acquired Rights Revisited*, April 1998.

Kahn-Freund O. (1954), in Flanders and Clegg (eds.) *The System of Industrial Relations in Britain*, London: Blackwell.

Kahn-Freund O. (1972) *Labour and the Law*, Stevens.

Local Government Management Board Survey, *Local Government Chronicle*, 15 August 1997.

Lorber, P. (1997), 'The Renault case: the European Works Council put to the test', 13 *Int.Journal of Comparative Labour Law and Industrial Relations*.

Lorber, P. (1997), *An Attempt to Assess the Curious Impact of European Works Council Directive on the United Kingdom System of Industrial Relation and Labour Law*, Jagiell. University Yearbook L.L.S.P, (9), Cracow.

Marchington, M., Goodman, J., Wilkinson, A. and Ackers, P., *New Developments in Employee Involvement*, Employment Department. Research Series No.2 May 1992.

McGee and Weatherill (1990), 'The Evolution of the Single Market - Harmonisation or Liberalisation', 53 *Modern Law Review*, 578.

McMullen, J. (1992), *Business Transfers and Employee Rights*, Butterworths (2nd Edition).

McMullen J. (1996), 'Atypical Transfers, Atypical Workers and Atypical Employment Structures – A Case for Greater Transparency in Employment Issues', *Industrial Law Journal*, 25, 4, 286.

McMullen, J. (1998), *Business Transfers and Employee Rights*, Butterworths (3rd Edition).

Millward, N. *[et al]* (1992), *Workplace Industrial Relations in Transition. The ED/ESRC/PSI/ACAS Surveys*, Dartmouth.

More, G. (1995), 'The Acquired Rights Directive; Frustrating or Facilitating Labour Market Flexibility', in *New Legal Dynamics of the European Union*, OUP

Morris and Fredman (1993), 'Is There a Public/Private Labour Law Divide', 14 *Comparative Labor Law Journal*, 115-137

Morris, G.S. and Archer, T.J. (1993), *Trade Unions, Employers and the Law*, Butterworths.

Napier B., CCT, (1993) *Market Testing and Employment Rights*, Institute of Employment Rights.

Neal, A. C. (1990), 'The European Framework Directive on the Health and Safety Workers: Challenges for the United Kingdom', 6 *Int.Journal of Comparative Labour Law and Industrial Relations*, 90.

Neal, A.C (1995), 'United Kingdom Point of View', in Blanpain, R. and Hanami, T. *European Works Council. The Implementation of the Directive in the Member States of the European Union*, Euro-Japan Institute for Law and Business, Peters.

O'Hara, J. (1996) *Community Law and British Industrial Relations*. Institute of Employment Rights.

Ogus (1994), *Regulation - Legal Form and Economic Theory*, Clarendon Press.

Pichot, E. (1995), *Employee Representatives in Europe and their Economic Prerogatives*. Report conducted for the European Commission.

Pollert, A. (1987), 'The Flexible Firm, A Model in Search of Reality', *Warwick Papers in Industrial Relations*.

Radford and Kerr (1996), 'Acquiring rights - Losing Power: A Case Study in Ministerial Resistance to the Impact of European Community Law', *Modern Law Review*, 60, 1.

Report of the Committee of Inquiry on Industrial Democracy (Chairman Lord Bullock), Cmnd. 6706. 1977.

Report of the Royal Commission on Trade Unions and Employers' Associations. Cmnd 3523. May 1968.

Rideout R. (1982), 'The Great Transfer of Undertakings Hoax', *Current Legal Problems*, 233.

Rood, M. (1992), 'Workers' Participation: New Initiatives at European Level' 8 *Int.Journal of Comparative Labour Law and Industrial Relations* 320.

Sargeant, M., 'New Doubts about Transfers', 26 *Industrial Law Journal*, 265-269.

Schofield, P. (1983), 'Protection of Employment on Transfer of Undertakings', 18 *Journal of Business Law,* 18.

Shanks, Michael (1977), The Social Policy of the European Communities, 14 *Common Market Law Review* 375.

Sharland J. and Isaacs S. (1996) *TUPE and the Acquired Rights Directive*, Trenton Publishing.

Skidmore, P. (1996), 'Worker Rights – A Euro litigation Strategy?', *25 Industrial Law Journal, 225-229.*

Slot, P. J. (1996), 'Harmonisation', 21 *European Law Review* 378-397.

Snyder, Francis (1990), *New Directions in European Community Law*, Weidenfeld and Nicolson.

Streit, M.E. and Mussler, W. (1995), 'The Economic Constitution of the European Community: From "Rome" to "Maastricht"', 1 *European Law Journal* 5.